THE
SILVER
EYE

SUSAN BRIND MORROW studied Classics, Arabic and Egyptology at Columbia University. She has travelled extensively in Egypt and Sudan, working as an archaeologist and studying natural history, language and the uses of poetry. Her first book, *The Names of Things: A Passage in the Egyptian Desert*, was a finalist for the PEN Martha Albrand Award for the Memoir in 1998. She is also the author of *Wolves and Honey: A Hidden History of the Natural World* and is the recipient of a Guggenheim fellowship for her work on the Pyramid Texts.

Also by Susan Brind Morrow

The Names of Things
Wolves and Honey

THE SILVER EYE

Unlocking the Pyramid Texts

SUSAN BRIND MORROW

First published in the USA in 2015 by Farrar, Straus and Giroux

First published in the UK in 2016 by Head of Zeus Ltd

Copyright © 2015 by Susan Brind Morrow

9 7 5 3 1 2 4 6 8

A catalogue record for this book is available from the British Library.

ISBN (HB) 9781784972387
ISBN (E) 9781784972370

Grateful acknowledgment is made for permission to reprint excerpts from Alexandre Piankoff's *The Pyramid of Unas: Egyptian Texts and Representations*, volume 5. Copyright © 1968, 1996 Bollingen/Princeton University Press. Reprinted by permission of Princeton University Press.

Designed by Jonathan D. Lippincott

Printed and bound in Germany by GGP Media GmbH, Pössneck

Head of Zeus Ltd
Clerkenwell House
45–47 Clerkenwell Green
London EC1R 0HT

WWW.HEADOFZEUS.COM

for K.R.

*"How can we talk about netchers?" he said, by which he meant
primary hieroglyphs, pristine archaic nouns, words
that would be drawn directly from nature.*

Contents

THE
SILVER EYE

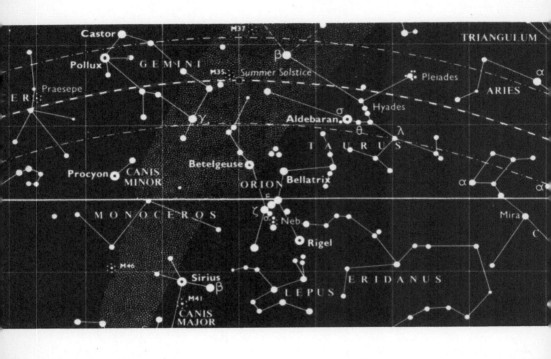

Prologue

You can see this any day. It is both time and place at once. It is of transcendent beauty. It is the agent of all transformation. It is the origin of all things. It is so familiar that it is known by all. Yet so familiar it is forgotten and unseen. But even forgotten it is the one essential thing: the dawn.

But to go back, or forward, to the night: Orion rises in the sky, a giant man of light. There is an implicit angle in his rising, a diagonal, a path. In a single night on this path he will sail across the sky. There are the unmistakable brilliant three stars, Al Nilam, the string of pearls, that are his belt, and beneath it the short clustering dimmer line that goes down, Orion's sword, the great Orion nebula, the green swirling clouds of space.

Above Orion on the diagonal is the red star in the root of the horn of Taurus, and below on the diagonal is Sirius, the sapphire star, the brightest star in the sky.

Anyone can see them, the jewellike stars going around the sky night after night, year after year, marking with exact geometrical precision, slightly altered each night by moments in time and geometrical degrees on the horizon that equal them, the progression of the night, of the season, and, coming back to its same coordinates, the year.

Thus the sky is an elegant clock, turning with visible arms, the Dippers swinging around the North Star, marking the deeply and gorgeously integrated life of everything on earth. If you were in China tomorrow it would mark the hours in precisely the same way that it does in upstate New York today, for the hours, *horae*, are stars.

This is a geometrical grid that anyone can see. Geometry in the truest sense: It measures the earth minutely. It has a life of its own. It is not abstract. It is not human. But you can know it. And to know it, to see it, belongs to a deep aesthetic sense that transcends what is human. The wail of the wild dog rises with the moon in the cold night air.

There is no need to look to anyone to explain it, this numinous world. The properties that extract us from it and render us back into it—the miracles of conception, birth, and death—are properties belonging to all that exists. Pure energy, the nature of light, underlies all. We emerge from and dissolve back into this radiant ground. Not only can you know this, you are this.

Poetry and religion arise from the same source, the perception of the mystery of life. Early Egyptian writing belongs to this universal language. The vehicle at work is associative thinking, in which metaphors act as keys to unlock a primeval human sense of the integrated living world. The meaning may not come across on the pedantic level, but on the poetic level it is transparent. Animal-headed gods, for example, seem alien, indeed ridiculous. When you think of them not as gods but as signifying the qualities of the animals themselves, they take on a different meaning. They resonate with an innate sense of animal motion, symmetry, force, color. What is *al-chem-y*, literally "the Egyptian thing," or, as *The American Heritage Dictionary* defines it, "the Egyptian practice of transmutation"? What or where is the gold? One looks to the writing of Egypt to find out.

The task is to take a medium that is proverbially indecipherable and to enter it, as though entering a pyramid with a lamp that gradually illuminates what is there. The first step is to look at the words themselves, and then in the second step, through them, as though through an uncovered lens, to see what is written on the walls of the hidden book. The third step is to ask what it means, to seek the deeper design that is the key to this primary early religion. Hence this book has three parts—the language, the translation, and seeking the deeper design.

I

THE LANGUAGE
OF BIRDS

Hieroglyphic means "mysterious," yet hieroglyphs themselves are instruments of absolute clarity that present a pellucid record of the natural world. This is writing as it first was, a mirror of life. Eliminating the dimensions of time and place and decay, it was a holy thing because it worked.

I began the study of hieroglyphs with the mind of a child raised with a keen awareness of nature. I was a freshman in the Classics Department of Columbia University at the age of sixteen when I stood in line at Salter's Bookstore on Broadway to purchase Sir Alan Gardiner's massive *Egyptian Grammar* for eleven dollars on a whim. Hieroglyphs were still offered as a course at Columbia in those days, though they were being phased out for lack of interest. I was one of three students of Roger Bagnall, a papyrologist working in Egypt, sifting through remnant shreds of Greek words. Immersed as I was at the time in Catullus and Pindar and Sappho, my thoughts were primarily on the construction of the line, how each one of these masters, in their own distinct way, crafted a line as though it were a physical thing, an instrument made to have a deep and palpable effect:

> *sophos o polla eidos phua,*
> *mathontes de labroi*

> The one who knows
> Is one who knows much in his own nature,
> Those who learn are like crows

> > —Pindar

Looking at Greek, you come to see words as tactile and alive. You are looking at words branching out from a phonic core, like the root of a plant. Though spelling varies, the root persists through root, red, rust, rose. The essence of writing was to get at the root and prod it into subtle tendrils of meaning.

Vivid imagery from nature, rhyming and elision, the beautiful construction of the line, were tools the Greek and Latin poets used to capture life in words. These devices were present throughout the literature of hieroglyphs. Yet hieroglyphs had a further dimension. The letters themselves had a living quality. They were composed of living animals and plants. In Egypt the phoenix is the blue heron rising in the swamp at dawn. The sky is green. The stars are flowers. In Egypt heaven is a wetland.

I was devoted in those days to Henry Fischer, the curator of the Egyptian collections at the Metropolitan Museum of Art, because of the beautiful books he wrote. In *The Orientation of Hieroglyphs*, he had the unusual insight that the words themselves were like the tableaux on the walls of tombs. Hieroglyphs were miniature paintings and sculpture; tomb reliefs were giant hieroglyphs. The pictures and letters were the same thing. Fischer so knew and loved Egypt that when I would run into him over the years at an annual New Year's party in Sherman, Connecticut, where he lived, he would turn to me at midnight and say, as though we were in Egypt, *kuli senna inti tayyiba!* He told me once that *susan*, a word that appears in the Pyramid Texts, was, he thought, the blue lotus of the Nile—for he was particularly interested in the hieroglyphs themselves, what they actually *were*, their humor, the charm of the verb *msbb* (to turn), written with the oryx characteristically bending back its head along its flank, as the curlew with its scimitar beak in the sand was the verb "to find." The letter was a study of the animal. The words were living pictures.

The years of my late teens were given over to transcribing and translating the literature of Egypt, the philosophy, the love poetry, *The Dialogue of Trees*. But what I was instinctively drawn to was the brilliance of these individual poetic conceptions, in the lines, the use of words, and in the words themselves. As Ezra Pound insists in his *ABC of Reading*, I knew that you had to see the original language, the original formulation, for the meaning lay not only in the content but in the structure. Writing was not simply about a thing: It contained the thing. It was the thing. This layered richness of meaning works on a level that is beyond analysis. It awakens the mind, as Yeats observed, in the realm of heightened perception, like falling in love. It should clearly be said that writing as we think of it today does not come close to the mastery in the formulation of words and imagery that was achieved in antiquity.

In Egypt the construction of the line was everything. When I lived in the Nile Valley in my twenties, village men and women who could not read or write would walk for miles to listen to a blind poet sing all night, or go to a holy man to have a poetic line scrawled out on a scrap of paper. They would put the scrap in a cup of water and drink the ink for the medicinal power of the words. Years later, Fischer, who devoted his retirement to writing books of poetry, sent me a poem that ended, "the words, the words, the words."

At Columbia as an undergraduate, and continuing into graduate school in classics, I worked at the Brooklyn Museum for the German Egyptologist Bernard von Bothmer, whose preoccupation was trying to break through the conventional understanding that Egyptian sculpture was inferior to Greek, that it was idealized and bland. Bothmer tirelessly pointed out the brilliance and skill of the Egyptians, that they showed real things, real people, weariness, complexity, sorrow. Bothmer had a few years before finished the work of the Russian Egyptologist Alexandre Piankoff on the earliest version of the Pyramid Texts, in the Pyramid of Unis in 2323 B.C., for the Bollingen Series.

Piankoff died before finishing his exhaustive study. His commentary begins with a quote from Goethe, to paraphrase: "They pull a thing apart, and in so doing drive its life away." In his first paragraph, in his very first sentence, Piankoff admits that the Egyptological approach, the dry cataloging of historical facts as they were understood, was not adequate to figure out the Pyramid Texts. Other Egyptologists have begun their books in exactly the same way: Rundle Clark in 1960 argues that although it is believed that the Egyptian religion is different from that of the rest of the world, "this cannot possibly be true." The English Egyptologist Christopher Eyre, in his 2001 book on the section of the Pyramid Texts that Egyptology has labeled the "Cannibal Hymn," laments on his first page, "The inaccessibility of Egyptian literature is not simply a matter of incompetent translation."

Great minds over the ages, among them Plato and Newton, had heard that hidden within the pyramids was a treasured body of writing, long sought for the scientific observations and philosophical insight it contained. Yet the actual discovery of the Pyramid Texts made barely a cultural ripple in the world. When the director of the Egyptian Antiquities Service, Gaston Maspero, heard that the small Old Kingdom pyramids at Saqqara were opened in the winter of 1880 and 1881 and that their inner walls were covered with incised columns of minute hieroglyphic writing that had been buried in the dark for nearly four thousand years, he wrote, "The so-called 'dumb' pyramids at Saqqara had spoken." The newly created academic discipline of Egyptology dismissed the hieroglyphic text as a disconnected collection of magic spells about snakes mixed into an incoherent myth involving the dead pharaoh with various animal gods, Osiris, and a sun god named Ra.

I became familiar with the Pyramid Texts by copying out the numbered lines of "utterances," as they were called, in the German Egyptologist Kurt Sethe's *Die Altaegyptischen Pyramidentexte* from the 1920s. The practice that I was taught as a student of Egyptology was to copy out the line recorded in the book, often reversing the letters in order to read it, combing through grammatical analysis and parallel lists of the usages of hieroglyphic words. The beauty and power of the individual lines were unmistakable:

Sew emerald, turquoise, malachite stars
And grow green, green as a living reed

When I received a Guggenheim to translate the Pyramid Texts in 2006, and spent the subsequent years studying every line, I looked for the most recently published translation:

Pull back, Baboon's penis! Open sky's door! You sealed door, open a path for Unis on the blast of heat where the gods scoop water. Horus' glide path TWICE . . . Unis becomes a screeching howling baboon . . . Unis's anus on Unis's back and Unis's back-ridge on Unis's head. Unis will make ululation and sit among the youngsters . . .

Unis has come to you, falcons, in your enclosures—become peaceful to Unis—with his bent tail, of the intestine of a baboon, at his rear . . .

Plait has been entwined by Plait, the toothless calf that emerged from the garden has been entwined . . . face has fallen on face, face has seen face. The dappled knife all black and green has emerged and swallowed the one it has licked.

—James P. Allen, *The Ancient Egyptian Pyramid Texts*
(Atlanta: Brill, 2005), 60, 52, 17

A reader might conclude, as I did, one of two things. Either Egyptian hieroglyphs were coarse, stupid, and pointless, or, to paraphrase the biochemist Karl von Frisch, it is easier to believe that Egyptology has come to a false conclusion than that Egypt has made an absurd mistake.

As I looked at the original in depth, I saw what the problem was: two foreign ideas are being superimposed on the Egyptian original. The first is that the writing is primitive. The second is that it contains a myth. The English does not track because the translator is following this preconception rather than the actual hieroglyphs, and the translation does not make sense because the myth is not there. Yet the hieroglyphic work is far from unreadable. The words themselves are clear and simple, the vocabulary familiar, and the sense readily made out.

I began to realize, almost in shock, that the columns of hieroglyphic writing formed a progression of complex, interrelated poetic verses. Plutarch wrote that the Egyptian priesthood used the poetic riddle, the word in Greek for which is *enigma*, as a vehicle to convey religious secrets. That this method was known in antiquity is captured by the story of the riddle of the Sphinx, which stands for the larger tradition. You have to solve the riddle to pass the threshold and enter this body of knowledge.

Puns and riddles depend on concealed meaning, a double sense that opens up a word or a phrase the way a hidden spring opens a box, revealing what is within. Indeed this is what hieroglyphs themselves are all about. The astonishingly naturalistic hieroglyphs that comprise the Pyramid Texts belong to the realm of empirical observation that is the basis of both science and poetry. They are both things, and metaphors arising from the astute observation of the intrinisic qualities of things. This is what enabled written language to develop: abstraction developed from metaphor. As Emerson wrote, "Language is fossil poetry."

In considering this one might look to Piankoff's realization about the pervasive use of symbolism in Egyptian representation. "For the Egyptian," he wrote in his *Wandering of the Soul*, "every so-called physical fact of life had a symbolic meaning, and every symbolic act had a material background. Both were equally true and real." Henry Fischer's insight reveals what is essentially the economy of the Egyptian execution of art, architecture, and writing, that they are, in his words, interrelated to a degree that is unparalleled in any other culture. Everything has a meaning. Temples are marshlands cast in stone, the field of rushes, the luminous marshland of the dawn.

The star-covered ceilings of the pyramids in which the Pyramid Texts appear conjure the vivid and stunning reality of the night and twilight sky, in which the opening line, *the penis of Babay*, is not the penis of a baboon but a familiar sight: the sword of Orion. *The sword of Orion opens the doors of the sky*. The *sharp falcon* is a hieroglyphic formula for the star Sirius, much as we recognize the constellation Aquila, the eagle, and within it the bright star Al Tair, the bird.

In other words, this extensive poetic work opens by stating the place and the time. It presents this not as we would today, as an abstract historical notation, but as a truth of the physical world. The text begins with the coordinates of a star map, embedded in a visual image in the form of a riddle, a four-line verse ended by a horizontal line across the vertical column of hieroglyphs.

The four-line verse is followed by a second verse, a poetic line so vividly illustrated that the reader can easily make out the meaning of the words. Although the words are spelled out in hieroglyphic letters in a phonetic alphabet much like our own, each spelled-out word ends with a hieroglyphic picture that defines it. This is how hieroglyphs work: they are a combination of pictures as letters and pictures as pictures. The defining pictures of the bull, the fingers, the horizon, and the horns are all clearly there to see in the line *Would that the bull break the fingers of the horizon with its horns*. Taurus is told to rise, to get out of the way of Orion and Sirius on the rising diagonal.

What is conjured is motion. One is actually entering the night sky. The language that conjures this imagined and mysterious reality is not the language of myth but of metaphor. To think about how the poetic riddle is used as coding in English, one might look to *The Four Quartets*:

> Garlic and sapphires in the mud
> Clot the bedded axletree

The hidden meaning is presented as a cryptic image, and then the image is explained:

The trilling wire in the blood
Sings beneath inveterate scars
Appeasing long forgotten wars
The dance along the arteries
The circulation of the lymph
Are figured in the drift of stars

In the coded language of a riddle, Eliot presents the ultimate question: What is a human being? What is the body (its flesh, the mud embedded with garlic and sapphires, its skeleton, the tree)? What survives death? And then the answer: the eternal nature of the body, of the human being, resides in its dissolution. It is a paradox, an *enigma*.

This is both the subject and the method of the Pyramid Texts. There are two streams of subject matter in the compendium of mystical poetry that covers the walls of the pyramid beneath the peaked ceiling's gilding of stars. The first is the night sky, the moon and its phases, the movement of stars, violent sudden storms with their thunder and lightning. The second stream is the dissolution of the body. The life energy that resides in the body, as in all living things, is light, like starlight, like lightning. The medium by which the energy is freed is death. The two streams come together within the numinous representational atmosphere of the monument as the absorption of the freed light energy rising into the sky.

The task of this book is to demonstrate that far from being alien and incomprehensible, religious thought, and with it writing as high art in deep antiquity, is superbly lucid. That far from being ugly and stupid, it is supremely intelligent. The plan is to provide a map of the verses, as ideas and images are introduced and elaborated upon, to talk about the natural history of the hieroglyphs themselves, the poetic devices used, and to track throughout the presentation of religious thought, the ultimate focus of which, then as now, is truth: What is life on earth, how does it relate to time and the interrelationship of all things, what is death, what survives death?

This is what written language, perhaps not far removed from the paintings on the walls of caves, is for: to capture and conjure a reality that stands outside of time. The Pyramid Texts are irrefutable proof that this is what writing is, and that it is a sophisticated, multifaceted device, meant to work on different levels at once, not simply a method of note taking that emerged to preserve a longstanding oral tradition, as is generally taught. It is a separate stream of human creativity and insight, where the visual component is as strong as the aural component in speech. The beginning of written language is language *as writing*.

But do not take my word for it. See for yourself.

•

We regard grammar as superfluous, because it does not need to be known. It is embedded in the mind. Its analysis is thought to be merely a mechanical exercise, and inherently dry. But the opposite is true: the life is in the grammar, and it is there that you look. The way in is to proceed down a trail or a track or a corridor of grammar, which has the effect of breathing life into the apparent artifacts that are hieroglyphs.

I found this in an old notebook the other day. I don't know why I copied it down, but seeing it years later I was struck by how easy it was to read, and how it could be used to quickly illustrate the arrangement and grammar of hieroglyphs. It is a short poem that reads in columns from right to left. The first and last words are left out. The poem is set up as a pattern of the same words repeated, with subtle variation, as new words thread through them. The refrain, repeated in the first, the third, and the fifth columns, is *Death is before me today*.

> Death is before me today
> Like the smell of myrrh
> Like sitting under sails in the wind
> Death is before me today
> Like the smell of lilies
> Like sitting on the shore
> Of a drunken land
> Death is before me today

If you wanted to think about it further, you might look at the mix of pictures that are letters and pictures that are pictures which make up the range of hieroglyphic signs. There is nothing dated or stylized about them. There is some overlap between the pictures as letters and pictures that are meant to mean something in themselves. You are looking at something that is familiar

and simple, and yet highly intelligent and able to convey a deeper meaning. It is not archaic. It is not alien.

The real pleasure in hieroglyphs is looking at words in all of their dimensions of meaning; the sound, the image, the range of associations arising from the common experience of the physical world, and in the surprise recognition that you know it already. These are associations drawn from the poetic underlay of language itself, the tactile sense of the world that everyone knows.

Look, for example, at the birds. The owl is one of the most common hieroglyphs. It is the letter *m*. It is the same owl I saw and heard on the barn roof last night. The letter is the sound the owl makes, the name of the owl in Egypt, bu*ma*. The owl as *m* alone functions like the *w* in shorthand, for the small directive words that begin with *w* in English, what who while when with, begin with *m* in hieroglyphs as in their close relative Arabic: *maa*, with; *min*, from; *min*, who; *ma*, what; etc. (a variation on this sound, for example, is *manna* from heaven, *ma-na*, literally, "what is it?"). The word *death* is spelled with the owl and a loaf of the rounded peasant bread of the Egyptian countryside, the letter *t*. The word is spelled out, *mut*, the Arabic word for death; as in *checkmate*, from the Arabic for "the king [*sheikh*] is dead [*mat*]." In hieroglyphs there is often a visual dimension to the written word. Here for example one might note the relationship between the owl and the bread. There is a belief in rural Egypt that owls bring death, and that you ward it away by putting bread, the name of which is *aesh*, "life," on the roof of a house (thus Lilith is the long-winged nightbird that sucks the life out of the infant's mouth). After the word is spelled out there is often, though not always, a picture that has no phonic value but visually reinforces the sense of the word: here, a man with a stick raised to kill something.

The following word is a composite of a picture as a letter and a picture as a picture. It is made up of the owl—here, not as an owl but simply the letter *m* as the preposition *in*, and the face as the *face* itself. The meaning is literally "in your face," "right in front of you." The hieroglyphic face becomes a metaphor for what a face is, the preposition *upon* or *above*—the metaphor and the thing itself are blurred, only the context tells you which is which. In hieroglyphs the context, the progression of the phrase as verb subject object, will usually make it clear what a word is meant to do, as in the case of the columns here.

The vowels, which pattern clusters of hard consonants into nouns and

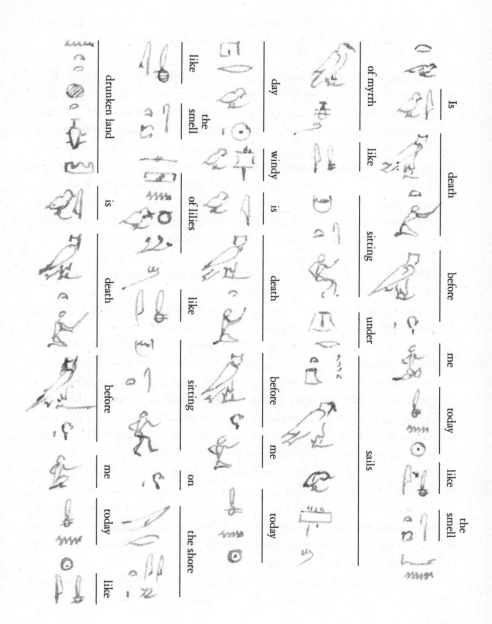

Is death before me today like the smell

of myrrh like sitting under sails

day windy is death before me on today

like the smell of lilies like sitting on the shore

drunken land is death before me today like

adjectives and verbs, are left out, leaving the consonants to stand for the word. Yet grammar resides in the vowels. Why are the vowels not written down?

Who has seen the wind?

The grammatical element that brings the words to life is the tiny chick beside the reed near the top of the column on the right, the hieroglyphic particle *iw*. This particle, tiny and subtle, like a tiny chick whose hidden movement gently moves the reeds, is not a word in itself. Its presence indicates the construction of a nominal sentence, a standard sentence construction in hieroglyphs as in Arabic, where it is often preceded by the conjunction *w*. The particle signals two nouns, or a noun and a phrase, placed together in apposition. There is no verb, but an affinity between two things arises simply in placing them together. This is not a common construction in English, except in poetry (the sky, a haze; sound, the sea), and the easiest way to translate the *iw*, generally, is as "is."

The bird in the word for "myrrh" is one of the most common carrion birds in Africa, the ashen-gray kite seen everywhere circling over cities and garbage heaps. The shrill sound it makes, *tiu*, is the sound of the letter that is a picture of this bird. Myrrh, *myrrh sweet bleeding in the bitter wound*, is the Arabic word for "bitter." In hieroglyphs the word is spelled out, *antiu*, but the meaning is signaled with an echoic effect: the letters themselves contain both the image of the bird and its sound. One is on familiar ground, the ground of the physical world. The sight and sound of the kite, now, as five thousand years ago, signals sadness, the gloom of mourning. The words are after what any true artist or poet is after: to capture, to conjure the living thing—to capture the sense of a thing as it relates to the living world.

Hieroglyphs are fluid, associations are signaled in inconsistent ways, yet the vocabulary of images that signal the qualities of words is universal. It belongs to the timeless realm of the sense field, of things that are known by heart: the disc is light, the sail is wind; *hst*, the stark landscape of desert hills and valleys, is a word that means both "desert" and "mountain," the desert hills, the out there, the desolate land.

The poem is so accurate in its tactile sense of the exhaustion of illness, the exhaustion near death, that it does not belong to any place or time.

Osiris

Words, are they alive or dead?
Osiris, is he alive or dead?
What is Osiris?
Osiris is anyone
As a rotting corpse.
Osiris is the life in all things,
Plant and animal.
Osiris as a word is the seat of the eye.
The dead thing is life.
What is the eye?

This is the territory of the mental magic trick that alone is strong enough to hold the truth: paradox. Plutarch wrote that Egypt hid truth in the vehicle of paradox: the riddle, the enigma. Osiris, he wrote, conquered the world with words, with the vehicle of enigma: poetry. The people who initially figured out hieroglyphs in the West were brilliant visionaries who understood what Plutarch meant, like the man whose pioneering work preceded Champollion: Thomas Young, the early nineteenth-century physician and polymath who discovered the prismatic nature of the eye, and the wave nature of light. Young understood instinctively that hieroglyphs were both pictures and words at once, that, like the eye itself, hieroglyphs are not flat artifacts but multifaceted, prismatic, with layers or angles of perception, and within them the power to carry the life of something that has died.

Hieroglyphs as Nature

The Pyramid of Unis

The outer shell of the pyramid complex on the Saqqara Plateau is dun-colored mud and stone abraded in the desert wind. But hidden within is a vividly illustrated study of the living world: the early attempts to domesticate wild animals, the catching and corralling of migrating cranes, and the solitary scimitar-horned oryx of the desert hills; marshlands where kingfishers hover in the reeds above the fish below, while concealed between them waits a watching otter. Buried within an outwardly collapsed pyramid, a nondescript heap of stone and sand, is a radical new vehicle for the preservation of life: a book. The detailed manuscript is inscribed from beginning to end on the hidden stone walls, from the entranceway to the innermost chamber. Where or how old the original composition is is not known, but this is the earliest version of the work that has yet been found, in the Old Kingdom Pyramid of Unis.

This is a riddle that has not been solved, although the words are simple. The wall is the page of a book. The columns are lines on a page. It is worthwhile looking hard at this wall, looking at every word, for this is the earliest surviving body of written poetry and religious philosophy in the world. It is important to say that what is written here presents a series of open questions. No one has figured out the meaning or the purpose of the Pyramid Texts. The questions presented are questions in the religious sense: the answers are not necessarily knowable; the object of contemplation is the question itself.

The columns read from left to right. The first line is missing where the wall was broken by forced entry into the tomb. The jagged wall of broken stone shows how fragile the lines of carved words are, words made of meticulously recorded objects, of animals and plants. The light of the mind sweeps over the stone to find the living thing. And there it stands, as it stands today: the peregrine falcon.

Entranceway, West Wall

But first draw back and look at the wall. You might find at once a patch of mental ground from which to probe this unfamiliar form of writing. The columns show the same structure that appeared in the poem on page 14: repetition. The first two surviving columns of hieroglyphic signs are nearly identical, and the third column takes signs from the prior two. The hieroglyphic words are repeated with subtle progressive variation in each line. The writing in the columns is unmistakably in the form of a poem, in the traditional sense. It is four lines long, and the first line is missing. Repetition draws the mind into an evolution of meaning, as though turning the object in the light.

Three primary elements are introduced in the first surviving column, then repeated in the second column and the third:

Fire

The first is fire, the word that appears at the top of the first and second columns. The word is spelled out *bkhkhw* (*b*/foot, *kh*/lined disc, *kh*/lined disc, *w*/chick), then marked with a picture, defining what it is. The picture shows a fire drill, a cord attached to a stick placed upright in a flat piece of wood with a hole in it—the cord wound around the stick will, as it rapidly unwinds, spin the stick to throw off sparks to start a fire. This hieroglyphic determinative is the standard designation for words having to do with fire. The fire is in a definite place, for it occurs between two prepositions, the face, *hr*, on or above, and the footstool, *shr*, beneath.

Netcher

The second primary element in the first column is the word *ntr*, netcher. It is a prayer flag. This word has been translated "god," as though this were a mythology, a story with characters engaged in actions such as scooping water on a fire. But really it is what a prayer flag is. It is a marker, a designation for something that is holy. There are three prayer flags, meaning three or more holy things are above the fire.

This is a riddle. It describes something real.

The Falcon

The third primary element that appears in the first column, and is repeated in the third, is the focus of the verse: the falcon, distinguished by the vivid black feathers that surround its eye like a marker. Hieroglyphs are dense composite metaphors. An animal is what it does. The peregrine falcon is the fastest animal on earth, clocked in flight at nearly three hundred miles per hour. The falcon's distinguishing pattern of flight is embedded in its name. In hieroglyphs the name is *qher*, in Arabic sa*qher* (*sagr*), in Greek *kirk*e (Circe). The related word in English is *gyre*, circle.

The falcon has long been translated as the god Horus, the Egyptian word *qhr* as spelled two thousand years later by the Greeks. But what is here on the pyramid wall is simply the picture of a falcon. The picture stands alone but conveys compounded meanings: Horus, meaning the falcon, is the child of Osiris. Osiris is the corpse. The falcon is its child, rising away in peregrine circles from all that dies: the universal shamanic image of the spirit rising from the body in the form of a bird. The soul rises in a gyre. DNA rises in a helix. How closely related the meaning of the hieroglyphic text is to some absolutely fundamental design of life: turning is transformation.

The sense of turning is implicit, in the falcon as in the fire drill—the prehistoric device that miraculously spins fire, heat, and light into being, out of thin air.

O Sages standing in God's holy fire
As in the gold mosaic on the wall
Come from your holy fire
Perne in a gyre

Yeats turns *perne*, a Greek word for "falcon," into the verb "to turn." He uses the image of a living thing to signify its characteristic motion, applying the sense of the animal's motion to another thing. This is the ingenious method the Egyptians devised in the development of writing. It is a trick of mirrors, capturing an image and reflecting it onto something else. And it highlights a question that arises on this wall: What is a noun? And what is a verb? And what is the difference between them? Like the vowels that activate the words, the verbs that thread through them are the movement that activates the line. In the Pyramid Texts, as in Yeats above, the verb is often the motion that rises from the thing itself, the noun, by repeating the name of the thing with a prefix or a suffix for a tag. Or it repeats the name in a verb that sounds the same, indicating the close relationship between the verb and the noun in a pun.

The language is deliberately repetitive; the same words are used as concepts are introduced and elaborated upon. The words are the basic hieroglyphic vocabulary, simple and clear, as clarity is critical for the valid representation of an actual thing. Clutter merely obscures it. As in Plato's Greek, or Auden's English, the sophistication of the language lies in the skillful arrangement of familiar words. The complexity lies not in the words themselves but in the meaning. Here the failure to recognize the verb as a simple familiar word is the key to the mistranslation.

The verb, appearing in the first column and repeated in the second, is *iknt* (*i*/reed, *k*/basket, *n*/wave, *t*/bread), instantly recognizable as a verb form, precisely as in Arabic today, by the addition of an initial *i* and a final *t*. Because *iknt* has not been recognized as a common word it has not been successfully defined. Allen, assuming that the prayer flags are gods in a myth, and that they must be doing something that has to do with fire, sees it as a spelling variant of the word *cup* (*qnt*) and translates the word *scoop* (with the idea of water implied). Piankoff also made the assumption that the prayer flags are gods and guessed that the word might mean "assemble"? (Piankoff politely puts in a question mark).

Yet the verb is not a mystery, and the translation of the word is not arbitrary or difficult. *Kn* is a common root in hieroglyphs. It is the word for "dark" (as in *knh*, dark, darken; *knhw*, darkness; *kni*, be sullen; *knmt*, darkness). This verbal form of *kn*, *ikn*, appears again within the monument on the east wall of the antechamber in verse twenty, with the unmistakable meaning *grow dark*. (*ikn hay*, grow dark O serpent).

The holy things grow dark is the literal translation of this, the earliest known poetic line:

Over the fire
Beneath the holy ones as they grow dark
As the falcon flies, as the falcon flies
May Unis rise into this fire
Beneath the holy ones as they grow dark

The verb that defines the falcon's action is *sbn* (*s*/knotted cord, *b*/foot, *n*/wave). This word appears throughout the Pyramid Texts with things that rise up away from the earth, away from death. It appears here before the falcon and is immediately repeated before the name of the dead person, who thus takes on the action and identity of the falcon. The name is within a knotted protection cord (for that is what the "cartouche" is). Like a blank in a legal document, the cord could contain any name.

The Path

 The netchers, the prayer flags, the things marked holy, make a path. The hieroglyph for "path" is a stretch of road between three trees or bushes. This is the first written use of the word for "path" in the religious sense. The netchers make a path for the spirit to rise through the fire. At the top of the third column a causative *s* is added to the word for "path" (*wat*), turning it into a verb (*s-wa*), as Unis takes the path.

The Eye

What makes the path is the eye. The eye here serves grammatically as a verb. But one cannot say, in the reading of this multilevel religious text, that it is just a verb, that nothing else is meant. As a verb the eye means to create, to make out of thin air, but there is an element of seeing involved in creation. The eye creates the concept in the mind.

Over the fire
Beneath the holy ones as they grow dark
As a falcon flies, as a falcon flies,
May Unis rise into this fire
Beneath the holy ones as they grow dark
They make a path for Unis
Unis takes the path

 The last words of the verse are *Unis is*, or *becomes*, *qhr spd*, "the sharp falcon"; *spd* means both "sharp" and what is sharp, the triangle. The picture of a triangle is what defines the word. Here it forms part of an odd composite hieroglyph, a hapax legomenon, a compound word that does not appear again but is created just for this place in the text. This composite, beneath the name of Unis, is the hieroglyphic letter *p* (the square, a reed mat) and, affixed to the *p* on the right, the letter *i* (the flowering head of the marsh reed phragmites). Affixed to the *p* on the left is a triangle. Beneath this unusual conflated notation, *pi + triangle*, stands the falcon. The notation alters the falcon itself, for the triangle in hieroglyphs is the sign of a star, Sirius.

The meaning of the missing first line was inferred from the tomb of Senwosret-Ankh hundreds of years later, where there is a similar but not identical version of these beginning verses. There the first words are *djed medw*, the formula for the beginning of a verse, the cobra and the walking stick: *say the words*.

The Thread

The word that follows is a standard geometrical notation: *sta* (*setcha*). The determinative is the picture of string being unspooled. This word is commonly used to describe the measuring out of a grid, as in the yearly remeasuring after the flood of the boundaries of small square plots of land for fields, using string pulled tight around posts hammered into the ground, much as one would measure out a garden plot today. As a verb it means "to pull," "to unspool a thread." The word that follows is *qhnn*. It is the common word in hieroglyphs for "penis."

This image is defined by the word that follows it, in the genitive by virtue of its position. The word is *ba*. It is the word for "soul." The *ba* is a long-legged waterbird. In the Pyramid of Unis this bird is the white stork. On their seasonal migration north and south the white storks are seen in the Nile Valley in huge numbers funneling up into the sky, an indelible sight, no doubt what is meant by the white bird as the image of the disembodied soul drawn up into the sky.

The hieroglyph comes to be drawn with a mark on its throat, a conflation with the wattled crane, a similar migratory waterbird. In the Pyramid of Unis the hieroglyph appears as both birds, though predominantly without the mark as an unmistakable miniature of the white stork. Three storks or cranes together form the hieroglyph that represents the power or force of a living person.

The wattle becomes a hieroglyphic flag emphasizing the throat of the crane, which is known for its beautiful sound. The sky filled with the sound of cranes, like the sound of wild geese, is a marker for the turning of the seasons.

The emphasis, the mark, flags what is relevant in the animal. The raised tail of the dangerous wild dog is lightning. A halo of silvery fur is the mind.

In Arabic the action of a verb or the quality of a noun becomes emphatic, is intensified, by doubling the sound: *wuswus*/whisper, *rufruf*/flutter, *loglog*/babble. *Hubbub* is a doubling of the Arabic word for "love." *Ruckus* is the Arabic word for "dance." In the English version of the word the sound of the central consonant is intensified to intensify the action conveyed in the word. *Alfalfa* is Arabic for "a thousand thousand," the best fodder crop; "pepper" is the English pronunciation of *felfel*. This kind of linguistic doubling is a common device in Egypt, and it is a common device in hieroglyphs.

Here the word *ba* (soul) is doubled for emphasis in much the same way: *Babay*. The tail feathers of the standing stork, and the two reeds together that comprise the final letter *y*, are all that can clearly be made out on the broken wall in the Pyramid of Unis.

The spool can either be a transitive verb, *pulls* (the thread), or a notation for measuring out a grid. The beginning of the reconstructed missing line has two possible readings:

Say the words,
The penis of the great soul
Pulls (the thread) open(ing) the doors of the sky

or

Say the words,
(On the grid:)
The penis of the great soul
Opens the doors to the sky

The sky is the picture of the bar of the sky, *pt*. The door of the sky is the picture of two facing swinging doors. But the gate to the path is a rebus. The word for "gate," *liw*, is the picture of a lion, for gate and lion are the same word. They are homonyms. It is a pun. And yet, the lion is the gate. The gate is dangerous. It is guarded. It is sacred. It is sealed. The word for "seal," *htm*, the picture of a seal on a cord, is the word for "seal" in Arabic today.

The penis of the great soul
Opens the doors to the sky
The doors seal again
The gate to the path over the fire
Beneath the holy ones as they grow dark
As the falcon flies, as the falcon flies,
May Unis rise into this fire
Beneath the holy ones as they grow dark
They make a path for Unis
Unis takes the path
Unis becomes the falcon star, Sirius

There is a sense of astonishment as the iconographic riddle clarifies before one's eyes. The solution to the riddle comes with a clarity that sweeps away all of the dust and fog that has surrounded hieroglyphs for centuries. This is a densely compounded but highly precise reading of astronomy. It is a star map:

The fire is the dawn
The holy ones, stars

The path, the thread of stars rising
In the door of the sky: the eastern horizon
Babay is the great soul, the great man of light, Orion,
The *qhnn* Babay is Orion's sword.

The Orion nebula is in the door of the sky. It is rising. The Orion nebula directly precedes Sirius on the path of rising stars. The soul rising like a bird becomes the star.

This is a moment in time, not a historical moment but the dawn of a day in mid-July when the dawn rising of Sirius signals the rising of the Nile.

VERSE 1
Say the words:
The sword of Orion opens the doors of the sky.
Before the doors close again the gate to the path
Over the fire, beneath the holy ones as they grow dark
As a falcon flies as a falcon flies, may Unis rise into this fire
Beneath the holy ones as they grow dark.
They make a path for Unis, Unis takes the path,
Unis becomes the falcon star, Sirius.

•

Taurus

That the Pyramid Texts are astronomical in nature is confirmed immediately by the second verse, which begins beneath the line across the fourth column that marks the end of the first verse. The subject of the second verse is visible at once. It is the picture of a bull with very long horns. It is the bull of the distinctive African longhorn cattle. Its name is spelled out with the wave (*n*) and the clay oven (*g*), *neg*. The verb following the bull is the word "to break"; it is spelled in exactly the same way, with the wave and the oven, ending with the Egyptian vulture (a semivowel guttural *a/r* sound), *nega*. The verb is a pun on the animal's name, as though the action, the sound of the verb, arises from the name of the animal itself, as though the animal is inseparable from its action.

Say the words:
Would that the Bull break the fingers of the horizon of
        earth with its horns.
Come out. Rise.

On the most basic level the sense of the line is easily
made out just by looking at the words. It is a clear and simple
poetic line, with wordplays in puns. The literal elements are
visible at a glance: the fingers holding back the bull below the
horizon are the pictures of the three fingers. The hieroglyphic
pair of horns is a noun, *wpt*, marked by the picture of the
horns of the bull. But a pun is implicit in the horns: as a
verb this hieroglyph means "to open." The horizon of the
earth is the word *Akher*, often though not here (as ending
pictures vary considerably) marked with the Sphinx as a
sign determinative. R. O. Faulkner's *Dictionary of Middle
Egyptian* draws the word with two lion heads to define it; the
lion heads look both ways.

Akher is the Arabic word for "the end," "the edge of the
earth." In Greek the word is *Acheron*, "the gate of hell." Is
the Sphinx itself the riddle, the lion that is the gate? The treasure
within is the meaning, hidden in poetic code: Hell is the fire
from under the edge of the earth. It is the light of dawn.

Ikher is the imperative form of the verb "to fall" or "to
come out of something," *kher*, which occurs throughout the
Pyramid Texts paired with the verb *sbn*, "to rise." *Come out. Rise*. It is used
here as a pun on *Akher*.

The verse unmistakably describes the rising of the constellation Taurus:
the head of a bull with very long horns. Taurus is told to rise, *sbn*, the verb
used of Sirius rising in the previous verse. Taurus is told to get out of the
way, to break the fingers of the horizon with its long horns. To open the door.
For Taurus directly precedes Orion and Sirius on the diagonal of rising stars.
This is an extremely valuable verse, because it is the earliest written reference
to the constellation Taurus.

•

The Moon

The third verse begins at the bottom of the fifth column. Following the opening formula, *Unis pi*, "Unis becomes," is the word *i'n*, the Hamadryas baboon. In the first verse Unis becomes the rising falcon as the star Sirius. The rising soul of the dead next appears as the baboon, not the animal itself, for if the falcon is Sirius, what is the baboon? What does the baboon mean in Egypt? This animal is not a coarse or comic figure but rare, revered, remembered from long ago and far away. It is the Hamadryas baboon of the desert grasslands, with long, slender humanlike hands and a face of strange, watching intelligence. With its distinctive halo of diaphanous long silver fur about its head, the Hamadryas is the avatar for the mind. This iconographic conception carried over from an earlier time, for the Hamadryas is not an animal of the Nile Valley but of the old days, when the inhabitants of the Nile Valley lived in the vast grasslands of what became the Sahara in the rapid desertification of the Neolithic, when people fled the growing desert in search of water and came down to the Nile. Like the hermit ibis, the hieroglyph for the light body, another animal with a haloed head, the Hamadryas belongs to the remembered landscape of semiarid scrub. It is a shy animal that lives on the pods and flowers of the acacia tree, the smell of which is almost intoxicating in its dry, faint sweetness. It is the smell of the Egyptian desert. The pod of the acacia is the hieroglyph for "sweet," *ndjm*. Its flowers are called *nuar*, "lights." Where this tree grows in the desert there is water. It is the tree of the sweetness of knowledge. Out of its wood the arc of the covenant was made. The name for the tree in both hieroglyphs and Egyptian Arabic today is the *sant* tree.

Thoth is the name Plato used in the *Timaeus* for this avatar, a Greek rendering of its hieroglyphic name, *Djehuty*. The early representations of Thoth are of a Hamadryas baboon with a moon on its head. This is because Thoth is the moon—not the moon as a god but what the moon represents. Like the word *Buddha*, from the Sanskrit word *buddhir*, "to know," Thoth is the subtle but real radiance of the electric awakening of intelligence. The awakened mind understood the patterns in nature and saw, then created, a system of signs to mark and predict them: mathematics and written language. The phases of the moon taught time and, inseparable from it, the intricacy of measurement, the fractions added and subtracted to the luminous body of the moon each day. The moon is both understanding and what is understood, *the silver eye* that sees and illuminates what it sees at the same time. Unis is absorbed into this composite metaphor for nonduality, *the dawning moon of the mind*, the radiant eternal eye.

The words that follow the baboon are *htt ptt*, spelled out here without pictorial determinatives. Piankoff sees the words as the names of different kinds of baboons: Unis is an *ian* baboon, a *hetet* baboon, a *patet* baboon. Allen sees them as participles: *Unis is a screeching, howling baboon.* The evident meaning on the wall is simpler than either interpretation. In the later, parallel text in Senwosret-Ankh (shown on the right, contrasting the spelling of the word in the Pyramid of Unis on the left), the word *htt* is marked with a pictorial determinative: the desert landscape discussed in the poem cited at the beginning of this book, making clear that this is simply a spelling variant of the common word *hst*, *the desert hills*, the home of the Hamadryas. Spelling variants are common in the Pyramid Texts where the hieroglyphs are fluid and not standardized, and reversals and regional variation in spelling and pronunciation are common in Egyptian even today. The likely answer is that, as in Greek lyric poetry, words have both prose forms and poetic forms, and here *htt* and *ptt* (of old; spelled with the pintail duck taking flight, the letter *pa*) are made to agree with each other both for the aesthetics of the visual construction and for the sound and rhythm of the passage.

Unis becomes the baboon of the desert hills of old

The following word, *'rt*, is a participle from *'r* ('/arm, r/mouth), the verb "to rise." It is the common description of and name for the cobra, and appears as such in the bottom of the first column on the opposite wall. The

word *cobra* is a description of an animal. It is the feminine of the Arabic word *kabir* (large). The cobra is the largest venomous snake in the world, *kabra*. The word *'rt* similarly is a description of a different aspect of the same animal: it is the snake that rises up. In this third verse something else is rising up. The hieroglyphic determinative tells you what it is. It is the circle, commonly used to indicate a source of light: *The rising circle of light is Unis.*

The word at the bottom of the column is *sa* (*s*/thread, *a*/vulture) marked with the looped bowstring as a determinative. This is the word for wisdom in hieroglyphs, where it is written both with and without a final *r*. This word appears in Arabic for knowledge, and for poetry (*shaar*: v., to know; n., poetry). Here it is used as an adjective, following the noun it modifies, the picture of a face: *The wise face is Unis.*

How can this simple image, with a kind of stately loveliness expressed by the simplicity of the hieroglyphs themselves, be misconstrued to mean the anus of a screeching baboon? The verse has an incantatory quality that is built around a visual image and the use of repetition to state different aspects, different views, of what the image is: the luminous disc of light in the sky is like a watching face, like a detached head, like a radiant eye.

The word that follows *wise* in the progression of stated qualities is a key word in Egyptian religious thought. Like the word *omphalos* in Greek, it is a word that means the center of a thing as both its essence and its eye. It is the mysterious word *imakh*. As an adjective this word means holy, radiant, shining. What it is is shown in the hieroglyph: it is the spinal cord, visible hanging down from the spine and a section of ribs. The disembodied spinal cord is shining, shockingly white, and in this tradition it has a very potent meaning: it is the cord of life itself. The spinal cord pulled out of the spine looks like a glowing white headless snake.

The hieroglyphs in the progression could not be clearer and more straightforward; the face is the face itself, followed by the head itself, the eye itself:

VERSE 3

Say the words:
Unis becomes the baboon
Of the desert hills of old
The rising disc of light is Unis
The wise face is Unis

The shining one is Unis
The face, the head is Unis,
The eye is Unis

What is described is the rising of the luminous haloed moon: it is "the Man in the Moon." The following word is one of the most common expressions in Egypt today, *haneean*, "rejoice." As *neg* (bull) is a pun on *nega* (break), *haneean* is a sonal pun on the word for "baboon," *i'n* (*eean*); the action is encoded in the animal's name.

•

I would like at this point to pause and state the purpose of going over the hieroglyphs themselves in depth, as I am doing in the verses presented on this first wall. I am asking the reader to consider the hieroglyphic text itself, to really look at it, in order to see its simplicity, its clarity, and its intelligence, and with me to probe what it means. For the meaning has not yet been understood. It is important to understand right at the start that the familiar interpretation of Egyptian religion, an interpretation that has long made Egypt seem archaic, strange, and, more important, irrelevant, is based on the institutionalized mistranslation of Egyptian religious literature demonstrated in the excerpt on pages 10–11, a convention of mistranslation that does not hold up if you look at the hieroglyphs themselves.

But the relevant question is much larger than that. It is an enormous question. What is Egyptian religious thought? What did the Egyptians know? And how has their perception, a perception that dates to and is embedded in the formation of written language itself, affected the development of culture and philosophy as we know it, the very way we see the world?

Taurus, Orion, and Sirius rising in the light of dawn, the moon becoming full, are among the most beautiful sights on earth today, as they were five thousand years ago. This first wall presents them as the progression of celestial phenomena key to the mechanism that underlies life itself. That mechanism is time. The Egyptians invented time as we know it. And they did so by means of the empirical observation of the night sky.

The hieroglyphic name for *The Egyptian Book of the Dead* is the *Am Duwat*, literally, "Among the Stars at Dawn." Yet the obvious fact that the primary work of literature and religious philosophy in Egypt is astronomical has been completely missed. Part of the reason for this is simply the mistaking of poetry for prose. Poetry predates prose. It is telegraphic and fragmentary by nature. Poetry is dynamic: the meaning is signaled as a glimpse of the active hidden layers of reality. Prose is static: the meaning is historical, hence inert. The view that this text is a prose narrative means that it is merely a historical document in which Unis, the historical figure, is understood to be the subject. Unis is and does this and that. In the poetic form Unis as a subject is unimportant. The subject is the writing itself. Unis is merely a name, placed as an afterthought in a finished work. The verbs and actions do not cluster around him. He is placed within an imagined reality and takes on its atmosphere.

The problem of mistaking what are essentially poetic conceits as prose has given rise to the idea of myth, the Greek word for "word." The institutionalized misassumption is that earlier religious systems are based on ignorance and play out in childish stories characterized by an anthropomorphized understanding of the world. But the simplistic view that sees existence only in human terms arises in an alienation from nature that belongs not to an ancient but to a modern society. Egyptian systems of thought and technology, one of which is written language, do not draw on the mere ephemeral dramas of human life. What they are after is what lasts: the essence of physical reality, not only to understand it but to work with it, to make things that work.

For more than a century different thinkers have tried to correct the misimpression that earlier religious systems are based on myth. Frazer's primary insight in *The Golden Bough* is that Christ is Osiris, and that Osiris is death. Harrison's *Themis* is an explanation of nature as the underlay of all of Greek religion. Graves's *The White Goddess* is a study of poetry as code for the interpretation of the natural world. In *The Marriage of Cadmus and Harmony* Calasso dissipated the concept of myth by placing what were obviously different versions of the same motif together in such a way that the reader saw that they were not merely stories but different presentations of the same communication of a historical event or religious idea. Though stories derive from the formulation of ideas, and continue on simply as stories, the insight lies in the original formulation.

In the Pyramid Texts one does not have to peel back layers of derivative story to find the original idea. There is no story. Isis and Osiris are not characters. They are not personalities. They are words. As such they are what words are, they are concepts. Isis is *the throne*, the numinous ground of space itself. Osiris is the active principle within this radiant surround, this pervasive inevitability of disintegration and resurrection. The active principle is the eye, the disembodied ordering intelligence of the universe, the paradox that is the mind of space, the mind of being as dissolution and manifestation, omniscient in the inevitability of its profound order, an order that spins everything predictably out to the last detail.

Much as hieroglyphs themselves represent both concrete things and their metaphorical dimensions, a religious text can be read on different levels. It can be read on the surface as the composition itself, or one can look for the deeper meaning within. The meaning of the Egyptian religious tradition is a familiar yet undiscovered country. We are in the territory. Now to define the map: the sequence of poetic tropes that track the journey into and out of form, from mortality to immortality, the trail of the falcon, the serpent, the eye, and the star.

This trail can only be followed poetically. It is not straightforward but circular, and dense with layers of meaning. Mistakes in interpretation are inevitable. Some words and phrases can be translated in different ways. Some things cannot be known. But the highly refined poetic stucture and the astronomical nature of the text are unmistakable. In this earliest version of the Pyramid Texts inscribed in columns on the twelve inside walls of the two corridors and two rooms within the Pyramid of Unis, each wall is a distinct chapter, leading the reader through a logical argument expressed in an unfolding series of poetic riddles. The primary concept of Egyptian religion is introduced in the first verse, embodied in the sense impression made by the motion of a bird of the prehistoric desert world. The bird is not a myth but a suggestion that conveys a numinous, multilevel metaphor. It is at once the vivid, newly freed motion of the infant child of the dead body: the wild energy that rises from the shell of the corpse back into the sky; and it is the continuous motion of rising itself, the dappled wings of rising and setting stars that are the variegated wheel of time as eternity. The resolution of the antechamber, the room beyond the entranceway, is the paradox that defines what rises from the body: it is a bird, and yet it is a snake, the snake that casts off the skin of death. In the sarcophagus chamber the description is refined as the snake emerging from the body becomes the disembodied eye.

This loose range of metaphors describes something real: the eye in the body is the snake of the central nervous system in the channel of the rising spine. As it leaves the body at death this serpentine current of energy is "thrown out"; rising like a bird, it becomes pure rising light. The subject of the text is the ultimate nature of the human body and mind. At death this essence, the light that is in fact the ultimate reality of a human life, is reabsorbed into the universe with its fluctuations of infinite light, the stars, the moon, their paths, their harmonious eternal movement in the sky. Hence the work is an investigation of the truth of the physical world, a truth that can only be apprehended through the associative imagery of poetry, which triggers a deep recognition on the physical level. What, after all, is the eye, defined as "an outpocketing of the central nervous system"? What is seeing, the essence of which is pure awareness? This awareness illuminates its object. It sees and shines as light. Is the mind, the nature of which is like a live electric current, the light energy that leaves the body at death? Is it indeed one with the light of the universe? In the antechamber doubts begin to be expressed: the person is dead, *find his mind*. Whatever leaves the body at death, the person ceases to exist.

Every wall has a different quality of language and presents a different aspect of the argument as it unfolds. The most significant passages are on the gables, the triangular sections within the monument that point upward. On the east gable of the antechamber is the "Cannibal Hymn," a name given to this section because of an Egyptologist's translation of the phrase *ankh m* a century ago. The owl as the letter *m* is the common abbreviation for hieroglyphic words that begin with *m*, among them the words for "with," "from," "in," and "as." In the "Cannibal Hymn" Egyptologists have agreed that instead of the obvious translation, *lives [ankh] with [m]* or *as his ancestors*, the phrase here means *lives on them*, an English colloquialism that one would hardly expect to find in hieroglyphs, meaning, incredibly, *eats them*: a classic example of how this critically important body of writing has been misunderstood, misrepresented, and marginalized.

For far from being obscure and strange, the verses in the Pyramid of Unis resonate with the familiar motifs of later religions. The virgin birth appears in the pyramid not as a religious mystery but as a riddle, *the one who gave birth but didn't know it*. It is the mother of all things, the sky itself, empty space. *Mary* is a hieroglyphic word for this all-embracing reality, a word that means "beloved." The soul leaves *the garden*: the earth itself, where the tree with the sweetness of knowledge is the human body, and within it the serpent, the name of which is *hayy*, "life." The infant soul rises away from the garden to heaven through *the field of rushes*, the eastern stars at dawn; *moses*, the word for "infant" in hieroglyphs, is itself the bright star in the east, the soul becoming Sirius as it rises in the dawn. *The three wise men* that presage its appearance are the three stars in the belt of Orion. The verses on the pyramid walls elaborate the concepts of esoteric Buddhism: the two truths (*maaty*), emptiness (*shu*), omniscience (the eye), the emanation body (the *ka*). The serpent rising within the human body is *the third eye*, the fire-breathing dragon of heat and light.

Others have long speculated that this is the original, universal religious text. Yet far from being primitive, or even archaic, it is clearly the work of accomplished writers (for stylistically there seems to be more than one), writers who are playing with words, raising the radical question: Is it possible that what is conventionally thought of as religion is not a record of historical events but is based on poetic formulations of the actual world? Auden wrote that poetry makes nothing happen. But in this religious system, that is where the power lies. The soul as an initiate in the process of immortality is *the one who knows the words*, the poet who wanders off into the dark to be torn apart by the glittering stream of stars. The cult of the poet, the cult of Orpheus, which pervades the writings attributed to Pythagoras, the poetic lines of Heraclitus, Pindar, and others, would seem to be the Egyptian cult of life in death, *the golden flow of falcon flesh* that is the rising snake of fire within, the *ophis*. The Orpheus symbology introduced into Greece in the sixth century B.C. is present throughout the Pyramid Texts: death as snakebite, the journey into and out of the land of the dead, death as reawakening, the questioning of the newborn soul, the lake of memory, the holy transforming fire. The Orphic formulas of Classical Greece appear in the pyramid as hieroglyphic palindromes, as the soul is introduced to the entities of the sky with the singsong *you know him, he knows you*, for the soul must remember itself and where it comes from. "Who are you?" the soul is asked. The answer, "I am a child of the starry dawn."

VERSE 4

                     The North Star as the Axis Mundi

O Star that sits shining,
Does Unis not give you his life force,

That he remain ever after as a holy thing,
That in the axis of the wheel
Unis may float to the sky

Astronomers in the past have noted the geometrical correspondences with the stars in Egyptian religious architecture: that the great pyramid at Giza, for example, is perfectly aligned with the North Star. They have speculated that Egyptian temples were created for astronomical purposes—and have assumed that Egyptian religion was essentially astronomy. Egyptologists have refuted these informed conclusions on the basis of philology, meaning the authority of their translations, and have insisted that the subject of the Pyramid Texts is a sun cult in Heliopolis, "sun city," some distance away from the pyramids themselves. The argument for this interpretation resides in the translation of a hieroglyphic phrase that occurs in verse 4 on the west wall of the entranceway. The reader can evaluate the validity of the claims on both sides by examining the hieroglyphs in this verse. The subject of the verse is a star, a hieroglyph that appears at the top of the second column. It is introduced by the first word in the verse, the flowering marsh reed, the hieroglyphic letter *i/y*. This is one of the most familiar expressions in Arabic, *ya*; like *oh* in English, it is the formal address:

ya qhmy sqhd
O Star that sits (*qhmy*) shining (*sqhd*)

The opening line signals the identity of what is conjured in the poetic lines of the verse, for it is a pun on the name of the North Star: *ihm* (the one who does not know) *sk* (destruction). As the moon and Sirius are similarly conjured though not named in the previous verses, the North Star as a prominent feature of the night sky is introduced in a trick verbal formula.

The key phrase that determines the validity of the refutation that Egyptian religion is not a reading of astronomy occurs at the end of this verse. It consists of three common hieroglyphic signs: the picture of a column, *iwn*, a jar, the letter *nw*, and a circle that contains four triangles, one apparently defining each direction. This marked circle is the hieroglyph *nywt*, a sign that becomes the designation for place in the general sense, as though the picture is of an X marking a spot, or a crossroads. This hieroglyphic phrase has been read as the city Heliopolis. The way to test out the validity of the translation of this phrase as the name of a specific city is to examine its use in a parallel verse, verse 7 in the antechamber, where the meaning of the phrase is teased out in the conventions of Egyptian poetry: repeated over and over with subtle progressive adjustments in the words that surround it. To test out the meaning of the phrase as Heliopolis, consider Allen's translation of the verse:

> Recitation: There is a Heliopolitan in Unis, god: your Heliopolitan is in Unis, god; There is a Heliopolitan in Unis, Sun: your Heliopolitan is in Unis, Sun. The mother of Unis is a Heliopolitan, the father of Unis is a Heliopolitan, and Unis himself is a Heliopolitan, born in Heliopolis . . .

Then read the hieroglyphs as what they represent, a column in a circle, an axis in a wheel:

> The axis is in Unis, the holy falcon is the axis in Unis,
>   light of the axis, you are in Unis,
> the light is the mother of Unis, the axis is the father of
>   Unis, Unis himself is the axis,
> the axis creates and the axis destroys, the light of the
>   stars, and the light of men.

The literal reading of the verse is an elegant description of

the fixed point around which the sky turns, the North Star. The soul of the king becomes the center of the universe, *the still point of the turning world*. The holy falcon with its glittering wings is the sky as revolving time, the arising and dissolution of all living things. The repetition in the verse mimics the physical reality of the turning sky. The noun remains constant, as the words around it change, embodying the concept of the turning wheel.

> Because I do not hope to turn again
> Because I do not hope
> Because I do not hope to turn
>
> —T. S. Eliot

Is the text meant to convey a meaningless myth or a profound insight? The answer lies in the hieroglyphic star in the pun that begins verse 4 on the west wall of the entranceway, *ya hmy sqhd*, signaling that the reality embedded in the lines is *ihm sk*, the North Star.

This introductory phrase is followed by a picture of shrugging arms, the negative, which modifies the verb *to give*, the pyramid, or specifically a pyramid-shaped bread, sometimes placed in an open hand as the designation of this pervasive verb *to give*: di (Greek: *di/domi*; Latin: *do*; Sanskrit: *do*; Arabic: *di*). What is requested to be given is the first representation in the text of the *ka*, the upraised arms, preceded by a twisted thread (*h/q*, a suffix for the causative). This word has been translated as *magic*, as though this were the work of primitive people who believed in magic, but the idea really is that of the energy in the body that survives the body at death, the chi.

The final image uses the implicit suggestion of the sky as a wheel to introduce the subject of the next verse. It is the water skin, *shd*, an object that brings to mind the connection between the wheel and water. A water skin filled with air rises through the water, suggesting the rising of the water itself. As a verb it means "to bob up." May the soul bob up on the turning wheel of the sky, as a water skin bobs forcefully up through the water. As a noun the water skin is the standard epithet for the animal that does precisely this, the crocodile. *Seshed*, the doubling noun from the causative form of this verb, is the lightning bolt, the defining picture for which in hieroglyphs is the crocodile, a dangerous animal that moves with lightning speed. This animal metaphor is the vehicle of the sense conveyed in the following verse.

·

The Nile

Say the words:
Unis comes today before the rising, swirling flood
Unis becomes the crocodile, green, floating up, face watching,
    chest raised,
He rushes out, rising as a leg and great tail within the shining
    light,
He goes to his banks of silt in the great swirling flood,
To the still place in the reeds on the rim of the sky.
He greens the green reeds on the banks of the sky.
He brings his precious green to the great eye in the heart of the
    reeds.
He takes his place on the luminous rim of the sky.
Unis rises as the crocodile, son of the water, Unis eats with its
    mouth,
Urinates, copulates with its penis. Unis becomes (the life-giving
    water of) semen itself,
Seizing women in their husbands' arms, wherever love arises,
    according to its nature.

A glance at the wall shows the subject of the fifth and final verse: water. Hidden in the waves is the danger of the rising water, personified by the danger rising in the water, the crocodile. The verse is a dynamic description of both the element and the animal. The swirling throb of rising water is conveyed by the word *kbb*, a word like *ebb*. The economy of the previous verses gives way to a kind of wild fluidity that conjures both the sight and the sound of the rushing flood that brings the miraculous greening of life. The crocodile is the rising of greenness itself. The intensity of the motion as the meaning of the animal is embodied in a visual pun on its name that contains the typical sweetness of Egyptian humor. The name of the crocodile is *sbk* (*s*/thread, *b*/leg, *k*/basket). *Unis pi sbk. Unis becomes the crocodile.* Beside the word *sbk* on the wall is the word

for "leg," *sbkh*, with the same letters but a different, aspirated *k*. Both words are spelled with a leg, which is the letter *b*. The second word ends with the leg, not as a letter but as a defining picture drawn slightly differently. Immediately below this picture is the word *khbs* (*kh*/lined disc, *b*/leg, *s*/knotted cord), the word for "tail," spelled out and followed by the picture of a tail. The word for "tail" is the word for both "leg" and "crocodile" spelled phonically backward. It is a hieroglyphic joke. Yet, by means of the words, the animal is dissolved into and hidden within its parts. There is a sense of the sliding meaning of things, of the drifting quality of the recognition of things, of the drifting quality of language forming words like the flow of mud forming banks in the river.

The first wall begins with fire and ends with water, the essential formula of alchemy applied to the dramatic reality of the flood rising with the star in the fire of the dawn. This final verse stands apart from the others, as ingeniously constructed on three different levels at once: the meaning,

the sound, and the words as images on the wall. The primary hieroglyphs are pictures of water and green reeds. The three reeds standing together form the word *sekut*: the hieroglyph for "marsh" is the Arabic word for "silence," an incidental pun that conjures the whispering sound of the marsh reeds in the wind. Everything is in motion, the motion of the water forming the precious banks of rich black mud, the name of which, *chem* (chemistry), is the hieroglyphic word for Egypt. Does the feather hieroglyph mean *feather-green* (like the green bee eater with its brilliant green feathers)? Or is the color green *floating up like a feather* (the meaning of the hieroglyphic feather as a verb). The feather grammatically applies to the crocodile, *rushing, rising, floating up through the water* as the green serpent that is the life in all things, water and seed at once, *pure semen* (*semen* is the Latin word for seed). The verse is filled with echoic devices: *mrr* (loving) echoes *r mr* (to [*r*] the shore [*mr*]). The leg and great tail are within the *iahw*, the *shining light*—the light that manifests as life itself, suggested by the phrase *the great eye in the heart of the reeds*, the

hidden intelligence that makes things grow. The cryptic phrase is echoed directly across the entranceway on the east wall, reversed in a mirroring sequence of the words: there *iahw, the shining light*, is in *the heart of the eye, ib ir*, rather than in *the eye of the heart*.

In hieroglyphs the word for "green," *wadj*, is spelled with things that are green in different ways: the cobra and papyrus. The papyrus is a picture of the vivid embodiment of the color, the floating fields of papyrus that fill the Nile. The cobra, the letter *dj*, is the essence of greenness, of newness, because it sheds its skin. The wall typically ends with an image that introduces the verse that begins on the following wall, and refines and examines the meaning of the image, a hinge between the first wall and the second. The first wall presents a description of the elements of the sky as markers in time that relate to the rising of the Nile flood: the dawn rising of Taurus, Orion, and Sirius, the full moon, their rising keyed to the sky turning around the North Star. As though going back in time, the soul goes back into the night to be born as a star in the dawn. The subject of the final verse on the first wall is essentially rebirth, the unstoppable rising of the inherently green, inherently serpentine life force.

The verses establish the eternal principles of geometry: the circling of the sky, and within it the triangle as Sirius rising and descending, pulls with it the life force on earth. With the stars that set beneath the edge of the earth, the greening of life will go down beneath the ground.

Breaking the Code

Babay = Orion; the fire = the dawn; the holy ones = stars; the falcon = Sirius; the bull = Taurus; the Hamadryas baboon = the full moon; the column at the center = the North Star; the crocodile = the greening life force in the flood, the semen that engenders life on earth.

Themes and Devices

Iconographic Riddles

The snake and the walking stick are an abbreviation for two words: "say," *djed*, spelled with the cobra, the letter *dj*, and the hand, the letter *d*; and "the words," *mdw*, the walking stick, in which the picture itself is the word for "word," as though hieroglyphs began as figures drawn in the sand with a stick. This phrase is used throughout the monument to signal the beginning of a verse. The phrase appears on this first wall two times and is the beginning of the text itself in the restored missing line. These two hieroglyphs together are a good example of the ability of hieroglyphs to signal the concrete and metaphorical dimensions of an image at the same time. As an iconographic riddle they suggest the *Hawy*, the Egyptian snake handler, who walks through mud-brick villages, pulling cobras out of houses by poking them and prompting them to coil up a walking stick—a living illustration of the caduceus, the snake or snakes on a stick that is the symbol of the medical profession, and the wand of Hermes, whose purpose is to lead one somewhere: into or out of the land of the dead. That the walking stick in the hieroglyphic phrase refers to this practice is clear from the position of the stick: it is upside down. The tip is pointing up toward the cobra.

In Egypt the word for "snake" and the word for "life" are the same word, *hayy* (the double meaning is implicit). The stick resembles the snake but is not alive. The snake is the spoken word; the stick, in sand an instrument of writing, is the written word, inert, but, as with Aaron's rod, with the potential to come suddenly to life, the magic wand that makes something suddenly appear. The cobra is the animal metaphor for the internal serpent, the current of life. The inner snake is understood as both invisible and having an anatomical reality, the spinal cord. The spinal cord resembles a long, headless white snake (and is a common hieroglyph). This snake is sensual awareness (a reality), the inner eye (a metaphor). The cobra has an eye pattern on the back of its hood (the actual animal). The snake is the life in the tree of life. The answer to the riddle: the ultimate purpose of this religious text is to pull the snake of life out of the dead body with the stick, with the words.

The Rebus

As you read across the three columns of the first verse horizontally, there is a hidden equation. Beneath the falcon in the first column there is a disc with two lines beneath it. This could be the designation to say something twice, *sp*. That is how it has been translated, and that is how I have translated it here: *as a falcon flies, as a falcon flies*. But the structure of the verse itself is the visual repetition of signs and letters, and it seems odd that a shorthand notation such as *sp* would be prominently included in it. The hieroglyph could be instead read as the disc of light, the two discs of light, for in Egypt the eyes of the falcon are the two discs of light, the sun and the moon. The line then would read: *as the two falcon lights rise, may Unis rise into the fire.* An iconographic riddle reads horizontally across the columns:

the falcon + the disc of light =
the prayer flags + the eye = the holy eye of the falcon

The rebus: the falcon eye, presented here at the very beginning, is the ultimate resolution of the poem. The dead becomes the holy eye, rising in the circling sky, the falcon. The notation would refer to the sun and moon as the two falcon eyes rising on their path, the ecliptic. Similarly the three prayer flags as stars could be a specific reference to the three stars in the belt of Orion, Al Nilam, the rising of which precedes Orion's sword and Sirius.

The Question of *Pi*

The hieroglyphic word or formula *pi* (*p*/reed mat, *i*/reed) follows immediately after the name of the dead person whenever a transformation takes place. It has been translated as a spelling variant of the definite article *pn* (this), as in *This Unis is Horus/This Unis is a screeching howling baboon.* But why would *this* be applied to Unis? Is there another Unis? The definite article is almost never used elsewhere in the text, and *pi* occurs only after the name when a transformation takes place. Otherwise the name stands alone. Hence one might conclude that *pi* may not be a word at all but is included instead simply as a sound. It occurs on this wall at the end of verse 1 as Unis becomes the falcon, in verse 3 as Unis becomes the baboon, and twice in verse 5 as Unis becomes the crocodile, and then semen, both the rising life force. That it cannot be the definite article is confirmed by its frequent appearance throughout the monument by itself, modifying nothing, as it appears at the end of the gables, like the word *amen* at the end of a hymn.

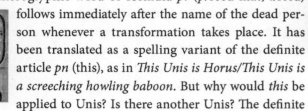

That *pi* is not a translatable word but may be something like a mantric sound is apparent in the sequence on the west gable of the antechamber, where the dead Unis is prompted back to life: *See Unis* pi, *Look Unis* pi, *Hear Unis* pi, *Exist Unis as Unis* pi. Is *pi* the inclusion of an unusual and irrelevant definite article in a description of a character, or is it a prompt? The question it raises is this: Is the text descriptive or is it dynamic? Are the words meant to make something happen, in the ceremonial religious sense, as in a cathedral, where in the imagination of the assembled religious community wine is transformed into blood, and bread is made flesh, and consumed? This does not actually happen, and would not happen in the outer world. It is made real in the mind of the congregation in order to be sanctified, much as in a mandala, where objects, presences, and, associated with them, things that would not be done in real life are imagined and, prompted with mantric sounds, arise, are transformed, sanctified, and then dissipated, in order to sanctify both the geometrical space within and the religious community or individual reading the text. The words and sounds in both cases are what make it real.

Is the pyramid similarly a vehicle for sanctification, in which words, imagination, and sound all take part? Throughout the monument the pyramid is called the *nywt p*, the place or circle of *p*. A green serpent called the *mistress of p* keens over the dead king on the west wall of the antechamber; *pi* as a prompt, a sound prompting dynamic transformation, suggests that in the ceremony, and in the mind of the religious community, Unis is not described but imagined: rising with the rising star Sirius, made holy as his eternal life becomes one with the motion of the sacredly ordered timeless life of the universe.

Reincarnation

The nightmare life in death was she,
Who thicks man's blood with cold

—S. T. Coleridge

Circe sits on the edge of a wood. Her green cloak falls away from her white knees. Her hand runs over the stone tablet she reads as she looks away, explaining the words. The falcon sits on a branch above her head, on another the owl; a spoonbill drinks from the water at her feet. At her feet is an open book where the circle as a geometrical figure is drawn. Men turned to animals surround her, a standing and a reclining dog, a stag—the strange branching miracle of growth that is the male, the bull. Dossi's later Circe is adorned in silk and gold, but the man-faced dog and the book with the circle and the triangle remain.

Circe (circle), Kali (time), St. Katherine, and the wheel are all the wheel, the turning that is transformation. Poetry is a language that is shorthand for the life and death of the turning year, the deep internal sense of the inevitability of life in death that makes your hair stand up. The life in death that is not the eternity of the soul but the dissolution of the body itself:

> You will be torn apart on the wheel
> I am a stag with seven tines
> I am a flood on a plain,
> I am a wind over the deep water,
> I am a hawk on a cliff,
> I am a tear in the eye of the sun
>
> the transformation is inevitable
> reincarnation
> release

Merlin passing shamanistically through the elements and animal forms is literally the falcon. Proteus, the old man of the sea, passing rapidly through animal forms to escape the clutching wishes of Telemachus, is from Egypt.

> I will not let thee go except thou bless me.
>
> —Genesis 32:26

Paradox

The womb of night: It does not exist. It is a geometrical configuration derived from the patterned movement of stars. The great soul, too, does not exist. Orion is an empty pattern of light, or, if Babay is a baboon, it is Thoth, the mind itself.

Tantra

The occult aspect of Neoplatonism is not much discussed in modern scholarship. But its general similarity with the . . . practices known as Tantric cannot be denied. The diffusion situation is obscure and, in a way, surprising . . . it would most likely be from the Near East into both Greece and India.

—Thomas McEvilley, *The Shape of Ancient Thought*, 592

Neoplatonism is a distinctly American thing. Emerson's sensibility is permeated with the awareness of the pervasive underlying light and its emanations, "the light hardening to ruby"; the Luminist painters made the rugged American landscape a place where mountains come and go as rainbows. Whitman's vision of the sacred and the profane as the same luminous multifaceted entity, and of language as its living reflection, is a Tantric vision. In Tantra words are alive. The world is a vivid, moving interwoven fabric of word and light and thing. The question of where this human stream of thought comes from is not really a historical question. It is an irrepressible native awareness that is always to be found, even or especially in the midst of chaos and war and dissolution. It does not matter if one is right or wrong in the details. The sense of the thing pervades. It is not learned but felt, and as such it is not a matter of fact but truth, as Emerson wrote, "I am weary of surfaces."

Emerson's idea of emanation, of things streaming out from the light, arising and dissolving in the light, with time as the medium, is the thought of Plotinus, who did not write much, who could not spell, who would not be painted or drawn. Emerson studied the work of this Egyptian who taught a small circle of men and women in Alexandria in the third century A.D., who set off to study in India and ended up teaching in Rome, and is associated with Plato, Pythagoras, and St. Augustine. Plotinus and his Neoplatonism are found at the heart of Jewish and Christian and Islamic mysticism. This heart, his thinking, *is the religious sensibility of Egypt*, with its pellucid awareness of life as a sudden ephemeral flood, of plants and animals popping out of the mud as the water recedes and birds wheel above in an echoing pattern of color and water, and cry, and soil and air resound with sound and movement and light. *Netcher, is it nature?*

Egyptian Religious Philosophy

Entranceway, East Wall

The Generation of the Light Body

VERSE 1

Unis becomes the primary serpentine life force
That absorbs his seven serpents
That manifest as the seven yoked attributes at his seven vertebrae
Nine times three sanctified attributes obey these words
Unis comes back as he absorbs myrrh, he receives myrrh,
He is blessed with myrrh, he is brought back with myrrh
Unis takes on your power sanctified attributes
As he turns he yokes your spiritual faculties

The west wall of the entranceway presents a sequence of vivid descriptions of
the physical world, introducing the primary forces in the night sky as if they
were in motion, turning the sky to the moment of the unstoppable rising of
water as the greening force of life rising on earth. The force of the water is then
conflated with semen, the rising water that brings life. The first verse on the
second wall pursues this idea, turning the text away from the outer world to the
inner body. The life force in the sky and in the water is now within. The
language in this opening verse is clear and precise. Something is happening.
The verse follows and refines the meaning of what the crocodile is. It is the
primary serpentine life force: pure brilliant light, *iahw*, burning, shining
brilliant light. It is the animating energy of life. Here this energy as it exists in
the body is not only conjured but mapped. The verse goes at once into

specifics, visible at a glance. This is a mathematical schema, and it has to do with snakes.

The first verse on the east wall of the entranceway presents the major clue to this earliest historical religious system. The verse announces that there is a primary serpent, and that it absorbs seven serpents and yokes them at seven vertebrae, and that the serpents are awakened and activated by the reading of the text itself, and by the burning of incense. These are recognizable instructions, and they indicate that this is a ritual text with a practical purpose, for the detailed map of internal serpents is a familiar one. It unmistakably presents the esoteric physics and physiology of Tantra, which uses the serpent metaphor in a geometrical schema in which pat-

terns of energy in the body are arranged as seven primary nerve centers called *chakras* (Sanskrit for "circles") along a central channel that correlates to the spine. The Tantric practitioner attempts the manipulation of these bodily energies, keyed to the reading of a religious text and the burning of incense. The goal of Tantric practice is to awaken the serpent sleeping within the central channel and draw it up through the chakras to the crown of the head, in order to release it as practice for the moment of death, an exercise intended to open the mind to omniscience, a capacity to see all things as jewellike, interrelated, and pure.

In the Egyptian text the serpent is awakened in the body and rises to the top of the head, where it is prompted by ritual words to leave the body at death. The final verse in the antechamber describes the jewellike diamond realm where the serpent will dwell, having become the eye, pure perception. A later verse within the pyramid describes the nature of this eye:

It is created for him from the fire of his serpentine light body . . .
Its essence is an eye thrust out.
With it we see the holy aspects revealed. You it burns.

And elsewhere:

Rise, rise, the serpentine light body burns in your skull.

In both traditions the rising of the inner serpent generates tremendous heat within the body. This is what is described in verse 2 on this wall as the rising of *the shining, burning life force* that is *the essence of the eye*. It is well documented that enough people have achieved the result of Tantric practice in life to demonstrate that the Pyramid Texts describe something real. In the early twenty-first century American researchers are wiring Tantric practitioners in the mountains of North India to track the rise of electrical energy to the head as the practitioners pass the threshold of death.

That Tantra is the religious system that came out of Egypt is captured in the name itself. *Tantra* is a hieroglyphic phrase: *ta* (earth), *ntr* (sacred), *ta-ntr* (the sacred ground, the pure land). Tantra is *al-chem-y*, the Egyptian (*chem*) thing. In its essence it is physics: the perception of the hidden background of all life as pure energy, in flux, like golden light, like fire. It is the cultivation and refinement of the flow of energy within one's own body, the inner serpent, the refinement of the energy in the human body into light. The flesh is the lead, the light is the gold. The name *ta-ntra* is used to describe this process in a ritual formula in verse 8 on the west wall of the antechamber:

The ritual words for the *ta-ntr*, the holy ground,
Dam the dam of the reassembled reassembled joined to the light
    within the canal canal.
Secret are the ways to take, not broad the banks for rising, the bank
    is scorching hot,
To cross the beaten Milky Way

The canal as the channel of the electrical energy in the spine is conflated with the Milky Way, the river of light in the sky, for in Tantra you do not go to heaven, you become it. The light body's absorption into the universe is expressed in a variety of tropes and images, a microcosm/macrocosm schema where it "lives in the form of every star." The *macranthropos*, the mystically expanding human form, is both diffuse, as the entire universe, and specific, as the headless giant body of light, Orion. The "union with the mother" that takes place within the monument is union with the sky itself, Whitman's "the merge," a metaphor for absorption into infinity. The power of the metaphor lies in the reversal of an essential taboo, much as the central metaphor of Christianity is not actual cannibalism but a mystery involving the absorption of the divine essence. In this earlier religious system the divine essence is not external but within. It is the composition of one's own body.

The *Vajra-yana*, the lightning vehicle, is the Sanskrit name for Tantra. The crocodile as the picture that defines the hieroglyphic word for lightning is the Egyptian word for *vajra* (lightning). The lightning in the Egyptian version is both metaphorical and real, the desert thunderstorm, "the bull of double brilliance" that prompts life out of the dead land. Thus, although the missing first words on the east wall of the entranceway, restored from the parallel text in Senwosret-Ankh, have been translated

Unis is the nau snake, the leading bull.
He swallows his seven snakes

it is appropriate that the lines be reinterpreted as:

Unis becomes the primary serpentine life force
That absorbs his seven serpents

For the snake *is* the bull. The bull *is* the life force. Bull and *ka* are the same word. This iconography does not belong to a primitive alien world of ancient Egyptian animal gods swallowing snakes but to the highly refined Tantric practice of physical and mental concentration in which the force of the generative serpentlike nerve energy is awakened in the lower body and reversed up the spine to the crown of the head. As Robert Thurman, a scholar of the Vajrayana, recently observed, "The founder of Mahayana Buddhism in India was *Nagarjuna*. The name means *informed by snakes*. Where do the snakes come from? Are they from Egypt?" That Tantric practice was well-known in antiquity is demonstrated by passages in Plato and elsewhere:

In the Timaeus, Plato proceeds to describe . . . a channel which passes through the center of the spine . . . the false eros draws the seminal fluid down the spinal channel, the transcendence of false eros must end this downward flowing . . . There are seven seats, or chakras . . . along the way down or up . . . The Greek belief in the Timaeus can be traced to a period before Plato . . . connected with the Pythagorean and Orphic . . . schools . . . the Orphic poet Pindar . . . [and] Heraclitus himself influenced by Orphism . . . [and in Aelian where] the spinal marrow of a man slithers out of his body as a serpent when he dies.

—McEvilley, *The Shape of Ancient Thought*, 208

The procreative fluid with which the psyche was identified [is] the spinal marrow believed to take serpent form . . . in the Orphic version the serpent was called Chronos . . . when asked what Chronos was, Pythagoras answered that it was the psyche of the universe.

—R. B. Onians, *The Origins of European Thought* (Cambridge: Cambridge University Press, 1951), 249ff

The first verse on the east wall of the entranceway proceeds in a series of puns on the word for "myrrh," as though the quality of myrrh becomes active through the punning verb. From the bottom of the fourth column to the top of the fifth the word for "myrrh" is repeated over and over—*antiu, antiu, antiu*—as the incense is shaken over the body. A rapid sense of spinning and a rising current of sparking energy in the spine arise in Tantric meditation. Intuition associates this violent power with lightning, the agent of the creation of life on earth:

Lightning storms in the atmosphere provided energetic ultra-violet light which transformed methane, hydrogen, nitrogen and carbonic gases into the proto-molecules . . . deposited by torrential rains into the primal seas out of which life arose.

—Robert Lawlor, *Sacred Geometry*
(London: Thames and Hudson, 1982), 30

•

VERSE 2

Unis becomes the shining burning bull-like life force.

The brilliant light is the essence of his eye. His mouth is stable in
the heat.

The head of Unis has the horn of the Lord of the South, the falcon
of old.

Unis reveals the path as the holy falcon. Unis has the power of the
nine holy ones

He is the root of the azure field of flax. As the flowering twig lifts up

It is Unis who binds the winding growth of the acacia branch to the
sky

Unis is the power throughout the earth, north and south,

He spins into being his circular horizon. Unis becomes three as he
rises.

The Brilliant Light Is the Essence of His Eye

The disc of light hieroglyph streaming rays of light is doubled
for emphasis. Unis becomes the pure light and heat that is
the essence of his eye, the living energy within him. The bull
is conjured, the falcon now has its horns. The horns are
lightning. A hymn to the diversity of life on earth follows in
a display of delicate botanical hieroglyphs, *the root, the azure
field of flax, the flowering twig, the rising branch*. This
rich diversity of life is the immediate result of the
lightning flash and the flash flood, the terrifying
force of life-giving water in the desert.

Botanical Hieroglyphs

The Root

The word for "root," spelled out *rd*, is marked with
the detailed picture of a root. The *s* suffix makes it a
causative verb, Unis is the root (or as a verb, roots).
The word at the top of the next column is *hsbd*, the
word for "lapis lazuli," but here it is not the stone but

its color, azure. The field, *ag*, is marked by the determinative picture of a field of flax; flax in blossom is a deep cornflower blue.

The botanical hieroglyph is of an acacia twig with its symmetrical arrangement of tiny leaves. This is the subject; the determinative beside it *reswt*, is an adjective that means "flowering" (an epithet for southern Egypt), followed by the detailed picture of an acacia branch with its twigs, identical to the twig in column ten. In this vividly real description of plant life it is worth looking at the beauty of the hieroglyphs themselves. The leafy twig of the acacia is elaborated upon in the next column, in a complex netting of acacia leaves and branches, as though the hieroglyphs themselves have the developing complexity of the progressive grammatical forms of the words.

•

VERSE 3

Holy is the night Unis rises as the three powerful ones:
They are Orion, Unis as Babay,
Unis becomes the son of she who did not know that she
    gave birth,
Unis, whose face is full all three nights.
Great art thou, Golden One, hidden from people
    before.
Unis becomes Babay, Lord of the Night,
The Hamadryas, who lives although he does not
    know it.

Paradox is a variety of riddle in which something that cannot be true is true, hence it is an essential tool of religious thought. Here two familiar religious paradoxes are presented for the first time. The first is the Trinity. Three is the plural in hieroglyphs. What is underlined is the idea that a single entity can also be a plurality: one is not only one thing but multiple things, three things. The rising light body, or soul, of the dead person becomes *he who is three*. The meaning may be that the dead soul rising becomes part of the cosmic pattern as the three celestial markers presented on the west wall of the entranceway: Orion, the moon, and the wheel of the sky. Or one might take an even more specific and literal meaning from the hiero-glyphic phrase *he rises as the three powerful ones: they are Orion, Unis as Babay*, and read the line to mean the distinctive pattern of three stars in Orion's Belt. These three *netcherw*, the holy ones growing dark in verse 1 on the west wall, may indeed be the three wise men from the east bringing myrrh to presage the birth of the holy child, who is the bright star rising in the east, *the son of she who did not know she gave birth*, the sky itself. The rising of Orion is followed by that of the *Golden One*, the moon, whose fullness is hidden from people (three lapwings walking together), then visible for only

 three days. As such the soul is seen as taking form as the three great apparitions in the night sky: Sirius, Orion, and the full moon. Thoth, too, exists but does not know it because he is a mere symbol, a human invention, like a hieroglyph.

The line *holy is the night* is followed by the usual verb for the rising of celestial phenomena, *sbn Unis rises*, followed by the desert hare, defined by three stars, which can mean many stars, or simply three. The desert hare is movement, *wn*, the word for both "to run" and "to exist." Existence is move-

 ment, "to be" is to be in motion. The verb unfolds in related nouns. In this context *wnwt* is the hare marked with stars, meaning the move-ment of stars, the star precincts moving across the sky, *the stars are racing by*. This word means "hour," the Greek word for both star group and season, time as a visible aspect of the sky. In hieroglyphs this is also the word for "priest," whose work is to track the movement of the stars, like Hamlet's, then Steinbeck's *The Moon Is Down*, taken from Sappho, "*deduke men a selanna, kai Pleiades, meso de nuktis, para d'erkat' ora, ego de mona ketaudo*." The moon is down, so are the Pleiades, it is the middle of the night, the hours go by, and I lie down alone.

The Virgin Birth

Unis becomes the son of she who did not know that she gave birth.

The mother does not know that she gave birth, for she is the night itself. *Mary*, the passive participle of the Egyptian verb *mr*, "to love," is "the Beloved," the all-embracing ultimate reality of all things. The mother is *the throne*, meaning the space in which all things arise. The word for "throne" in hieroglyphs is the picture of a chair, *st* (seat, sit), the Arabic word for "lady." The Greek spelling of this Egyptian word is *isis*. Mary with Christ on her lap is the hieroglyph itself, taken from the standard representation of Isis as the chair that contains the falcon, the sky that holds the rising star Sirius in the east, the hinge of the year. In *The Golden Ass*, Isis emerging from the sea in the growing dark, adorned by a crescent moon, *is* the growing dark, as Sappho wrote:

> *Hespera panta pheron phainolis eskados aws*
> The growing dark brings back all that was scattered by the shining
>   dawn, brings the child to the mother.

The one who is three, the one who gave birth but didn't know it, the one who lives, although he does not know it, like words themselves, these are merely concepts: they exist but do not know it. The real mystery is that they exist as words, conjuring an approximation of what that power is like. Unis is not simply a baboon or a bull or a falcon, he is not one thing or another. He is or is one with the mysterious harmonizing, pervading power of the universe. *Trismegistos*, "great in three ways"; the intelligence of the universe manifests as three things, the falcon: time as the turning sky and the life of the year; the moon: time as the measurement of the month; Orion: a representative constellation that signals the calibration of time in a single night. This is the physical nature of time that is life. Its nature is light. Its essence is turning.

•

VERSE 4

Say the words:
Would that he would that he bring to Unis
The triangle (thorn) on the top of the spine of Osiris
That Unis might rise upon it to the sky

Osiris: The Central Paradox

The *ankh* sign appears for the first time in the text in the previous verse, *He lives although he does not know it*. Here the word is spelled out, backward as the columns read from right to left on this wall. The sign that defines the word now comes first, followed by the letters that spell out its sound: the wave as the letter *n*, then the hard *h* (the lined circle, the horizontal lines across the circle are invisible in the carving here). If you look at the *ankh* sign above carefully, you will see that it is a composite image. This cannot possibly be, as Gardiner defined it, a sandle strap. The lateral line is the picture of a vertebra, the *ts* hieroglyph. The sign for "life" is one of the most significant hieroglyphs; like the eye, it is a metaphor containing a multifaceted sense of something real. It is a riddle. Yet it is a simple familiar word that exists in hieroglyphs, in Arabic, and in English as the same word, *neck*. It is the word that means to bend, as a noun it is what bends: the neck. The word is related to the word *angle*, and *snake* (*anguis* in Latin) and *anguish* (twisting, being bent). The neck is the corridor between the body and the head that enables breath, and life. The *ankh* sign is a composite picture of the vertebra hieroglyph *ts* (which as a verb means to fasten something on, and as a noun means both vertebra and knot) and the hollow of the spine. Thus the hieroglyph may be an anatomical illustration of the channel of the empty spinal column from above with a side view of the vertebra attached at the top of the spine that connects the neck to the empty skull. On the wall at the bottom of the second column from the left the spine is shown in three sections with ribs attached and spinal cord hanging down.

The principle of paradox, introduced in the previous two verses, leads to the central paradox of Egyptian religion, Osiris, the seat of the eye, the meaning of which is the ultimate mystery: the reality of life in death. The corpse is death inevitably feeding life: the decaying body that releases energy trapped in form. And it is the form: the channel of the electricity of life, the spine. In this last verse in the entryway it is the spine of Osiris that will enable the soul to go to heaven, the life force to leave the body as light. The added dimension is the paradox of the hieroglyphic text itself, with its unique ability to conjure a vivid sense of the animation of living things. Embedded in stone for thousands of years, it resonates with the Tantric insight that it is the words themselves that are alive.

•

When the morning twilight is about to begin you can see, in some months of the year, the softly radiant zodiacal light rising obliquely in a rounded pyramid . . . two and a half or three hours before sunrise, the twilight glow becomes asymmetrical, rising in the east and descending from there more steeply to assume after a while the shape of a cone of light sloping upward: the zodiacal light with its axis having practically the same inclination as the ecliptic . . . The fainter stars have now faded, but the stronger ones are still percep- tible . . . The yellow twilight now begins to make its appearance, fad- ing away at the top into a green-blue tint. The twilight proper has begun . . .

> —M. G. J. Minnaert, *Light and Color in the Outdoors*
> (New York: Springer-Verlag, 1993), 312

In a desert country, life is a negotiation between the extremes of dark and light, like the oblique light that falls between them in prismatic momentary layers of jewellike color. Egyptian religion is the interpretive system of this harsh reality as a progression of multilevel metaphors. Night is the great mother, empty yet inexhaustible; it gives birth to infinite worlds. Woman is a vessel of water, the holy grail. In the desert the coolness of the dark is the coolness of water; the cooling, water-bringing moon is the great silver eye that sees and illuminates at once. In the glittering wetland of the stars wanders with crescent horns the golden calf. Hours in the original sense are studied precincts of the turning sky. The *Dwat* is the hour before dawn, when a luminous blue-green floods the dark. The silver speckling of stars in the east that brighten before they fade into the flood is the field of rushes, where the soul becomes a luminous eternal being, a wandering star on the wheel of the sky.

Antechamber, North Wall

The Arms of the Sky

The room beyond the entranceway was sealed and dark. Its walls were not meant to be seen. Yet the letters are painted the greenish blue of the first light of dawn. The ceiling of the room is covered with stars. The walls of the entire room are minutely inscribed with columns of words in a circular arrangement of text that moves from wall to wall, from north to west to south to east. The miniature re-creation of the starry sky is made real by the surround of words. One is entering the perfect eternal geometry of the vast intangible body of the night. Having entered the body by way of the male, the monument opens now into the realm of the female, the realm of creation.

The north wall of this room presents a sequence of riddles encoding the visible features of the north side of the night sky. The first verse introduces the primary constellation of the north, the Big Dipper. The riddle lies in the mystery of what the Big Dipper is and what it does. The Dipper is the mechanism that turns the sky like the hand of a clock. Hence it is a paradox: it is the arm of the night, real and active, yet as a pattern of stars it is diffuse and nonmaterial. The night is not a goddess. It is the night. The second verse presents *the two great holy ones in the cool dark*: Sirius, the falcon, and Canopus, the dog, the brightest stars in the sky. In the dense layering of poetic imagery that characterizes this wall these two primary stars as markers of the seasons cross what is called in this verse the square (*hat*) of the falcon (*hor*): the sky as a dappled cow, whose milk is the Milky Way. The third verse presents this *glittering stream of the marvelous sky* as a ladder of souls, a word (*mkt*, ladder) that is a pun on the hieroglyphic name of the Milky Way (*mskt*). In verse 4, in keeping with the macrocosm/microcosm nature of this religious system, the ladder, having been established as an entity in the sky, is now in the body. It is the spine. The soul climbs the ladder of the spine within, as in a tug-of-war among the corpse, Osiris, and its child, the rising falcon that is the soul rising as a star.

The sequence of riddles addresses the larger question of the riddle implicit in the monument itself, the unsolved question of the orientation of the text. The verses clearly read inward, into the heart of the monument. But the overall sense of the text reads outward. Taurus rises before Orion and Sirius, not after. The answer to the monument as a riddle lies in an odd hieroglyph on the east or final wall of the antechamber, the picture of a cow with a head at either end of its body above a door. This is the riddle of *the door that opens both ways*: *There is a door that opens both ways. What is it?*

The answer: the door that opens both ways is the entrance to the womb. It is conception, the going in, and birth, the going out. The verses begin with the imagery of conception, as the soul as a seed, a fragile winged infant, flies away into the great mother, the dark night. Reading inward, the verses continue to the innermost room, the sarcophagus chamber, the room beyond the antechamber that is called the womb of night, where the entire being of the dead person disintegrates and is reborn as light.

VERSE 1

The door of the sky: Sirius lives as Unis
Brought to life as the child of Sirius.

The eighteen holy ones are purified for him.
As the Dipper does not set,
The rising of Unis will not set in heaven.
The seat of Unis will not perish on earth.

Though placed in the tomb, men fly away to them, the stars.
Sirius makes Unis fly to heaven among his brothers, the stars.

Great Night uncovers her arms for Unis:
A hundred thousand twin falcon souls,
The sailing souls of the axis,
While the head of the sun sleeps below
She weeps these tears.

The shining falcon is yours, Unis,
He does not give it to another rising to him.
Unis goes to the sky with you falcon shining.

The face of Unis is as the falcon's,
His wings as those of waterbirds,
His claws in the shining night,
Are like the jaws of the desert lynx.

Is there not a poem for Unis from the earth among men?
Does not the bird dance belong to him in the sky among the stars?
Give the name of Unis his poem.
Unis himself is destroyed upon his ascent to heaven.

Wepwawet flies Unis to heaven
Among his brothers the stars:
Unis takes the arm of the wild goose
Unis beats the wing of the turtle dove,
Fly fly away man fly away Unis from your hand.

The most striking feature on the north wall is the range of classic poetic devices used, and the detail of the hieroglyphs themselves. There seems to be
more than one writer involved, for the voices and the style of the different
verses are so distinct. Verse 1 begins with a line that is a dense configuration

of doubling hieroglyphic words. The meaning of the first word has to do with the unsolved question of the orientation of the text, hence the orientation of the monument itself. Are the lines in the room to be read backward (east to north, toward the entranceway), making this the final sentence in the room, or forward (north to east, toward the inner sanctum), making it the first? Does the door of the antechamber go into the monument, or out of it? The entranceway is recognized by all as the birth canal. This first word has been variously translated as a verb (Piankoff, "to be serene," Allen, "to bleed"). The letters are *s* (the thread or string), and *b* (the foot), below which is a rectangle that could be a letter, *sh*, the artifical lake or lily pond. The word that follows is the familiar word for "sky": *p*/reed mat, *t*/bread, plus the edged bar of the sky as a sign determinative. These two words constitute a phrase consisting of either a verb and its subject, or two nouns, the second in the genitive: the sky either has or does something. Thus the first word may not be a verb but a noun: *sba*, the word for "door." This reading, with the word that follows it, *pt*, the sky, would create a word play on the name for Sirius: *sb-pt, the door of the sky=spdt, Sirius*. Thus the rectangle below the letters *s* and *b* may not be the letter *sh* but the picture of a door, oriented in such a way that it mirrors the bar of the sky directly below. This is, after all, the door. But there are other dimensions conjured by this simple familiar word. It renders a pun on another common word that is spelled in the same way. In hieroglyphs *sba* (*seba*) is the word for star, in Arabic it is the word for morning. The equivalence of the words *door* and *star* signaled by the pun in the hieroglyphic phrase would then suggest the imagined reality so far described: the entrance to the sky is as a star. The star is in the door of the sky. And the star is the door of the sky.

1. *sb*/door
2. *isankh*/cause to live
3. *pt*/sky
4. *ankh*/live
5. *sa*/child
6. *spd*/Sirius (m.)
7. *spdt*/Sirius (f.)

FIRST COLUMN:
The door of the sky, (elided) *sb-pt*

lives, *ankh*
Sirius, *spd* (the star defined by the picture of a needlelike triangle)

SECOND COLUMN:
    brought to life, *isankh* (*ankh* is stated as a verb, then morphs into
        the causative with the addition of the suffix *is*, like a fourth-
        form Arabic verb, "he is made to live")
    as the child *sa* (the goose)
    of Sirius, *spdt* (with the addition of the final *t* Sirius is now female)

The one thing that can clearly be said is that the meaning of the line is conveyed by the visual relationship between the hieroglyphs that spell out the words. It is not something that does not relate directly to the images. If you look at this first column, and the others that immediately follow it, you will see that the point of the first verse is a demonstration of the mastery of the use of the literary form of hieroglyphs. The favored device of mirrorlike repetition is visible at once. The other lines in the verse, too, are aesthetically crafted in a way that is rarely seen today. One thinks instead of the crafted lines of a master of imagery, elision, and sound such as Catullus.

Technique in poetry originally resided in the construction of the line itself. A line was like an object made by a trained hand and a gifted eye, like a beautifully carved flint knife, to have a particular effect. Catullus creates a poem that is not so much an expression of feeling as a loaded device made of words:

> *Odi et amo, quare id faciam fortasse requiris*
> *Nescio sed fieri sentio et excrucior*

> I hate and I love, why do I do this you may ask,
> I don't know, but I feel it and am torn apart

What Catullus is focused on is the architecture of the line itself. By eliding "I hate and I love" using *et*: *odyetamo*, he is merging two opposites that naturally pull apart. Then he caps the poem with a word he made up himself just for this occasion (elided, glued together, again using *et*, with the word *sentio*, "I feel"). The word he makes up is *excruciate, excrucior* (literally "I am on the cross"), placed like a stamp as the final word to indicate what he is doing. What he is doing is creating a cross, a chiasmus, a cross-like organization of contrasts. It is the construction of the line, rather than simply the meaning of the words, that says "to hate and love at the same time is excruciating," it literally *tears one apart*. As in the placement of the hieroglyphs here, the meaning of the words lies in their visibly interlocked arrangement. English does not easily lend itself to the kind of construction that plays with the skeletal structure of words, as in the lapidary effect possible in Latin and in hieroglyphs, although Hopkins tries:

> I caught this morning morning's minion king-
> dom of daylight's dauphin, dapple-dawn-drawn Falcon

The north wall of the antechamber is an illustration of the antiquity of this tradition of ingeniously structured poetry. The first poem consists of a succession of different kinds of classic construction in verse. It is obvious that what the writer of the hieroglyphic lines is after is the display of his technique in the composition of the line itself. Economy of words and density of meaning are, as in Catullus, paramount in this kind of writing. The very first line is elided, and it is a chiasmus or, more technically, *antimetabole*, a reversal or change of the meaning of a sequence of the same words. The most prominent subsequent devices used in the verse are:

> *Paradox*: establishing two opposing realities that exist at once or
>   as one and the same thing
> *Enigma*: a riddle encoded in a dense active visual metaphor
> *Paranomasia*: punning, in which a word suggests the quality of
>   a like-sounding word
> *Palindrome*: reversing the visual order of a sequence of words
> *Onomatopoeia*: here having the quality of shamanistic mimicry,
>   used not merely to describe but to conjure the living thing

The perfected use of these devices, valued and admired as a mark of skill up to the present time, raises the question of why. What are they for? Do they simply indicate mastery of technique in the writing itself, or are they used to create or refine a perception of reality, to create a perfected magical reality? To what extent are words themselves understood to create what is actually seen, and do they?

The use of language to blur the margins of things through puns, for example, making unexpected connections, reflects the truth that nothing is permanent, all things inevitably run together. The hieroglyphs elaborate the insight: it is the interconnectedness of things that releases their true meaning. One thing becomes another, and contains another, and thence unfolds in multiple hidden dimensions. The verse is a return to the catalogue of celestial phenomena that began on the west wall of the entranceway. It is as though one were in a planetarium, a miniature re-creation of the night sky. But the actual, accurate re-creation of the map of the night sky is effected not with a detailed visual imitation of it, as in Grand Central Station, or with a verbal description of the night sky, as in the beginning of the *Purgatorio*. It is done with iconographic riddles that contain not only the physical description of primary stars and specific constellations, but layers of deeper meaning that reveal their significance in the life of the universe.

To get a sense of how this works one can look at three familiar iconographic riddles. The first is the story of "the lady or the tiger." Behind the door is a beautiful lady or a ravenous tiger. Which is it? This is the same kind of iconographic riddle that begins the Pyramid Texts: a hidden calendar pointing to a specific date. The door is the door of the sky. Behind it, below the horizon, and about to appear in the door, is the helical rising of Virgo, the beautiful maiden, the rich harvesttime. Or will it be Leo, the fierce heat of summer? This can be an urgent question, as the rising of the horn of the new moon in the door of the sky might mark the end of hunger, as it does, for example, at the end of the month of Ramadan.

The scout ballad "Green Grow the Rushes, O" refers back to the Egyptian cosmology presented here: the rushes are the eastern stars at dawn. A recent analysis tracks the song as a sequence of astronomical references, "the eleven that went to heaven," "the April rainers," "the nine bright shiners," "the seven stars in the sky," "the lily white boys," and so forth.

A third iconographic riddle that comes to mind is the story of Samson (*shams*, sun), whose locks (rays) are shorn by Delilah (*dalila*, confusion), hence he is blinded: he cannot see without his rays. The formulation contains the subject/object nonduality that is presented in the Pyramid Texts: shining and seeing are the same thing. The sun and the moon are eyes. Samson pushes the wheel, the turning sky (*nywt*). But he is blind and, bound to the column (*iwn*), his repetitive circling motion stops and he pulls the column down, causing the roof to fall, killing everyone. The blinding of the sun as the eye of the intelligence of the universe stops the motion of the wheel, and the sky falls down.

The subtle shift in the mirroring sequence of words in the first line of the first verse on the north wall of the antechamber signals the transition from male to female, from the active manifestation of life to the mystery of nonbeing, the mystery of conception, the mystery of birth. The text, the idea, and the ritual have gone from masculine to feminine. The meaning of the verse is revealed in the lines that follow. You are looking at the imaginary night sky and being shown its wonders. Before you is the north wall of the night sky. The text then identifies its primary constellation: *mschtiu*, the name in hieroglyphs for the Big Dipper. In English the Dipper is also known as the Great Bear and the Wain. In Egypt there are different ideas and images that define it. *Mschtiu* is the name of the adzelike instrument used in the funerary ceremony of reawakening the corpse called *the opening of the mouth*. It is also called *khpsh, the foreleg of a cow*, for the sky is affectionately thought of in the elemental world of shepherds and herdsmen as a beloved cow, streaked with milky starlight. The verse begins by indicating the significance of the Dipper. Why is it important and what does it do? As the primary constellation of the north sky the Dipper is always there. It never sets. It swings eternally around the stationary axis of the sky, the North Star. Hence the verse immediately states, *The Dipper does not set*, and this means that as the dead person is being absorbed into the perceived and defined reality of the sky, *the rising of Unis will not set in heaven*. Then the paradox is stated. It is the pyramid itself:

> The seat of Unis will not perish on earth.
> Though placed in the tomb
> Men fly away to them, the stars.

The tomb is the sky; the sky is the tomb. The hieroglyphic determinative of the tomb in the column is the picture of a tumulus, a raised burial. The pyramid as a tumulus solves the problem of burial in the earth and absorption into an imaginary sky. *He rises, pr*; the hieroglyph is the picture of a house with an open door. As a verb the house with the open door means "to go out of the house," or "to rise." The tomb, the house will not perish, and the rising will not perish. Both exist at once, are the same thing, and, by residing in pure geometry, are made eternal. The pyramid is a geometrical formulation of eternity, pointed at the eternal axis: the North Star. What is more lasting than the pyramids?

What is more lasting than the pyramids? What is it that exists outside of time? What is inside them: geometry, and poetry, the patterned map of words. The paradox embodied by the Dipper is that eternity is not static but in motion. It is circling.

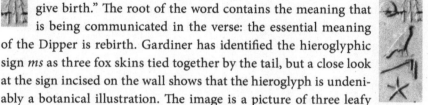

The name of the Dipper grows out of the word *ms*, "to give birth." The root of the word contains the meaning that is being communicated in the verse: the essential meaning of the Dipper is rebirth. Gardiner has identified the hieroglyphic sign *ms* as three fox skins tied together by the tail, but a close look at the sign incised on the wall shows that the hieroglyph is undeniably a botanical illustration. The image is a picture of three leafy branches or garlands bound together, and relates to the meaning of the word. The ceremonial and decorative use of branches or flowers to mark a place, occasion, or dwelling in which a birth takes place, or will take place, like a wedding, is universal. The word *ms*, birth, as it relates to the idea of birth among the stars, has multiple dimensions, one of which is turning: *Mschtyw*, "the Big Dipper"; *Mskt*, "the Milky Way"; *Mshn*, "abode of the gods"; *Mshnt*, "birthing place," cemetery; *Mshnt*, "serpent goddess of birth"; *msn*, "spin"; *msnh*, "rotate"; *mss*, "infant."

The hieroglyph may have its origin in the illustration of branches set up beside the female figure with raised arms on Negadan redware from the predynastic, formative period of hieroglyphs. Beside her is a diminutive male, and an erected display of branches and cattle skulls set up on poles. Around them are lines of desert mountains, and between them waves of water and flamingos, as though marking the seasonal storms and subsequent flash floods and rain-made lakes that drew vast flocks of migrating birds in their passage across the North African deserts.

A new poetic construction follows, a multilevel metaphor that will explain the overall meaning of the verse. It begins by refining the point that the Dipper does not set, with a precise visual reference: *Great Night uncovers her arms.*

This is a coded line that means night reveals its secret. The secret is that the night sky is a clock. The arms of the sky are the Dippers, which swing around the North Star like the arms of a clock, measuring the hours of the night. This is at once an astute astronomical observation, a poetic conceit, and a practical measuring device. The question of orientation is solved. The panels of text on the walls in the antechamber are arranged in a counterclockwise motion, matching the direction of the circular movement of stars in the night sky, the motion of the Dipper. The monument is a metaphor for time: conception, gestation, and birth. The second aspect of the Dipper in the paradox is now revealed. The corpse no longer has functional arms or limbs. The sky is formless and yet it has arms. The Dippers are the arms that turn the sky. The metaphor becomes the paradox of time as emptiness and manifestation. There is nothing there. It is space, and yet it is food, hence its nature intrinsically is growth, is greenness and water. The soul rises to heaven by means of the Dippers turning the sky, turning the seasons, bringing rain, pulling Sirius up with the water of the Nile, and making rise all the green things that rise with the rising flood.

> Great Night uncovers her arms
> A hundred thousand souls
> As the head of the sun sleeps below
> She weeps these tears

Any notion that the night is a goddess called Nut is dispelled at once by this image. What is being described is the actual night sky, *nut, nux, night*. The Dipper as an arm of the sky is presented in the layered meaning of a classic poetic line. There are two wordplays involved in the image. The first is the pun on *kfn* (uncover) and *khfn* (a hundred thousand), a word usually marked with the picture of a tadpole to illustrate what a huge number of things looks like: it looks like the tadpoles filling the pools and irrigation ditches as the Nile recedes. The verb again arises from the noun, with an implicit image that conveys the sense that the arms are not solid arms but are composed of countless diffuse particulate stars; the stars are the souls of the dead, the tears of mankind. The word for "weep" (*rm*) is a pun on the word for "mankind" (*rmt*), which appears near the word for "to weep" in another column on the wall, again implying a sense relationship between the verb and the noun: What is the nature of mankind? Sorrow. Then there is the pun implicit in the line itself: *Uncovering the arms* is a gesture of mourning. Yet the arms of the night, what are they made of? Thousands of glittering stars. *The stars are tears.* The core of the Dipper's hieroglyphic name, *mschtyw*, is *ms*, the hieroglyphic verb meaning "to give birth." The turning sky *is* the birth of all things. The verse itself resolves the question it raises, that of sorrow, of the grief of life, much as Eliot does in the verse from *The Four Quartets*: "The dance along the artery / The circulation of the lymph / Are figured in the drift of stars." "Uncover" and "a hundred thousand" as a pun turns the pain of grief and mourning into the multiplicity and beauty of the starry night.

> The souls are stars the stars are tears the tears are men.
> Mankind was born from tears.

Why? Because they are the same word. As with the pun on the lion and the gate, the story is contained in the pun itself. The words are magically related, take on the quality of the other through the like sound. Relation and distinction arise from the doubling of a thing. The doubling of hieroglyphs introduces the core Egyptian religious idea that is introduced in the image that immediately follows: twinning—*the twin falcon souls*.

The hieroglyphs of the two birds, the falcon and the crane, are doubled beside each other in the column on the wall, introducing the primary Egyptian concept of the eye, the logos, and the twin. The eye creates the logos. The logos is the twin. The dead becomes not the actual star but its twin. The twin is an *idea* in the literal sense of its origin in the Greek verb *eidw* (to see). An idea is something that has been seen, and having been seen remains in the mind a concept. The twin is the Platonic concept of the template: you exist before you exist, and you exist after you exist, because there is a pattern that is the template for your existence, the geometric essence of your existence. The pattern is eternal. The pattern is the twin. "All patterns are pure, and so am I" is the Tantric basis for becoming: it is the genetic code. The idea is the reflection of the thing as it is seen in the mind. The twin is the essence of perception as duality, mediated by the eye. It is language. The word is the twin of the thing. A thing lives on in its twin, the word. The twinning is now presented as an idea, both visually and linguistically in the following line as a visual palindrome, beginning and ending with the falcon of light, enclosing the pronoun *you* with the verb *rising*:

> The shining falcon is yours . . . yours the falcon shining

The letters are repeated and reversed in an almost mirrorlike sequence. The next construction is onomatopoeia: the living thing is conjured by its sound. On the wall are the pictures of wings.

> Though placed in the tomb
> Men fly away to them, the stars

The pun on the door of the sky is repeated, and here it becomes: *s-pa spdt. Sirius* (now female, *spdt*) *makes Unis fly* (*s-pa*) *to heaven.*

The verb for "to fly" is *pa*, the pintail duck taking off (here *s-pa*, the causative form of the verb: "makes fly"). If you stand back and look at this beginning of the north wall, you will see the word used over and over, over and over, the sound and the image of the rising duck beating its wings: *papapapapa.* A detailed progression of waterbirds follows, drawn from the vast array of beautifully colored waterbirds on the Nile, in astonishingly accurate naturalistic detail: the spur-winged goose, the wigeon, the Eurasian spoonbill. These are the *apdu*, the birds that make a rushing sound with their beating wings as their dense flocks rise at once from the water.

The letters are animate. They are living pictures. The living thing is conjured by its image. In *The Orientation of Hieroglyphs*, Henry Fischer observed that hieroglyphs were not simply letters but miniature tableaux like the detailed reliefs on the walls of tombs. Here the turtle dove as a hieroglyph predates a nearly exact representation of a turtle dove as an illustration in a relief in a nearby tomb. The hieroglyph of the turtle dove on the left is from the line *he beats the wings of a turtle dove.*

After the birds the word *itf* is spelled out. It is the name in Egypt today for the desert lynx, the sand cat.

The writer, having ingeniously created a sequence of vivid, lifelike metaphors, now reminds us that what we are looking at is this: *medw, muthos, mots* (words). It is a magical device made of words. It is a poem. The person no longer exists. What exists is the poem. Is there not a poem for Unis, is there not a dance?

Carmina sunt dicenda
Neget quis carmina Gallo

Then, like Catullus, the Egyptian writer tops it off with something he made up himself, a hapax legomenon.

A hapax, a fetish, a beautiful curiosity, a joke

The hapax is the bird dance, illustrated by a picture that is also a verbal phrase: it is the word for dance, *chb*, spelled out with the lined disc (*ch*) and the foot (*b*), and a novel sign determinative on the left: the foot of a bird. The word is introduced with the negative, *n*, the shrugging arms: *Is there not a dance?* The meaning is conveyed by both the picture and the word. It is a joke. And yet it says it all. The letters of the word form the picture of a headless person dancing as the human foot becomes the foot of a bird. The aggregates of the body have separated out and recombine as both a word and a thing, half-bird, half-human; a headless person, a faceless person is no longer a person. It is also, extraordinarily, a reference back to the subject of the verse, the disembodied limbs of the sky, the movement of the sky. The person is dead. He has gone to the North Star, to the still point of the turning world, where the dance is.

The final image on the wall is conjured by its sound:

Wepwawet flies Unis to heaven
wep=yip, the dog

Anubis

Onomatopoeia here has the quality of shamanistic mimicry, used not merely to describe but to conjure the living thing. *Wepwawet* is onomatopoeia for the wild dog's cry, the well-known coyote's cry at the rising of the moon. But in keeping with the tendency of hieroglyphs to contain layers of deeper meaning, this word is not simply a name. It is a verbal phrase. The hieroglyphic name is spelled with the pair of horns, *wp* (to open), followed by *wat* (path) in the plural, *wawat*: three pictures of the sign for path. Hence the action is implicit in the thing, the verb is hidden in the noun: the dog, conjured by the sound of its name, does something—it is the opener of the paths. The dog embodies a primary Egyptian concept, what we have come to call evil. The wild dog is a very dangerous animal. Yet the dog has a dual nature. It is its own twin: it is wild but can be tamed. Hence the wild dog is not a bad thing; it is, after all, a dog, the ultimate tracker, the animal that finds the path. The dog appears in the text in a gradual elaboration of this idea. It appears as Anubis (in verse 3), the wild dog tamed, ears back, tail down, black like the night, where it shows you how to find the way. Next the dog appears as Set (in verse 6), with ears up and raised tail forked like lightning, ready to kill.

Set is the universal embodiment of the wilderness, the wolf. This form of the dog means danger. It is the hieroglyphic determinative for rage, for storms, for suffering, for tearing things apart. A dog at rest in calm devotion lets its tail hang down. A loving dog will place its ears back. The quality of the dog is listening. It is both motion and sound. Hence the dog is marked by its ears, by the movement of its tail. In the hieroglyph for rage and storm, the tail is shown as split to mark rapid motion back and forth, as the tail of a wild dog ready to attack has the dangerous, erratic, fast motion of forked lightning. The dog embodies the purest love and the greatest danger, the mystery of good and bad in one. Chaos is tamed by harmony: the dog is tamed by the falcon, wildness is tamed by time, by patience, as the wild canids of the North African desert are tamed by desert nomads today to hunt in the age-old hunting method of the desert: falconry. The dog, released, runs erratically through the desert brush and flushes a game bird up into startled flight, as the falcon, released, circles evenly above, then descends with lightning speed to catch the bird and bring it to the falconer. Their relationship is a geometric formula for rising and turning. The dog is the erratic movement of bad weather, the falcon is the sweep of the stars, the circular motion of time, that sweeps the storm away. The first verse on the north wall ends with a classic image from falconry: the soul is set in flight as a hidden bird by the action of the dog, then told to fly up as a falcon from the hand:

> Wepwawet makes the soul fly to heaven among the stars
> Fly fly away man, fly away Unis from the hand

Looking beyond the metaphor drawn from animal motion, one finds again a specific star reference. The star is Canopus, a word that reads as *canopus* (dog face) in Latin, but on closer examination is simply *kanopis*, the Greek rendering of the Egyptian word *Anubis*. Anubis the dog is the star that rises just below Sirius the falcon. J. J. Hobbs, in his study of the Egyptian desert, offers this insight:

> Bedouin are born geographers and students of the heavens. Spend-
> ing their lives outdoors they lack walls and roofs that obscure views
> of their surroundings. Stars are most important to the Arabs as
> indicators of the seasons. If you see Canopus low on the horizon at

sunset with Sirius above it, they explain, this is the end of winter and the beginning of summer. When you see Canopus low on the horizon below Sirius at sunrise, summer is about to end and winter begin. Sixty days after Canopus rises (in the first week of September) is the start of "rain time," with clouds, thunder, and lightning. The nomads recognize a number of other constellations, the most important being Taurus with its principal star the Cow, Aldeberan; the Big Dipper; the Falcon; Orion, and the Pleiades.

—J. J. Hobbs, *Bedouin Life in the Egyptian Wilderness* (Austin: University of Texas Press, 1989), 43

The second key celestial formula of this text is now revealed. The falcon as Sirius is the marker for the flood. The dog as Canopus is the marker for the seasonal desert storms with their life-bringing rain. The falcon and the wild dog together supply the food of the desert world, just as the falcon and the dog in falconry bring food to the desert hunter. In the formula these two stars are the aspects of order and chaos manifesting in the sky.

The Egyptian perception has the simplicity of nature itself. There is nothing wrong with the weather. In an evocation of the thunderstorm in the "Cannibal Hymn," the soul rising as Canopus is *the detested wolf* who is *the most precious thing in the sky.*

The Devil Is a Wild Dog

Pursuing the devil purely in terms of iconography, the cloven feet, the split tail, the color red, the pitchfork—three-pronged like the *vajra* and the Egyptian *ws* scepter (the head of a dog mounted on a bolt of forked lightning), one arrives at the remnant statuary of the god Pan in the Roman countryside in the early Christian era. Pursuing the word *devil*, one comes to its origin in the English pronunciation of *diabolos*, the Spanish pronunciation of the Arabic word *Iblis*, the whisperer, the ever-whispering sound. Iblis is a satan, the Arabic word *shaytan* (sprite), a word typically used of mischievous children. The Greek translation of *shaytan* is *daimon* (demon). Socrates was informed by a daimon, an angelic disembodied intelligence, a murmuring voice that guided his reasoning. The devil, as one pursues its image and its name, runs off into the wild, uninhabitable places, to the name of its image, *pan*, the Greek word for "all" (pan-demonium, panic). Pan is the background fabric of all that exists, pure sound, pure vibration, the thrilling rush of wind in the reeds.

Set's title in hieroglyphs is *neb* (the all). This common hieroglyphic sign is the open basket, the thing that contains it all, the *pan*. It is the word in hieroglyphs for "lord." One might say that so close are the two conceptions that *pan* is *neb* spelled backward. They are the same thing. Thoreau wrote, "In wildness is the salvation of the world." How bad is it? How dangerous is the wild dog? A pack of African wild dogs tore apart an American toddler in a Pennsylvania zoo in the winter of 2012. A pack of American feral dogs tore apart an elderly couple in Texas in 2011. Set is the universal symbol of the wilderness and its unknowable, uncontrollable danger, the wolf. The dangerous wild dog is the wild sky with its storms, its lightning that splits the sky and falls to earth, setting the dry brush on fire, its thundering voice that shakes the ground, the howling wind, the howling wolf.

If you go back to the original idea of the wolf as the wilderness, an idea that is present even today, you understand at once that Set represents good and bad, fear and reverence, as one and the same thing, and that this is the life of the world.

One way to tame the wildness of a dog is castration, as in the allegory of Set and Horus. Horus, the falcon, is blinded by his uncle Set=the eyes of the sky, the sun and moon, are hidden by the raging storm with its blinding clouds. Set is then castrated by Horus=the wings of the sky sweep the storms away. Chaos (Set) is tamed into Time (Horus). The story becomes Kronos (Time) castrated by his son Zeus (the eagle/falcon), and plays out in King Lear, the embodiment of the doddering old year, whose three daughters are the harsh extremes of summer and winter, which leave him out in their brutal weather, and the gentle constant spring. The conflict lies between the two sons of the blinded/castrated old year: the illegitimate wild one (Set/chaos/Edmund) destroyed by the new order (Horus/harmony/Edgar).

How the Dog Comes into Hieroglyphs as the Storm, as the Wild Sky

The hieroglyphic word on the right is *nshny*, "the storm," marked with Set, the wild dog, ears and tail up, over which streams falling water. Beside it on the left is an odd composite hieroglyph that appears in verse 5 on the east gable in the sarcophagus chamber. The verse tells how the dangerous stormy sky creates all that is beautiful in the world. The central hieroglyph in the composite is the *ws* scepter, the dog's head on a bolt of forked lightning, over which arcs a three-barred rainbow and above it a feather, the air. For the storm tamed by time is a thing of unsurpassed beauty. Anubis is the bridge between the human and the wild, the domesticated dog. Its blackness is the blackness of the benign night. As the avatar for intelligence is marked by what is understood, the moon, the dog's vocal recognition of the moon on its path makes the dog the one who shows the paths, the trajectories of heavenly bodies moving across the turning sky. From the modern perspective one thinks: What's it called? From the ancient perspective the question is: What's it like? The ancient original taxonomy is based on similarities, not differences. The dog as an idea does not go into genetics. Anubis is an idea rather than a specific animal, exoticized by the name given to it by European translators, *jackal*, the Sanskrit word for "coyote." There are two wild canids in northeast Africa: the golden jackal, a large, light-coated animal that closely resembles the American eastern coyote, and the slight, slender, long-muzzled Abyssinian red wolf, a canid so gentle that it is adopted by Bedouin as a hunting companion even today, though it is now listed as an endangered species. This swift and beautiful wild dog is the parent of the lightning-quick tracking dogs that came out of Egypt: the saluki, the greyhound, the slender red vizsla.

In getting to the heart of a thing, imagery is elastic. Language is much the same. What is a wolf? It is the Latin word *vulpis*, "fox." We have come to believe that words and things exist in flat categories, and that language is static. But life is fluid, it moves beyond categories. And language is a living thing, in which words rearrange themselves, and sometimes flip. One can easily see that the Greek word for "leaf," *phyl* (as in chlorophyl, green leaf) is the English word *leaf* spelled phonically backward, just as *phil* is the word *love*. The Arabic word *zeug* (Greek, *zeug*; Latin, *iugo*; Sanskrit, *yoga*; English, "join") in Egypt occurs most commonly in reverse, as *gawaz* (marry) and *goz* (husband). Another common example is *nefs*, which occurs both in hieroglyphs and Arabic as the verb "to breathe." In Arabic the noun means both "self" and "soul." The word appears in English as *sniff*.

The image of the wild dog occurs on a number of predynastic slate palettes from Egypt, rimmed with two African hunting dogs holding hands; between them is a circle, or a tree, the axis. This recurrent motif of wild dogs holding hands could easily be read to indicate the sky. Beneath the dogs on one palette is a chaotic mix of real and imaginary animals that might seem to be the constellations. Among them is a dog with the exaggerated ears of Set, and human feet, playing the flute: the music and vibration that underlies all life and movement. Is this Pan, the All, the dog who calls the tune, who recognizes the patterns in the vast chaotic starry sky? Is Lucifer, light-bearer, the dog star, the "fall" or descent of which prompts the season of death? The wild dog Set tears Osiris into twelve parts=the wild sky is divided into twelve months. Set devours the eye=the gradual erosion and disappearance of the circle of the moon, the closing of the eye, which is time itself. Pan is born on wolf mountain, the son of the Greek Anubis, Hermes, the messenger who knows the way into the land of the dead. The story of Pan chasing Syrinx into a whispering bed of reeds is the story of the background murmur of sound, as Syrinx ceases to exist and becomes the wind, *iw seshu sw*. It is the rebus rather than the icon, the tactile signal rather than the story, that the Egyptians are after. If it works it makes your hair stand up, because you are approaching something real.

> Turning and turning in the widening gyre, the center cannot hold.
> The falcon cannot hear the falconer. Everything falls apart.

The earliest cult sites in Egypt are for the falcon and the dog, and raise the unanswered question: Who were the "ancient Egyptians" and where did they come from? The flat surfaces of rocks in the deserts on either side of the Nile all the way to the sea in the east and Tassili in the west suggest an answer in the drawings that presage the formation of hieroglyphs, drawings of the falcon and the dog, the wild bull and the dappled cow, the subject of the verses on the north wall of the antechamber, animal metaphors that embody raw nature as the hinge of the life and death of the nomadic year.

•

VERSE 2

The Sky Is a Dappled Cow, Hat-hor: The Square of the Falcon

Say the words:
Stars of the west, east, south, and north, the four embracing horizons,

are purified for you for Osiris on his ascent to heaven. He crosses
the cool dark as his son the falcon
With two fingers he lets him live and makes him rise as the great
falcon star in the cool dark.
They have made you, Unis, into the falcon son of Osiris,
Unis, into the falcon star, the older son of the square of the falcon.
It is the command of Osiris that Unis, though seed of the earth, rise
as the falcon twin
Thus it is written of these four: the shining souls within the axis,
Regarding the instruction of the two great holy ones in the cool dark.

The square of the sky is established in a seemingly mathematical
configuration as a celestial square, the limits of which are the four directions, perhaps defined, just as today, by the limits of movement in those
directions, the solstices and the equinoxes. The Osiris mystery is now introduced: Osiris crosses this quadrant not as himself, the earth-bound disinte-
grating body, but as what rises from it, his "son" the falcon. He crosses the
hat (the square) *hor* (of the falcon): the sky as a dappled cow with the precious
jewels of stars under her feet as she wanders through the wilderness of the
dark benign night, beloved as the one refuge from the parching sun. The stars
flow across this cool, dark sky; the stars sail across the sea of the sky.

This is *the instruction of the two great holy ones in the cool dark*, Sirius
and Canopus, the brightest stars in the desert night.

·

VERSE 3

The Ladder to Heaven: The Milky Way

Say the words:
O Daughter of Anubis, (you who are) the watching of the sky
As it was presented by Thoth,
(You who are) the rungs of the ladder, open the path for Unis, that
Unis take the path.
O winding stream of the glittering sky, open the path for Unis, that
Unis take the path.
O bull with four horns: your horn in the west, your horn in the east

Your horn in the south, your horn in the north [wall broken] . . . in
    the west,
For Unis that he take the path
Unis, you are the pure falcon of air, rising with the falcon of the
    circular horizon
O rich green fields [wall broken] pure are the offerings within

"Daughter of Anubis, (you who are) the watching of the sky" is the hieroglyphic pun *pt ptr*: *pt* is the sky, *ptr* is the pair of eyes. The watching of the sky is
the way into the sky: the eyes in the sky, the eyes of the sky, the eyes on the
sky=the sky as it is seen is the sky.

The concept of the measurable, traversable night sky is the daughter of
the realization that there are paths, and that they can be opened, understood,
entered, and traveled, and that they were presented as such, understood as
such, by Thoth, the human mind. This verse presents the first appearance in
religious literature of the concept of the ladder to heaven, as in the vision of
Jacob, "and behold a ladder set up on earth, and the top of it reached to heaven:
and behold the angels of God ascending and descending on it. And at the top
of the ladder there is a column, and at the top of the column is God." In
the Egyptian version the ladder is a visible feature of the night sky. It is the
ladder of souls, the Milky Way. This familiar celestial marker appears in
the poem midway through the verse, precisely as the Dipper appeared as a
vivid metaphor for a constant feature of the night sky in the middle of verse
1. Like the Dipper and the North Star, the ladder appears first encoded in a
pun. The word for "ladder" in hieroglyphs is *mkt*, a pun on *mskt*, the name of
the Milky Way, which is then named and described as *the winding stream of the
glittering sky*. The hieroglyph is a picture of a winding stream.

The daughter of the dog with its three natures, or heads—Set, Wepwawet,
and Anubis—guards the river in the underworld, the Milky Way, raising the
inevitable question: Are the River Styx, the punishing wheels, the devouring
monsters, and Elysian fields of the Greek underworld, and their derivative, the
Christian hell, a confused misreading of Egyptian astronomy? The "under"
world is the night sky with its constellations slipping continually down below
the horizon of the earth. The Milky Way is later described as pure milk of
white light, *glittering, like metal*. The concept is contained in the word *galaxy*,
literally "milky."

Mazzaroth, "the path of the goats," *maaz* (goats)+*wat/rot* (path), is what the desert nomads call fondly after their flocks, the animals one milks: goats, sheep, cows, the *milky* way. As seeing *is* the sky, so the Milky Way is the ladder of souls.

•

VERSE 4

The Ladder in the Body

Say the words:
Tie the ladder (make the ascent possible) by (means of) the
　　light,
In accordance with Osiris.
Tie the ladder by means of the falcon in accordance with his
　　father Osiris
As he moves into his light body, one of them is on this side,
　　one of them is on that side
Unis is within the empty space between them.
You are made into a star, a pure falcon among the constellations
　　that rise, purified.
Unis is lifted by the falcon, Unis is set in place by the wolf,
Taking his hand by means of the light.
Thus the light body goes to heaven, as the corpse goes to the earth.
What men receive when they are buried: a thousand (loaves of)
　　bread, and a thousand (jars of) beer
On the offering table, is a poor inheritance
As it cannot be consumed (by a corpse).
So write (about it instead. Make writing the offering instead). Write
　　the name Unis in a large hand, not in a small hand.

Tie the ladder by means of the light is a concrete image of leaving the physical body, Osiris, the corpse, and moving into the light body, the falcon. The soul rises from the corpse and becomes the star. Unis, the person, is in the empty space between the two forms, between the material earth and the celestial light. The text on this wall switches back and forth between the sky and the earth, between the stars and the body. The ladder is the means of ascent. The energy leaving the body, the nature of which is light, is the word *akh*, the sound of *ka* spelled backward, as though it were a mirror, a twin. It is the haloed bird, the hermit ibis. Upon entering the realm of light, the body is washed away. Unis is lifted up by the falcon, the turning of the sky, and set in place by the wolf, nature.

The one thing that survives is writing.

The verse makes it clear that the belief is not that the actual person survives: the offerings are in fact pointless, they are simply a ritual. What survives is writing.

VERSE 5

The Star in the East

Say the words:
How beautiful the sight, how pleasing to see, by means of them, by
        means of the stars
The rising of him, as a star, this falcon to heaven, the rising of him,
        of Unis, to heaven
His power, his head, his entire body, his nerve centers upon his legs
The spun form the earth made for him, goes forth as the souls made
        stars
In the circular horizon P, the holy souls are in the protection of the
        circular horizon
The stars up in heaven, the stars near the earth, make them lift up
        Unis upon their arm
As you rise, Unis, to heaven, leap up on it

Beauty

The word for "beauty" is *nfr*, the picture of a stringed instrument, the Egyptian *oud* or *rababa* (known in English as al oud, the lute). In hieroglyphs this image contains a range of related meanings, beauty in the sense of both sound and silence. The hieroglyph signifies completion, the mathematical concept of zero, emptiness. It conveys both the beauty of music and the music's having stopped, completed; it has vanished.

The image of the soul leaping up onto the arms of light as the arms of the stars reaching fondly down is a paradox, a reversal. The soul no longer has arms, but the formless sky has moving arms that reach down. The body and life of the person are then broken down into their aggregates, the attributes of what an individual is composed of—head, body, legs, life story, life energy, all spun together as the soul enters the eternally spinning sky.

•

VERSE 6

For in You Is the Wheat

In this its name of ladder,
Give Unis the sky, yet give him the earth.
Is it not said about this: the earth is the green sprouting
    mounds
Green green the falcon, green the wolf, the green fields they
    are stars.
Thus your name is falcon of the ascent, for in you is the wheat.
Thus you are its wild bull, as is said of its essence:
Your death is its death, behold, for you, your form is its form
In secret, the wild bull, hide, hide the secret of the bull.
So, Unis, you unfold, as you remain among them,
The shining souls of eternity, as they sail, as they sail

This mystical verse clarifies the primary message of the poem: the essence of wild nature is growth, the essence of time is green, *for in you*, these two pervasive intangibles, is the tangible, long-sought thing: food. Thus you are the wild bull, the wild, dangerous invisible life force. The picture here is of the falcon now with a crown on its head. Before, the falcon is the needlelike pyramid that appears in the first verse with *pi*, as Unis became *qhr spd*, the falcon of the triangle, of the triangular path of the ascent and descent of Sirius. In the first verse the dead soul is becoming the falcon, now the soul is crowned, for it has become the falcon. Below this charming and complex image of the falcon with the crown and the pyramid in this verse is the word for "wheat," spelled out with the picture of three grains of wheat beside it. This verse on the north wall is the key verse, for it brings together the principal actors of the sky: the wolf as wild nature, the falcon as time that tames it. Together they are the mystery—food. The essence of the mystery, the thing that makes it work, is water, the bull, both in the sense of flash floods from seasonal storms, and the Nile flood that destroys everything in its path. The bull is an astute metaphor for a thunderstorm. The ranging approach of the violent, unpredictable thunder sounds and feels like a wild bull erratically running to and fro, pounding the ground, threatening to strike at any moment. The falcon and the wolf are equally responsible for the greening of the mounds of mud left by the flood, and the greening of the desert after the rain. The words in the verse are *yatyat* (green green), a doubling verb that is also used of the stars coming out, for, as is stated in the verse, *the green fields they are stars*; *iarw* is the hieroglyph of waving grass.

Directly below is the first use in the text of the word *Dwat*, the hand, the lasso, and the star, signifying the realm of the greatest beauty and mystery, the dawn as the momentary layer of light that appears just before the sun rises, for as it rises, the yellow sun washes out the blue-green light with its fading silvery stars— suggesting the transitory moving nature of the Egyptian sense of what the sky is: a great flood, a blossoming. Here one has the strange parallel conception of *phws*—the Greek word for "light," as in phosphorus, photosynthesis—the creation of life through light in the greenness of a plant, for *phws* in Greek means the essence of the human soul as it resides in the body, as in Emerson's "we are placed into our bodies as fire in a pan."

The Secret of the Bull

Hide the secret. The word for "hide" is *amn*; as a noun it is *amnw— amnamnamnw*, thus the verse mimics the sound of *the thunder, the bull is the thunder.* It is also *the thunderstone*, meteoric iron, the double-headed axe thrown from the sky, resonating with the idea that lightning is a sword, *he has loosed the fateful lightning of his terrible swift sword.* The secret of the bull is the thunder that causes the desert to bloom.

Why Emerald Is More Valuable Than Gold

The Emerald Tablet of Hermeticism begins with the inscription *as above so below*, and brings to mind the unsolved etymology of the word *emerald. As green as emerald.* The word appears as a foreign word in Latin: *sma-rag-dos*, which comes into English as *emerald.* A proposed etymology: *sma* appears in this verse as the hieroglyphic word for the picture of a bull with arced horns and a tossing head, looking very much like the rock drawings left by cattle herders throughout the Egyptian desert on the east and west sides of the Nile. It is the Arabic word for "sky." In Arabic the sky is also called *Al Akhdar,* the great green. As the verse states, it is the wild bull that greens the sky: *sma* followed by *raq* (Arabic, *raq/g*, ascend with *dos,* the Greek patronymic ending plastered onto a foreign word) means *the wild bull ascends* greening the sky. *Copt,* from which the word *Egypt* derives, is the hieroglyphic formula *ka-pt,* "the bull [*ka*] of heaven [*pt*]." This lovely verse ends:

> So, Unis, you unfold, as you remain among them
> The shining souls of eternity
> As they sail, as they sail

The final image: Unis unfolds, opens, as the flower. Here the verb *to open* is represented by a four-petaled flower that opens from within.

The Stars Are Sailing the Cool Watery Dark

The boat is the vehicle in which one crosses over the lake of the sky. That the boat is a metaphor is apparent from the fact that it is made out of letters, of two hieroglyphs: the verb *to see,* the sickle, is the cradle, and the verb *to perceive,* the prayer shawl, is the stern. Within the boat are two falcons, the falcon star and its twin, the soul. Between them are the hieroglyphs for "to create," the boomerang, and "to follow," the sled. In a later version of the boat in the text, the two falcons appear with the *imakh,* the spinal cord, as the stern, for the vehicle in that verse is the spinal cord.

.

The Axis of the Sky

Say the words:
The axis is in Unis, falcon star you are the axis as Unis
The falcon star is the axis as Unis, light of the axis, you are in Unis
The light is the mother of Unis, the axis is the father of Unis
Unis himself is the axis.
The axis creates, and the axis destroys
The light of the stars, and the light of men
There is no equal to his inheritance on earth as the falcon star,
Its condition is entirely given over to Unis and under his
    control,
For you are its star. Is he not then until eternity, Unis, the
    falcon star?
Thus he grinds not bread or cake but as the holy falcon
With his companions the stars he does not tread a trodden
    path
Nor leap up from among them, nor does he open the doors of
    the little boat
Nor does he open the doors of the boat of the dawn
Nor is the spell broken within his circular horizon
Nor does he open the doors, lest it be destroyed.

Unis comes from you. Unis becomes the wild cow, O bull-like
    life force above,
Rising in the axis. Unis comes from you wild cow
Unis becomes the ancestor that gave birth to you who give
    birth

That the turning sky is what is meant by the *nywt* hieroglyph is made clear in this verse. The first image is of the central axis with the wheel turning around it. Then the wheel becomes the mill wheel that doesn't grind bread or cake but is the turning sky itself, producing food. Then the image becomes the sky as a wild cow, embodied by the tongue-twisting pun *mstw msstw*. The core of the word *ms*, "to give birth," is "to turn." *Mstw msstw*, *gives birth to you who give birth*, is a pun on the name of the Big Dipper, *mschtw*, the turning sky as the cow, Hathor, the leg of which is the Dipper.

The verse ends with a Tantric image: Unis merges with the mother and becomes the child. Unis merges with the sky and becomes it.

•

The Two Daughters

Say the words:
O falcon [m.] of the green falcon [f.] mounds,
O wolf [m.] of the green wolf [f.] mounds,
O reeds of the green fields of reeds,
O essence of the two daughters of the four primary holy ones
In the great shrine (of night), you rise as a sound to Unis revealed.
Unis looks at you as the falcon looks at the sky,
Unis looks at you as the life force looks at what enables breath,
Unis looks at you as the crocodile looks at the water,
Unis looks at you as the wild dog looks at your heart.

This is a coded astronomical reference in keeping with the rest of the text. It has to do with the mystery of the polarity of male and female. The verses on the north wall of the antechamber progressively spell out the shift from male to female in the words themselves, as in the first verse from Sirius as male to Sirius as female, in Anubis cast as his daughter in the third, and in the dead becoming first the wild bull, the fructifying power in the sky, and then the wild cow, the turning sky itself in the previous verse. The characters in this body of writing are ideas. Much as with a theme in a musical composition, an idea is introduced, and then activated by being reintroduced and elaborated upon. And ultimately the entire thing fits together as a gradual elaboration of parts of a greater whole: the falcon and the wolf and the bull, and the greening of the fields. The two holy ones that arise from the four were presented in verse 2, *Thus it is written of these four, regarding the two great holy ones.*

The method used throughout the text is that of hiding the meaning in an embedded pun in the beginning of a verse. Here the buried phrase is the Egyptian religious concept of the *ma'a herw.*

Maa, the sickle and the eye, is the verb "to see," as though one were clearing reeds with a sickle in order to see beyond, across the river. The word ends with the white Egyptian vulture, with its bright yellow face and beak, a stunning sight against the blue desert sky. The letter indicated by this bird is called the *aliph*, but its sound is like the Arabic *ghain*, a glottal sound between *a* and *r*. Hence this is a word like *mira* (admire/mirror), a verb that means "to see" in Arabic as it does in Latin. The verb appears four times in the verse, as the repeated phrase *he looks at you, as . . .*

The hidden pun in the verb "to see" is the similar word *ma'a*, the Egyptian word for "truth," which comes into Greek as *moira*, "fate." The hieroglyphic word is spelled with a ruler, indicating that measurement is the ultimate truth, the cosmic order, the invisible underlying pattern that manifests in geometry, in astronomy, and in sound. This key word appears first in the text here, as a pun on the word for "to see." It then becomes the focus of the text on the next wall, *give him truth* (the eternal geometry of the stars with their essence of fire), *leave the false to the earth* (what decays and is impermanent). That the pun is intended here is made clear by a word that follows in close proximity. The word is *herw*, "sound." The hieroglyph that defines this word is the picture of a lion's tail, suggesting that the essential meaning of the word is not simply sound but the essence of sound, vibration, as the tail of a cat vibrates like a guitar string before the cat strikes its prey. The hieroglyphic word *herw* is commonly paired with the word *ma'a*, "truth," as the noble goal of life: one strives at death to have accomplished *ma'a herw*, not to speak the truth or have a true voice but to be true to the clean underlying pattern of what one is, the *ma'a herw—the true vibration, the vibration of truth.*

Hence this verse is a truth being revealed. It is addressing the essence of the two daughters. The question is, what are the two daughters and the four holy ones? Are they the sky as wild and benign, as in Lucretius when the laughter of the nourishing mother calms the wild sky?

He Looks at You
As the falcon looks at the throne: the sky
As the snake looks at the scorpion

The scorpion with its ribbed body resembles the esophagus and in hieroglyphs is a metaphor for the windpipe. Hence the scorpion is called *what enables breath*. The meaning in the riddle here may be that as the serpentine life force leaves the body, it looks at the limitations of life in the body, what animates the physical body, breath.

As the crocodile looks at the water: as the liberated fierce greening life force looks at the mother that gave birth to it, water.

As the wild dog looks at your heart: how the wolf became a dog no one knows, but what everyone knows is this: the dog belongs to the heart. Perhaps what is meant throughout is that the male is the free energy, and the female binds it, enabling manifestation—catches and contains the rising life force in form—or that the male is drawn inevitably into the larger realm of the female. Or perhaps what is meant is that the principle that underlies both the harmonizing of chaos and the miracle of the manifestation of form is love: that is the underlying vibration revealed.

•

VERSE 9

The Living Words

Unis is an offering to the stars. The tomb a rising light.
Born in a prayer to the stars, in a boat of light
Unis sits in its presence. [followed by instructions:]
Open (Unis) the boxes. Hand out (Unis) the instructions.
That Unis live in the living books.
That Unis send out its message that does not die. That Unis
    enact what is said of him.

The verse makes clear that this is not a description or an artifact but an instruction manual. As elsewhere in the text, the verse switches abruptly to the imperative and gives instructions for transformation.

•

VERSE 10

Threaten Not the Twisted Threads

Say the words:
Shenuunis Shenutemshenthethunis Shenthethtemhu
Unis is encircled with protection. This is protection.
Do not threaten Unis. Threaten not the twisted threads

Beat not the legs of Unis on this path not for legs
Unis becomes a falcon. Unis goes out from his father. Unis goes out
    from Osiris.
His face in front of his head within his hair and his eyebrows, the
    entire makeup of Unis
Which is in the tomb, Unis brings as he flies up from his nest

This is one of several verbal formulas the meaning of which is essentially the sound. Still, the sound is a series of words with real meaning. The meaning here is the tying of the protection cord. The ritual is proceeding. The instruction has been read aloud. The first thing that must be done is the tying of the protection cord, so that the subject will be protected, precisely as in a ritual initiation in the Vajrayana, a religion of knots and cords. Here the protection cord is placed and knotted around the name, which stands in for the person. The words themselves are twisted together as a tongue twister, forming a protective spell, with the ultimate resolution *threaten not the twisted threads*. The same formula with slight variation is repeated in the beginning of the verse that begins the west gable in the sarcophagus chamber, the text above the body itself. There the formula reads *surrounded by the serpent, by the serpent surrounded*, as the protection cord becomes the serpent of life that threads throughout the universe.

The Birth from the Head

As Athena is born from the head of Zeus, Unis rises from the head of his corpse as a bird.

•

VERSE 11

Orion

Say the words:
See the light of Unis, Orion is Unis the king.
You who know know him.
As all of him goes out does he not know peace?

Let the doors of the horizon open for the rising boat.
May you know the hall of the shrine in its innermost part
As you hasten your rising from it, as you go down in your little
   boat.
Command Unis command him command him
Say this four times:
Column of these four,
Would that you would that you be seen
(kahawhawka—the word runs backward and forward,
the following words containing their echoes)
Upon upon the words words [*mdwdw*] of death death [*mutut*]
For the name has the power to enter.
Is it not is it not with it you them?
Do they not stretch out their arm to the tomb of Unis? for Unis is
   going with you.
As you say the name the great flood rises with the great one.
Is Unis blind to your hand in the dark?
Is he deaf that he not hear your voice?
Come take Unis to you, with you with you.
You drive the rain
You drive the clouds
You cause the storm to break
Your eye is Unis, rejoice, rejoice [*haneean*]
His eye is yours, green, green,
Grant Unis the form of the bird of the mother
Say the words:
And may the bread fly up to the houses the houses of Egypt.

Orion Is Invoked by Name and by Echoing Words

Unis has become Orion, the calendar sign for water. The hieroglyph shows
the bar of the sky pouring rain. Orion is named, *sakh*; the determinative is
three flags together with a line through them at the base, signifying Al Nilam,
the brilliant arrangement of three stars that are Orion's Belt. In Egyptian
religion *akh*, with a slightly different but typically substituted *h*, and the
hermit ibis as a determinative, is the light body. With the causative *s* this
usual name for Orion can be read literally as *he who makes the light body*.

In this verse is the first mention of the importance of knowing and re-membering *you who know know him*. The formula is picked up on the south wall: *you know him he knows you*. The patterns of the sky are the essence of memory.

The text abruptly switches to the imperative, as though the action is happening and suddenly the words are frightening, as an actual presence is invoked. The power of the invocation lies in doubling the words in an echo, *the words words of death death*. The name conjures the thing. *The name itself has the power to enter.* The living numinous presence from outside is called at last by name and reaches in its hand to the dead man, *as you say the name, the water rises*, and the eerie voice, *is he blind to your hand in the dark? Haneean*, the Egyptian word *rejoice*, appears again and again.

The Eye

The wall ends by introducing the primary element in the Pyramid Texts, the point of the whole thing: the emergent eye.

The Eye Is Green

The eye is given to, or prompted in Unis by, a mysterious presence in the dark. The eye is green: the eye in the heart of the reeds, the azure fields of flax, the root, the tree, and the twig, the creative force that resides in the patterns of the world. Seeing, knowing, and creating are the essential elements that pass into the realm of the eternal, through and beyond sense impressions, beyond memory, through and beyond words.

May the Bread Fly Up to the Houses the Houses of Egypt

The dead is absorbed into the eye, the energy that manifests life, as though death were merely a transition from the particular to the universal, from a limited existence to the great formative wave of life. The physical entity is gone but remains alive as light in the realm of nonstory. Perhaps the question is whether the greatest good is simply what is inevitable: death as the purification that enables one to pass beyond story, to become complete, calmed, eternal as peaceful nonstory, feeding with freed energy all that comes into being and passes away. This is the organic Egyptian perspective, anchored in a profound knowledge of nature. The language of hieroglyphs is purely Egyptian, instinctively captured by Egyptian poets five thousand years away, echoed unknowingly, in a line by the Egyptian poet Salah Jahin, in *Ghenut Baramhat*, (The songs of spring):

> *rufruf ya tair qalbi ala byut byut,*
> flutter flutter o bird of my heart over the houses the houses

and in the final poem of the Saidi poet Amal Dunqal:

> Go round winged falcon go round
> The year passes and the end will come
> And when my death comes it comes around
> Like the ravenous falcon.

Thus the north wall of the antechamber presents the idea of time and nature in terms of the turning sky, and how together they relate to what is on earth. The method of the text has been established. The first easily identifiable device is the use of animal metaphors to conjure principles of motion and to capture the essential qualities of things. This use of metaphor works on the level of ideas, on the level of words, and even on the level of the letters themselves. It is not a standardized device and shows throughout the workings of human insight, intelligence, aesthetics, and delight. The Egyptian sensibility is both knowing and affectionate, and there is a great deal of humor in it.

The second easily spottable technique is that of refining the meaning of a thing or an idea through repetition, as though words and lines can be spun around and seen at different angles. The subject, although it is more than that, the thing that is conjured with words, is the principle of motion and change in the sky, flagged by visible entities: Orion, Sirius, Taurus, the phases of the moon, the North Star, the Dipper, Canopus, the Milky Way. The sense of the progression of images is one of pure motion. The motion of the sky relates to motion, to growth, on earth: the rising of the flood, keyed with eerily exact precision to the rising of Sirius at dawn on a specific day in late July; the rising of Canopus presaging the autumn rains; the green growth keyed to the rising of the water. This motion in its purest form is the moving integration of the sky and the earth, of death and life. The idea flows on to what life is in the body: electricity, seen, in the way that is characteristic of

Egyptian representation, as an animal metaphor, as an internal snake. That this electricity can be actively manipulated and concentrated within the body, and that this active concentration of energy opens a mystical quality of vision that is free-flowing and omniscient, is known. It works. It can actively be done. It is a reality. Whether this free-flowing omniscience, this third eye, leaves the body and continues to exist is a question that is still being asked. The idea of the immortal soul rising to heaven, and of a heaven inhabited by winged angels, is known to have come from Egyptian iconography. In the Egyptian conception, the rising serpent in the body that becomes the external eye is conflated with the disembodied ordering intelligence in the sky and on earth. In its purest form this reliable cosmic order that underlies both life and beauty is not beneficent or punitive, but the variegated sweep of stars that tracks the circular motion of the universe. It is time itself.

II

THE PYRAMID
TEXTS

OFFERING CHAMBER

East Wall and Gable

East Wall

North Wall

ENTRANCEWAY   ANTECHAMBER

South Wall

West Wall

West Wall and Gable

North Wall

PASSAGEWAY

South Wall

East Wall and Gable

North Wall

SARCOPHAGUS
CHAMBER

South Wall

West Wall and Gable

Entranceway

West Wall

1

Say the words:
The sword of Orion opens the doors of the sky.
Before the doors close again the gate to the path
over the fire, beneath the holy ones as they grow dark
As a falcon flies as a falcon flies, may Unis rise into this fire
Beneath the holy ones as they grow dark.
They make a path for Unis, Unis takes the path,
Unis becomes the falcon star, Sirius.

2

Say the words:
Would that the bull break the fingers of the horizon of earth with its horns.
Come out. Rise.

3

Say the words:
Unis becomes the baboon of the desert hills of old
The rising light is Unis, the wise face is Unis

The shining one is Unis, the face, the head is Unis,
The eye is Unis. Rejoice that he remain among you
On the path/as a child

4

O Star that sits shining,
Does Unis not give you his life force,
that he remain ever after as a holy thing,
that in the axis of the wheel
Unis may float to the sky

5

Say the words:
Unis comes today before the rising, swirling flood
Unis becomes the crocodile, green, floating up, face watching, chest raised,
He rushes out, rising as a leg and great tail within the shining light,
He goes to his banks of silt in the great swirling flood,
To the still place in the reeds on the rim of the sky.
He greens the green reeds on the banks of the sky.
He brings his precious green to the great eye in the heart of the reeds.
He takes his place on the luminous rim of the sky.
Unis rises as the crocodile, son of the water, Unis eats with its mouth,
Urinates, copulates with its penis. Unis becomes (the life-giving water of)
    semen itself,
Seizing women in their husbands' arms, wherever love arises, according to
    its nature.

East Wall

1

Unis becomes the primary serpentine life force
That absorbs his seven serpents

That manifest as the seven yoked attributes in his seven knots
Nine times three sanctified attributes obey these words
Unis comes back as he absorbs myrrh, he receives myrrh,
He is blessed with myrrh, he is brought back with myrrh
Unis takes on your power sanctified attributes
As he turns he yokes your spiritual faculties

2

Unis becomes the shining burning bull-like life force.
The brilliant light is the essence of his eye. His mouth is stable in the heat.
The head of Unis has the horn of the lord of the south, the falcon of old.
Unis reveals the path as the holy falcon. Unis has the power of the nine holy
    ones.
He is the root of the azure field of flax. As the flowering twig lifts up
It is Unis who binds the winding growth of the acacia branch to the sky.
Unis is the power throughout the earth, north and south,
He spins into being his circular horizon. Unis becomes three as he rises.

3

Holy is the night Unis rises as the three powerful ones:
They are Orion, Unis as Babay,
Unis becomes the son of she who did not know that she gave birth,
Unis, whose face is full all three nights.
Great art thou, Golden One, hidden from people before.
Unis becomes Babay, lord of the night,
The Hamadryas, who lives although he does not know it.

4

Say the words:
Would that he would that he bring to Unis
The thorn on the top of the spine of Osiris
That Unis might rise upon it to the sky,
That Unis be joined with the light in the sky.

Antechamber

North Wall

1

The door of the sky: Sirius lives as Unis
Brought to life as the child of Sirius.
The eighteen holy ones are purified for him.
As the Dipper does not set,
The rising of Unis will not set in heaven.
The seat of Unis will not perish on earth.

Though placed in the tomb, men fly away to them, the stars.
Sirius makes Unis fly to heaven among his brothers, the stars.

Great Night uncovers her arms for Unis:
A hundred thousand twin falcon souls,
The sailing souls of the axis,
While the head of the sun sleeps below
She weeps these tears.

The shining falcon is yours, Unis,
He does not give it to another rising to him.
Unis goes to the sky with you falcon shining.

The face of Unis is as the falcon's,
His wings as those of waterbirds,
His claws in the shining night,
Are like the jaws of the desert lynx.

Is there not a poem for Unis from the earth among men?
Does not the bird dance belong to him in the sky among the stars?
Give the name of Unis his poem.
Unis himself is destroyed upon his ascent to heaven.

Wepwawet flies Unis to heaven
Among his brothers the stars:
Unis takes the arm of the wild goose
Unis beats the wing of the turtle dove,
Fly fly away man fly away Unis from in your hand.

2

Say the words:
Stars of the west, east, south, and north, the four embracing horizons, are
     purified for you for Osiris on his ascent to heaven. He crosses the cool
     dark as his son the falcon
With two fingers he lets him live and makes him rise as the great falcon star
     in the cool dark.
They have made you, Unis, into the falcon son of Osiris,
Unis, into the falcon star, the older son of the square of the falcon.
It is the command of Osiris that Unis, though seed of the earth, rise as the
     falcon twin
Thus it is written of these four: the shining souls within the axis,
Regarding the instruction of the two great holy ones in the cool dark

3

Say the words:
O Daughter of Anubis, (you who are) the watching of the sky as it was
     presented by Thoth,
(You who are) the rungs of the ladder, open the path for Unis, that Unis
     take the path.

O winding stream of the glittering sky, open the path for Unis, that Unis
    take the path.
O bull with four horns: your horn in the west, your horn in the east
Your horn in the south, your horn in the north [wall broken] . . . in the west,
    for Unis that he take the path
Unis, you are the pure falcon of air, rising with the falcon of the circular
    horizon
O rich green fields [wall broken] pure are the offerings within

4

Say the words:
Tie the ladder by (means of) the light, in accordance with Osiris
Tie the ladder by means of the falcon in accordance with his father Osiris
As he moves into his light body one of them is on this side, one of them
    is on that side
Unis is within the empty space between them
You are made into a star, a pure falcon among the constellations that rise,
    purified
Unis is lifted by the falcon, Unis is set in place by the wolf, taking his hand
    by means of the light
Thus the light body goes to heaven as the corpse goes to the earth
What men receive when they are buried: a thousand bread, a thousand
    beer
On the offering table, is a poor inheritance
As it cannot be eaten
So write (as an offering instead). Write Unis in a large hand, not in a
    small hand.

5

Say the words:
How beautiful the sight, how pleasing to see, by means of them, by means of
    the stars
The rising of him, as a star, this falcon to heaven, the rising of him, of Unis,
    to heaven
His power, his head, his entire body, his nerve centers upon his legs
The spun form the earth made for him, goes forth as the souls made stars

In the circular horizon P, the holy souls are in the protection of the circular
     horizon
The stars up in heaven, the stars near the earth, make them lift up Unis
     upon their arm
As you rise, Unis, to heaven, leap up on it

6
In this its name of ladder,
Give Unis the sky, yet give him the earth.
Is it not said about this: the earth is the green sprouting mounds
Green green the falcon, green the wolf, the green fields they are stars.
Thus your name is falcon of the ascent, for in you is the wheat.
Thus you are its wild bull, as is said of its essence:
Your death is its death, behold, your form is its form
In secret, the wild bull, hide, hide the secret of the bull.
So, Unis, you unfold, as you remain among them,
The shining souls of eternity, as they sail, as they sail

7
Say the words:
The axis is in Unis, falcon star you are the axis as Unis
The falcon star is the axis as Unis, light of the axis, you are in Unis
The light is the mother of Unis, the axis is the father of Unis Unis himself is
the axis.
The axis creates, and the axis destroys the light of the stars, and the light of
     men

There is no equal to his inheritance on earth as the falcon star,
Its condition is entirely given over to Unis and under his control,
For you are its star. Is he not then until eternity, Unis, the falcon star?
Thus he grinds not bread or cake but as the holy falcon
With his companions the stars he does not tread a trodden path
Nor leap up from among them, nor does he open the doors of the little
     boat

Nor does he open the doors of the boat of the dawn
Nor is the spell broken within his circular horizon
Nor does he open the doors, lest it be destroyed.

Unis comes from you. Unis becomes the wild cow, O bull-like life force
    above,
Rising in the axis. Unis comes from you wild cow
Unis becomes the ancestor that gave birth to you who give birth

8
Say the words:
O falcon [m.] of the green falcon [f.] mounds
O wolf [m.] of the green wolf [f.] mounds
O reeds of the green fields of reeds
O essence of the two daughters of the four primary holy ones
In the great shrine (of night) you rise, as a voice to Unis revealed
Unis looks at you as the falcon looks at the sky
Unis looks at you as the life force looks at what enables breath
Unis looks at you as the crocodile looks at the water
Unis looks at you as the wild dog looks at your heart

9
Unis is an offering to the stars. The tomb a rising light.
Born in a prayer to the stars, in a boat of light, Unis sits in its presence.
Open (Unis) the boxes. Hand out (Unis) the instructions.
That Unis live in the living books.
That Unis send out its message that does not die.
That Unis enact what is said of him.

10
Say the words:
Shenuunis Shenutemshenthethunis Shenthethtemhu
Unis is encircled with protection. This is protection.

Do not threaten Unis. Threaten not the twisted threads
Beat not the legs of Unis on this path not for legs
Unis becomes a falcon. Unis goes out from his father. Unis goes out from
    Osiris.
His face in front of his head within his hair and his eyebrows, the entire
    makeup of Unis
Which is in the tomb, Unis brings as he flies up from his nest

11

Say the words:
See the light of Unis, Orion is Unis the king. You who know know him.
As all of him goes out does he not know peace?
Let the doors of the horizon open for the rising boat.
May you know the hall of the shrine in its innermost part
As you hasten your rising from it, as you go down in your little boat.
Command Unis command him command him
Say this four times:
Column of these four,
Would that you would that you be seen
Upon upon the words words of death death
For the name has the power to enter.
Is it not is it not with it you them? do they not stretch out their arm
Toward the tomb of Unis? for Unis is going with you.
As you say the name the great flood rises with the great one.
Is Unis blind to your hand in the dark?
Is he deaf that he not hear your voice?
Come take Unis to you, with you with you.
You drive the rain
You drive the clouds
You cause the storm to break
Your eye is Unis, rejoice, rejoice
His eye is yours, green, green,
Grant Unis the form of the bird of the mother
Say the words:
    And may the bread fly up to the houses the houses of Egypt.

West Gable

1

Say the words:
The eye in you is your child: the falcon.
The great ones tremble when they see you rise
With the book in your hand into the realm of stars.
Honor to you wise one,
Though the earth formed you
The nine gave birth to you.
Peace, falcon of your father
Peace, not limited to his years,
Peace stars of the east and west.
Manifested in the enclosure of the arms
The holy infant falcon
Unis *pi* Unis
See Unis *pi*
Look Unis *pi*
Hear Unis *pi*
Exist Unis as
Unis *pi* Unis

Raise yourself upon your side
Do as commanded
Unwilling, asleep, weary
Rise in the mill.
The eye is your bread:
The beauty in the circular surround of P.

Take up your life force in the axis
Become the falcon.
The eye of your father commands
The master of storms, Orion, to come back
That wild nature grant what lifts you
lifts everything that exists.

2

Say the words:
Unis becomes large as he rises between the thies of the nine.
Unis, conceived by power, of malachite born as Sirius,
Unis is foremost of the blessed dead that rise.
Carried high above on the path of light, the light of all
Unis goes to his seat in the sky above Egypt.
Unis rises as a star.

3

Say the words:
O aged shades,
Say to the noble one in this his name,
Unis becomes a pool of lilies glittering on the flooded land,
The light of Unis, made by his constellation.
Unis becomes joy of great force as he enters the surround of fire.
Give him truth within it, (give) the false to the earth.
Unis becomes the joy of the noble protectors, the cobras
That guard the night of the great flood that rises with the great one.
Unis rises as the beautiful one, as the lotus,
The shining joy, he rises on the horizon full of light.
Pure are the stars of his appearance.

4

Say the words:
Unis exists by means of the energies reassembled as essences
According to the great method within the holy book
Of the knowledge of the falcon of light.
Unis goes to his seat by means of the energies reassembled
As essences according to the great method.
Unis takes the form of the perception in the holy book,
The falcon of light, prompted by the hand of Unis, by Unis,
told within the heart of the great practice in the ritual book, hidden there.
Unis *pi* Unis *pi*

The concept of the holy falcon of light,
Its twin essence is before you: the arrival of the flood.

5
Say the words:
Among the racing stars,
Upon the arms of light,
The path of sprouting green is made, for Unis.
Unis takes the path in the middle of the turning
Of those rising above.
Unis goes to his place among the constellations.

Would that divine agency give back
The head of the blossoming time of sharp Sirius
Under the sharp knife [of the horizon] that cuts its throat:
The circuit with the head of the bull and Orion,
Placed in the dark of the powerful arc of time of the great holy flood.
Give to Unis the burning ones. Unis grasps their front,
Nor does the arm of Unis spin away from the horizon.

6
Say the words:
Lift up your face, stars in the dawn, Unis is coming.
You will see his transformation into a great star.
Unis flows forth as a white bird.
Unis is restored to you to eternity.

Declare, Unis, the words in the book for all mankind.
Open, Unis, the living words within the shore of light.
Speak, Unis, for this shore he is made pure, that he remain.
Open the two holy ones. Empower Unis.
Lift his scepter to his head. Unis, purify him,
That he sit among the shining sailors.
Command Unis that he accomplish the completion:
That Unis become a great star.

7
Say the words:
Pure is he who is washed in the field of rushes
Pure is the light in the field of rushes
Pure is he who is washed in the field of rushes
Pure is Unis in the field of rushes
The arm of Unis is in the bright arm of Night
Iw seshw sw
Iw seshw sw
Let him be free
Let him be free
Or,
He is the wind
He is the wind.

West Wall

8
[incense]
The greatness of the bull: flame and heat.
Mourned spirit of the tomb, O great unknown spirit
Upon the throne of the one lord, O Lord of the luminous horizon,
Osiris as Unis, if not you, Osiris as Unis, then the eye.

Unis is lifted up from his father the earth.
Earth, do not speak to him lest he fall.
Unis finding on his path his food:
The breath of the wind, and water water.

The pelican presages the rising of the nine: the great pelican twin.

The spell of the *ta-ntrw*:
The ground of the twenty-seven sanctified elements:
Dam the dam

Of the reassembled, reassembled
Joined to the light within
The canal canal.

Secret are the ways to take
Not broad the banks for rising
The bank is scorching hot
To cross the beaten Milky Way.

The vessel is in the mouth
Two sons flow out.

O terror of the marshland,
You, the rain star, at the head of the column of stars.
They see your column as the bull of the desert hills in the sky,
The green marshland of the bulls of old.
Ah the fear and trembling, the terrible stormy sky of old
Opens the earth as it washes the light.

He loves to go out in the tall grass
Of the field in the heart of the starry sky.
With you he goes out, he is in your spinning, beautiful falcon of air,
In your spinning, with its beautiful rain.
Ah, say, "Make it go out, soil born of the overflow."
His horn is the sharp pillar, the eye of the bull of heaven,
Lifted up, your lion eye, let it take the path in peace,
Washed, lifted up by the beautiful falcon.
As for Unis, he goes out, as you sail by,
To the fields with their offerings of bread and beer,
May you take the overflow onto the high ground
Where the field is planted.
You plow your seed into the earth at the right moment.
You let it rest. You watch the light in its windings,
The bright realm of stars in their winding ascent
In the great circuit. Within its garments
Are all the offerings it gives you, on your arm.

The monkeys in the circuit form the heads.
May Unis take the path with you in peace.
He ties the head upon his neck
It is the neck of Unis, under his protection.
It is he that ties the head, he ties the head.
The bull flows out within it.
It is the day of tying the plow ox,
That Unis give them food
In the vessel of the inundated land.

You do not know that Unis is within.
Seeing him delights you:
The green essence of the storm.
It is Unis that the wind bears up
And makes firm his place
In the column within the circular horizon.
In the column within the circular horizon,
In the column of the two lights
It is powerful, the precise moment the great ones set.
In the marsh of Unis, in the field of rushes,
Established, revealed is his earth in the fields,
The fields with their offerings.
Release, Unis, release the great flood
With its bull, its life force
Among the sailors and their powerful setting.

With the power of his eye, the ubiquitous falcon,
The eye of the falcon is his protection.
Unis, take these eyes.
His bread is taken in his hand, empty of him.
The taken new-made food is in his hand,
Empty of itself, for in reality it is taken by the wind.

Powerful were the ways of his day
When Unis lived among them.
Rising he turned back the enemy,
Their hearts in his fingers, cut out,

Their red blood poured to the ground.
For their heirs poverty, for their houses fire,
For their land, their homes the Nile.
It sweetens the heart.

Thus Unis is one with the bull of heaven.
He subdues anything done against him.
He destroys the weapon.
The earth below his seat in the north.
His father is the wind behind the storm.

9

Say the words: [incense]
The horizon of the falcon [incense]
The horizon of the falcon of all [incense]
Horizon of the falcon of flame
Mourned spirit of the tomb,
The flood, the fiery blast of heat are yours,
As the great one is lifted up [incense]
Horizon of the shining falcon, the falcon of all things.

Hateful its nature. Hateful what is done.
It destroys you in your home.
It lays down your flesh on the earth, as Unis,
Its purpose is not for you. It destroys you.

The life force of Unis goes out in it. It is great.
Every moment the power that is yours
Of the eye within it will manifest.
As it goes around you it prompts the storm.
Thus forms are made, as the flood rushing up assaults you.

The life force of Unis puts his arm on your breast
The arm rises toward him inside the tomb
As he receives the instruction:
The power of the perception of the falcon.

10

Say the words:
Unis is the heir of the earth. He is the heir, not his father.
Upon the seat of the older falcon, his eye with its power is his
    protection.
It is created for him from the fire of his serpentine light body.
Over these is the image of the rising cobra at his head.
Give to Unis his terrible one. Its essence is an eye thrust out.
With it we see the holy aspects revealed. You it burns.
As for Unis, with adoration, his mother, his fortress, rows him
    to shore.
Ah, your boat is tied.

11

A sailor in the sky sees the truth,
Indeed, the holy ones, those of the falcon,
The nine holy aspects of the distant falcon.
In its brilliant light give him protection,
You who make the turning for him.
Eighteen holy stars, do not let his seat be not in any place.
Let Unis have heaven, let his seat be the firmament.
Guide Unis on the paths of light.
Let Unis become at peace in the life of the falcon,
Following the starry realm of the falcon
May Unis shine, seen as he comes out in the east,
Taking his place as a sailor. Behold him.
Its protection give to Unis, ancient ones,
Powerful in his place. Let him take the rope
That brings one to eternity, made fast for him.
May his feet know the boat. May he reach the luminous horizon.

12

This Osiris Unis goes to his place in the fire.
This he does not enter as one from earth

For his earthly form is destroyed.
From the tomb he rises over the earth,
His bones broken open, His obstacles removed.
Purified is Unis with the eye of the falcon,
His obstacle removed in its entirety.
Osiris release Unis from his evil.
With the knowledge of the circular
    horizon.

His sister, the green serpent,
The mistress of the circular horizon of P,
Weeps for him.
Unis has gone to the sky
Unis has gone to the sky
With the wind
With the wind
It is not known,
You do not know
If he remains
Or makes the crossing
As a holy thing.
Unis becomes
one (who remains) after,
As the ancient stars,
His bread is high above in the light.
His food is the flood
Unis becomes a thing in motion,
He sets out with the light,
He embraces the constellations,
Unis harnesses their energies.
The energies seize him
They make him wake
For he sleeps
He calms the two threads
Among the racing stars of the turning sky
Nor does he cross on foot
Nor does his essence spin away.

13
Say the words:
O earth,
The bull of night becomes Unis,
Heir of his father. Unis becomes movement,
His movement is of these four bringing the flood.
Grant the purification of what has been done.

South Wall

1
O by the foreleg in the reeds,
Are they deaf to the truth of the voice in his eye?
There is a division of Unis, of the male moisture from the female
    moisture.
There is a hearing of the two truths. Emptiness is the witness.
There is an instruction of the two truths.

As he goes around the places of the earth
He is lifted up to his beloved country.
His inheritance is reassembled within the mystery.
He is reconstituted within the waters.
Give him the attainment of the words in the books
Regarding the axis of the circular horizon.
As Unis passes away may he rise on this day
In the true form of a living light body.
Break Unis open and drive him off as a rising sailor.

If the truth is brought to him, is it not with him as he departs
Raging as he goes around within the waters alive?

There is a refuge for Unis in his eye.
There is protection for Unis in the eye.

The strength of Unis is in his eye.
The power of Unis is in his eye.

O falcon stars of the south, north, east, and west
Protect Unis, make him grind,
Seat him with the dappled sail of time.

Rise, rise.
Your serpentine light body burns in your skull,
Pulling up your essences.
They go out as if Unis on his two legs were going.
Unis becomes himself—the self that is his father,
Green new shoot of his mother.

Unis travels into the dark unseen.
Unis rises, hanging in the sky, on this day,
The truth is brought to him,
It is with him, nor does it depart:
Unis is in your fire, O stars.

2
Say the words:
Unis becomes your departing
Essence of earth essence of wind,
Revered fierce glowing spinal cord,
Unis becomes fire in the wind.

To the end of the sky
To the end of the earth
To the end of the limits of space
Unis travels as the wind.

Again as he goes out
The horizon kisses the king
The holy forms open to him
Their swaying arms.

Unis rises,
His face to the east of the sacred vault of heaven.
He is carried on the distant ascending path
He becomes the open eye of the raging storm.

3

Stchtchw rchtsw stchsw rchtchw stchsw rchtchw
Stchtchw irchtsw stchsw irchtw

Do not not know Unis, holy star,
You know him, he knows you
He knows you, you know him
He knows you, you know him.

Do not not know Unis, sun,
You know him, he knows you
You know him, he knows you
He knows you, you know him
Do not not know Unis, sun,
It is said of you: greatest of all who set.

Do not not know Unis, moon,
You know him, he knows you
He knows you, you know him
Do not not know Unis, moon,
It is said of you: he fulfills the one.

Do not not know Unis, Sirius,
You know him, he knows you
He knows you, you know him
Do not not know Unis, Sirius,
It is said of you: he is pain.

Do not not know Unis,
You within the starry dawn,
You know him, he knows you

He knows you, you know him
Do not not know Unis
You within the starry dawn
It is said of you: the night wakes.

Do not not know Unis, Bull of heaven,
You know him, he knows you
He knows you, you know him
Do not not know Unis, Bull of heaven
It is said of you: he who quakes.

Who is Unis?
Unis is who is going.
Who are you Unis?
Rise.
Does Unis not go himself?

The opening effects his going out
That Unis take the path of his wide rising [wall broken]
For him, his emerging soul, the great void.

He takes no food.
Why within the great boat does he not spin away
From the palace of light of the great ones in the Milky Way,
the shining arc of the sky. Ah see Unis reach the heights of the sky
See him in his form in the vehicle of the spinal cord (*imakh*)
Unis is carried as a sailor within it
He knows his rising cobra is the boat that carries him as he bails out.
Witness him, equipped with the brilliant north light
Give him the storms of the sky. Make him rise in the light.

4
Say the words:
Grant that the two embracing celestial horizons of the light
Let him cross to the luminous rim of the sky.
Grant that the two embracing celestial horizons of the falcon

Let the falcon of the luminous rim of the sky cross with the light.
Grant that the two embracing celestial horizons
Let Unis cross to the luminous rim of the sky with the light.
Grant that the two embracing celestial horizons of Unis
Let Unis cross with the falcon of the luminous rim of the sky
With the beautiful light,
That Unis (cross) with his living life force, Unis with his life force, his soul.

His leopard-skin apron, his flail in his hand,
His scepter in his hand, his protection
Hurry bring him these four things.

Ancient souls who wear the forelock
Holy ones who stand on the eastern side of the sky
With their scepters: the lightning,
They say the beautiful name: Unis is in the light.
They announce Unis to the great serpentine life force
They grant him entrance to the northern fields of stars
That Unis cross the river of celestial light.

The lake of space:
Cross cross, Unis, to the eastern side of the luminous horizon
Cross cross, Unis, to the eastern side of the sky.
His sister is the star Sirius.
He is the child of the starry dawn

5
Say the words:
Your heart is yours, Osiris,
Your legs are yours, Osiris,
The heart of Unis is his own,
The legs of Unis are his own,
The arm of Unis is his own,
Dancing out on his legs
To the sky he rises over heaven
Having arisen in great clouds of incense.

He flies up as a waterbird
He alights as a beetle
He flies up as a waterbird
He alights as a beetle on a seat of air
In a boat of light.

O rising ancestors,
Those who do not know nonexistence.
Unis sits on your throne,
Sailing in heaven in a boat of light.
Thus Unis is separate from earth.
As you rise on the luminous horizon
You and he, his scepter in his hand.
As you sail, your light rises in the sky
On your distant path away from earth
Far from where the acacias grow

6
Say the words:
May he rise, this Unis, as the shining light rises,
O great holy nine, as the wondrous gold one is raised high
Before the shrine, taking Unis P,
Arm in arm, his heir with him,
Unis grasps the crown from the holy nine.
Isis nurses him, Nephthys suckles him.
The great one takes him with his two fingers,
And washes him clean in the lake of the wolf.
He releases the life force of Unis in the lake of the stars,
He wipes away the flesh from the life force of Unis,
From his body, with water from the arms of light
On the luminous rim of the sky.
May he shine with the light of the horizon,
May the holy stars open his sight.
He leads the life force of Unis from his body in the tomb.
His great eyes are the gates of the souls. He ties the knots.
He leads forth Unis among the indestructible stars.

He crosses the fields of rushes. He sails the luminous horizon
He sails in the cool dark.

This Unis is worthy of trust, worthy of trust.
He does not hold back his arm before his life force reaches him.

7
Say the words:
Set the fire. The fire glows.
Set the incense on the fire.
The incense glows.
The scent goes out to Unis.
The incense, its scent goes out Unis, to you,
The incense, its scent goes out as Unis to the holy ones.
This scent of Unis comes to you holy ones.
Unis is with you, holy ones.
You are with Unis, holy ones.
Unis lives with you, holy ones,
You live with Unis, holy ones
Unis loves you, holy ones,
Love him, holy ones.
Come cake come bread,
Rise on the knee of the falcon.
Come rise, come climb,
Come climb, come float.
It is the floating up that is the rising
Of Unis onto the knees of Isis.
Climb, Unis onto the knees of Nephthys,
To the limit of the father of Unis, the universe itself.
Let Unis be counted among the stars.
Count him precious, protected among the stars.
Mother of little Unis, give this your breast
That he may cross it over his mouth
That he may drink from you
Your milk of shining white light
That Unis may travel this land

And not thirst nor hunger there
Until eternity.

8
Say the words:
Watch in peace over him, behind him in peace,
Look behind him as he sails the water in peace,
As the holy stars sail in peace.
Unis goes with you as you ferry him across
As a sailor in the boat of the falcon
As your boat crosses, the holy ones are in it.

Go to Unis, to his side.
As you go, holy one, to his side
Go to Unis, to the very locks of his hair
As you go, holy one, to his very hair.
No one lives who knows anything against Unis
No one knows anything against Unis
No daughter knows anything against Unis
No bull knows anything against Unis.
There is no one against you, Unis,
You may cross on the wing of Thoth.
He ferries Unis across, at his very side.

9
Say the words:
Unis becomes the complete majesty of the earth
As he rises in the void.
Unis becomes the green lotus.
Unis becomes peace of the two lands.
Unis becomes the joining of the two lands.
United with his mother,
The great wild cow that is his mother,
The wild cow wife on the greening desert hill,
On the desert hill, shining, shining

The white stork rises
The column, the column,
Descending whitens the land, the land, the land
So Unis rises in the ascent.
His bright shining father, the falcon dog star
Made for him, for the souls going up to heaven.
He who gives this to Unis gives him the starry dawn.
O his eye is your protector. It is his.
He orders your protection.
O his eye opens the holy vision to Unis, of the wife,
Unis, the face of great Isis at the side of the holy one.

10
Say the words:
Raised up, united with her therein, the gate of the water.
Unis goes with you, grant your opening to him, Water,
Unis becomes a child there. Unis is the companion of the light
Is not Unis among the holy ones in your divine light.

East Gable

1
Heaven storms
The stars cry out
The vaults quiver
The bones of the horizon quake
They are silent
They are weak
They are weak.
They see Unis rise,
A living star in the reeds is he
(Or a living star, with his fathers)
The wild bull of his mothers

Unis becomes the all, the detested wolf,
Whose mother does not even know his name.
Yet Unis is the most precious thing in the sky.
Unis is the great power on the horizon.
The universe that gave birth to him
Gives birth to one more powerful than itself.
The energy forces of Unis are all around him
His female angels are under his feet
His spirit powers are above his head
His serpent rises on his crown
His guiding serpent is on his brow.
To see the white bird on the luminous horizon
For you is a mystery.
There are spirits around Unis for his protection.
Unis becomes the bull of heaven.
His heart throbs as he lives in the form of every star,
Feeding in their pastures as they come,
Their insides filled with spiritual power
From the encircling fire of the horizon.
Unis becomes the full vessel of its light bodies
Unis rises as the immensity of all that is within the throne.
Let him set his back to the earth.
Unis becomes an instruction of carved words,
With this, his hidden name of light, which to know, guides him.
Unis becomes the prince of peace, the revered shining eye,
He is himself the bread and wine. Unis becomes the food of
    mankind,
Who lives as the holy ones, everything that comes from the shining
    heaven.

Open now the books:
So seizing the hairs on the top of his head
In the dark, they tie them for Unis
Then the serpent's head rises, guarding him as he spins,
Then moving outside the bonds, he is free
Then moving on he is given his pervasive true nature.
He absorbs it. Let him be filled with it within

What is opened sends him spinning.
The known instruction as practiced for Unis.

He burns in the protecting fire.
His vessels are in the evening sky
Unis becomes one who feeds on their energy
And absorbs their bodies of light.
They are large, the two lights at dawn.
In the midst of their essence in the evening is he.
They are small in the hall of the night.

The ancient ones burn on his hearth,
As the falcon looms large in the northern sky,
Shooting out flame. The flood goes out beneath them
As these ancient legs turn in the sky, for Unis.

Thus he is the arrow,
And the vessels, the legs of their women;
As he goes around the entire sky
He turns the two celestial horizons.

Unis becomes great power, powerful among the powerful, Unis becomes,
The arm goes round the arm goes round the arm goes round, great,
Finding on his path his food: the breath of the wind
And water, water. His protection is on his brow.
All the noble ones are on the horizon.
Unis becomes a holy one, as ancient as the ancient
Thousand that go around with him.
Offered to him are the winding (paths)
For given to him is the arm of fulfillment
The great power of Orion, father of the stars.

Unis rises again in the sky.
His flesh goes out to the luminous horizon.
He has broken the knots of the spine.
He receives the essence of the stars:
He feeds on red. He absorbs green.

Unis is transformed into the branches of wisdom.
He is in bliss as one who lives on the essences
Of their life force. Ah he Unis
Licks the moist essence within the red
Until his flesh is flooded with it
And their life force is within him.
Thus not residing in his mummy or with it
Unis has absorbed the mind of pervasive holiness.
The light of Unis rises *pi* for all eternity *pi*
The body that is this, his mummy,
That he so loved, is made hateful to him
For it does not function within the realm of light.
What is eternal is the soul.

2

The light bodies are within Unis. They are with him.
Before Unis offerings are burned for the holy ones
For their bones. Their souls are with Unis
As are their shades as they rise.
Unis is among those
Rising rising remaining remaining
Doing what is done in the instruction in the books.
The seat of the essence of Unis dances
As one who lives on this earth
Forever and ever.

East Wall

3

Say the words:
Unis goes with you, falcons in your three mansions.
Ah weep for Unis. He was born
To attain your secret of the tomb
With the door that opens both ways

To carry Unis to the limit of the luminous horizon.
As he lies in his wrappings on earth
He is transformed into a great being
Placed in the north of the circular horizon.

4
Say the words:
Irk irk irtk irk sksk
You create your eye as it destroys you.

5
Within his burial
In the grave itself
The falcon in his eye goes out.
The life force in his testicles rises.
Go out. Rise.

6
Say the words:
The arm again the arm of Babay
Strikes within the thunder
Of the turning sky.
Ah it belongs to him, the outflow.
Ah . . . that you are loved, you are loved.

Release him, O serpent
Give him your protection.

7
Say the words:
Unis becomes a burning other,
Beyond the ways of Thoth,
Beyond O Unis

It is dark, it is dark.
Ti ki taha ti kki ti kki

8
Say the words:
Your eye, your eye
Is behind you, over you,
Around you, as your great protection.

9
Burn, house of the star,
House of the celestial falcons
Lion of P, your house,
Lion of P, you, you P, your house P,
You who are placed in the axis of the three falcons.
The secret flesh in the axis,
The vessel, is moving, moving,
The serpent, the serpent.

10
Say the words:
O light, bird,
This is in your mouth
Aeeee
As you become
A bird of light
This is in your mouth
Aeeee
The praised gold
You rise burning,
Praised, this is your life force.
This honor has been done for you.

11

Say the words:
For you Unis this is his fingernail
For you Unis this in the east is his hand
Catch with them the thunder
It is yours. Catch it if you can.

12

Say the words:
P Command him
Not to fill the mouth of Unis.
Give him this, a thread
Give him this twisted thread.
A centipede is in the two houses.
Rise, rise, twisted thread,
In the two houses, rise, rise.
The centipede P, he is the lion
Within P the lion
Two energies fight within
The light of the white bird.

13

Say the words:
There are in you two things made of alabaster.
There is of your alabaster two,
Your two alabaster cups, your cup.
O cup of water, O water, O eye,
Place of the book of the writer,
Sacred home of the gold-mine rain,
Your life force, the essence of the flood itself,
The lion of revered revered water,
The fertile field of your heart.

14
Say the words:
Glittering white as the vultures
You are free.
You take your wave
As the herons
Gliding back and forth.
The crowns, the kites,
The kites lift up the crowns
Going away from me.

15
Say the words:
This is for his mother
Excellent among them
Excellent among them
You are his lion.

16
Say the words:
O cry of the snake
O cry of the *kerawan* snake
Go, for you have two faces
On the path of the eye.
Unis does not see
That he has an eye within
It is not your eye
That is fully opened
Not Unis that seizes him within.

17
Say the words:
Slide out, life force bull plover snake

Slide out plover of the life force bull
Slide out, spin away.

18
Say the words:
Slide out, face upon face
Rise again, dappled feather
He absorbs him completely
He receives him.

19
Say the words:
Give praise to you, soul, shining white bird
That you rise from him, the serpent.
Receive praise for you, soul, shining white bird,
That you rise from him, for you are a serpent.

20
Say the words:
Ntktkkntkyk
Grow dark, O serpent
Draw near, draw near
You draw near,
Grow dark, O serpent.

21
Say the words:
Would that you be hidden
Nor that you be there
Nor that you be able to be seen,
Unis, within, nor do you go to that place.
Unis, there, there he is not.

Your mouth says this for you to me.
Cross over the earth in its winding path
Slide out as the shining pelican over the Nile
Leap away as the serpent sleeps.

22

The falcon becomes Unis
As he rises from the acacia
As he rises from the acacia
The serpent guides him.
You who are wise, as a lion rises
He is leaving, as a lion rises
In Unis, from his skull.
He that sleeps in his skull is rising,
Unis, at first light, from his skull.
He that sleeps in his skull
Is rising, Unis, at first light.

23

Say the words:
His appearance leaps up, is given
According to what is harnessed.
It prompts him to manifest the serpent.
Repeat it:
According to what has been set in place,
(Here is) the holy head of the serpent.
What remains of him, of Unis?
What remains of him?

24

Say the words:
The serpent takes you
Yet you do not go.

Unis becomes earth.
You, burning serpent, and your twin,
The burning (female) serpent.

25
Your father is dead.
Find his mind.
This is the end of Unis.
It comes upon you,
This, the emptiness,
This comes upon you.
Its appearance is set before one:
The life departing.
Ah thou, turn away from this
Turn away your eyes.
Better to fall into your own excrement,
And glide into your own urine,
Then to fall and glide into this sleep
And see your mother the night.
In the end this is all that is seen:
The bad deeds,
Your name,
Your writing,
And your children
These are the only four things that endure.

26
Say the words:
The light body rises.
It is a serpent.
The head is that of a snake rising from earth.
Under the fingers of Unis
Is a knife to cut off your head.
With this knife in hand
Its appearance is produced.

The face is raised.
Within those who follow in your shoes, Osiris,
The serpent sleeps,
The life force that glides away.

27
Say the words:
The serpent goes to the sky.
The centipede falcon under the shoe.
The falcon—he travels everywhere
As your life force.
The snake encircles you in your tree.
The tree of Unis is his tree.
The tree of Unis is his tree.
Rising as a light body, Unis,
On his path, he absorbs him completely.

28
Say the words:
O one beneath, daughter of the circular horizon,
You who are within,
Let the serpent cross.
Call the protected eye of the falcon.
Let this be brought to Unis
That Unis become the hawk
From the burning land.
Unis is for the place that is under your sway,
The far desolate expanse of the mirror world.
Brought to this mirror of sadness, this desert.

29
Say the words:
Primordial dark,
With those of the turning sky

Pray that when you die
You may join the holy stars,
The holy stars in their atmosphere
Of secret primordial darkness
That is the secret of the universe.
May you join the holy stars,
May you join the stars in the shadow
Of the primordial dark of the universe
With the two gates made holy:
They whose form is air, P, and moisture.
May you be remade in the image of the stars
And remain as the stars.
Ask your father to give you, Unis,
Water, that you be complete
In your manifestation, Unis, as a shining light.
That you cross with him to the numinous horizon.
Unis knows him, he knows his name in prayer
His name in prayer, his name in prayer.
Every year in his name the falcon rises on the shining arc of the sky.
As he makes the two lights shine, so may he make Unis,
Let him make Unis live as pure light,
That Unis come with you, the true falcon of the turning sky.
Unis comes out, the shining falcon.
Unis comes out, the shining falcon of the east.
May you be brought, Unis, your great eye in the east.
This light is yours, it is with Unis,
The green eye, the water within it,
Your green eye, the books that are in it,
The green eye, the throats that are in it,
The green eye, the power, the radiance that belong to it,
Take it, in this your name of king
Whose grave is under divine protection,
In this your name of light, given to you
It is yours. It is before you,
In this its name of finest alabaster
And your lion therein,

In this its name of willow tree,
And your gleaming therein as the stars,
In this its name of your great joy,
For the primordial sleeping serpent
Loves you. She rises she rises
In the great embrace of the opener of the paths
As you in your light body rise on the numinous horizon
And seize the great crown, the great wide snake of south Libya
The crocodile soul, the desert's eye.
You sail your green marsh through the canopy of trees
Your protector breathes the incense of the malachite land
You rise, falcon soul of Unis, at his side
You rise you cross you are washed, Unis,
White as the moringa tree in this your lake of the wolf
O wolf, O washed wolf, it is you,
The stars in it are your soul.
You are Sirius
The falcon lord of the green lake
The falcon lord of the green lake
The falcon lord of the green lake
The falcon lord of the green lake
The falcon the falcon
Is the green snake.

Passage to the Sarcophagus Chamber

South Wall

1
This is the eye
[wall broken]
In you,
About you,
From his mother
For you.

2
Broken, exhausted you go,
Unis P,
Into the night you go,
Unis P,
Into the night.
He was made for the earth
But leaves it as a falcon,
As his legs become wings.
As a falcon you are free, as a baby hawk.
His light body carries him, though he perish,

His life force is reassembled.
You open your place in heaven
Among the stars of the sky.
Like the ancient ones before you
Given to the night, flapping,
You will see the face, the head of Osiris.
He commands, he commands
Your light bodies to rise to him,
Though you are not in them,
You do not exist.
[wall broken]

3

See Unis rise in heaven with two horns on his head.
Who, who, what son, what child what white soul is nursed?
Distant four, who goes to you?
Falcon, whose azure eyes are your protection,
Falcon, whose red eyes are instant pain
His soul, it does not spin away.
What attributes are his as he rushes by,
He races by? They are flapping
To the holy face of the east.
This one may pass among you.
The falcon commands
Let his majesty be given to the fields of stars.
Be silent, stars.
The nine stars give their arm,
From their mouth, head/on legs
Saying, this one is among you.
The falcon commands
That his majesty be given to the fields of stars,
To rise through the doors of the luminous horizon.
Ah in the lake, the pure doors,
You rise among them, (as one from) earth.
Among the nine stars,
Their cormorant leaps up
Their bull restored to life.

They rise, they rise, with their eyes
They see you, the thunder,
The two houses rising behind you
As you rise. You in your rising
Would that you not be destroyed nor perish
Nor the light in you as you set,
As you come into being among the stars.

North Wall

1
[wall is broken for most of the column]
The twin of Unis descends . . .
[text missing]
[following column]
Say this four times:

Ah, the eye of light sees
You are purified
Osiris counts you as pure
(He) counts you
[wall broken]
Rise
As Unis rising goes from the earth
You rise with the falcon
Who goes to bring you the falcon eye
To wash white your essence
Having it brings you your milk your cream
Take to yourself what flows all around you as you rise
Nor will your heart ever weary possessing it

Say this four times:

As you rise a voice comes to you
Made pure as Osiris you take in what is said,

Unis, every word:
In his name of Thoth
Go take him to Osiris
Bring him the words
In the name of Unis Thoth
Give him your hand.

Say this seven times:

You are with him.
Protection is on you.

Seven times:

He is your protection.

Go go with his life force
Go falcon with his life force
Go wolf with his life force
Go Thoth with his life force
Go falcon with his life force
Go Orion with your life force
Ah Unis, the arm of your life force is before you
Ah Unis the arm of your life force is after you
Ah Unis the leg of your life force is before you
Ah Unis the leg of your life force is after you
Osiris Unis given to you is the falcon eye
Your face is destroyed
The faceless form of Sirius itself is yours
The eyes (alone) are on you.

2
Greetings divine one you who are three
Greetings divine twin
Greetings to you who are among the heirs

Of the great falcon father, thou stretched (across the sky).
In your mouth, your odor of incense for Unis
Your Natron for Unis
Eye of the falcon raised high, you who are great,
    for Unis,
Divine one you who are three.

The Sarcophagus Chamber

South Wall

1

O Unis you will not go on to die
You will go on to live.
On the throne of Osiris
Your scepter in your hand
You utter the words of those who live,
As you rise, your lotus scepter in your hand,
Uttering the words of the mysteries of the thrones:
Your hand is as the universe
Your shoulders are the universe
Your stomach is the universe
Your sides are the universe
Your legs are the universe
Your face is the dog star.
You go around the green mounds of the falcon
You go around the green mounds of the wolf
O Unis, your protection is empty space.

2
Say this four times:

The horns of your life force come out upon you
The horns of your father come out upon you
The horns of light come out upon you
Go with your light. You are pure.
Your bones are the bones of little falcons
Of holy serpents in the sky.
You exist at the side of the holy.
Leave your house, all that concerns you, to your son.
You of the name of Unis are called to rise.
The earth has ordered him onto the path of the turning sky,
Where he has placed him.
You are pure as the stars are pure.
O you in bonds, break free.
On the shoulders of a falcon, in his name,
Inside your vehicle of light,
For you are one of the beings of light.
You are raised up among the indestructible stars,
The ancient ones, for you are from the place below,
As your father was from the place below, the earth.
He places your falcon soul in front.
In it is your life force. In it is your being.
Foremost falcon of air, O Unis,
Your form moves, your feathers rush.

3
You set with the universe,
With the universe you rise.
It is all around you.
It is in your arms.
For are you not a holy star.
Your sight of it
Your sight of yourself

Are appearances you see
With eyes born of their fathers
And known only to them,
The imperishable stars.
As you see within the shrine
Of the falcon and the wolf,
You in the aspect of the falcon
Bring coolness
As the shining moon dispels
The darkness of the wild sky.
That you are given flesh
That you are born
That you are conceived
That you are born as a falcon in his name,
A great lion of earth that makes the sky tremble,
Is not from love, nor sexual intercourse.
You are born of Osiris, your soul is his.
You will not forget him.
You were conceived by the wolf of earth.
Your soul is his. You will not forget.
No divine child goes out to rise
[column broken]
In the front of your heart
Osiris, you will not forget him within.
You will not forget your son within, the falcon,
Nor will you forget him within.
Nor will you forget your father within
For you will remain as a holy being.
A son or daughter will say: the universe lifts you up
And they bring this about in your name as a holy being.
You become a spirit of the universe.
Everything upon you is as a falcon
In the realm of stars that do not set.
In front of you are the eyes
Of the falcon of old that does not set.
Your two ears are the son and daughter of the universe.

Your eyes the son and daughter of the universe that do not set.
Your nose is as the wolf (the dog star) that does not set,
The falcon star, lord of the heavens, that never sets.
Your arm is as a son of the stars embracing its mother.
Your celestial hand rises through the sky with your rising legs.
He is pure, his hand is your celestial hand
As you descend in the turning sky.
Descending, all your limbs are sons and daughters
Of the universe and will not perish, you will not perish,
Your spirit will not perish, for your spirit is the life force.

4
Say the words:
The whole sky moves with you, vehicle of light.
Truth goes with you in your depiction as a falcon.
The one who goes with you is she of a thousand souls.
You will remember him, Unis, the one Orion takes around
And brings to the pure realm of the stars
Alive on the numinous horizon,
Whom Sirius takes around
And brings to the pure realm of the stars
Alive, as a soul of earth.
Unis goes around, carried in the realm of stars,
Pure, alive on the numinous horizon,
His light body among them, washed white,
Among them in the hand of his father,
In the hand of the universe.

5
Say the words:
The light of the universe comes to you, Unis,
Indestructible spirit, lord of the fertile land,
The seat of the four greens.
Your son comes to you, Unis, a hawk goes forth,

Ascends to heaven into the dark,
Where you shine on the luminous horizon,
The luminous place where the sacred shrine
Of the stormy sky goes around:
The temple of the holy ones that blossoms with souls.

Unis goes there, an indestructible soul,
Whom he desires to die will die.
Whom he desires to live will live.
The light of the Universe goes with you, Unis,
Indestructible soul, lord of the fertile land,
Seat of the four greens.
Your son comes to you, comes to you, Unis,
As a hawk going forth ascends to heaven
Who shines in the dark, raised up on the luminous horizon
In the place of your soul, with Isis and Osiris.
Go then, flap up to the holy ones, among the shining souls.
You will get there, Unis, indestructible soul.
Stars above the Nile, praise him, shining souls in the waters.
Whom he desires to live will live.
Whom he desires to die will die.
The light of the universe comes to you, Unis,
Indestructible soul, lord of the light,
Seat of the four greens,
You go as your son, you go, Unis,
Travel as a hawk ascending to heaven in the dark.
You shine on the numinous horizon,
In the place of your shining soul, with Thoth.
Go then to the temple of the stars, falcon of air,
Their shining souls.
You will get there, Unis, indestructible soul
Clothed as a dog on your neck,
Near the high falcon of air.
He examines the hearts,
Whom he desires to live will live,
Whom he desires to die will die.

As the light of the universe
You go out as an indestructible soul,
Lord of the fertile land, seat of the four greens.
You go out as your light body,
You will go, you will travel as a hawk,
Ascending to heaven in the dark.
You will shine on the numinous horizon
In the place of your soul with the falcon go
To the temple of the power of the wind,
Their shining souls.
Now he comes to it, Unis, an indestructible soul,
Whom he desires to live will live.
Whom he desires to die will die.
Light of the universe, you go as your son, you go as Unis,
You will lift him up, you will surround him with your hand,
As your son forever and ever.

6

Say the words:
Osiris Unis goes to him, as nine lights, an indestructible soul.
He counts the hearts in his seat of the *kas*.
He harnesses the spirit powers as he lifts him up
Surrounding him with his arms.
He arrives without his wives, without his bread,
Without his spiritual food. His food is at an end
For the earth said to him, rise in the name of the holy ones
As a falcon so that they receive him.
See how shining white and strong you are.
Unis will come to it, as nine bright shining lights,
Indestructible soul, the thunder is yours.
This thunder is yours, this is yours, greatness, greenness
Thunder is yours. It is not your season of silence,
For with you is the eye of the storm,
With Thoth you go round and round,
The weeping stars of Isis and Nephthys
Gather round you gather round you,

Ascending to heaven around you,
Ascending to heaven around you.
Unis will come to it, appearing as nine bright lights,
An indestructible soul, falcon of the west on the horizon
So Unis will come to it, appearing as nine bright lights,
An indestructible soul, falcon of the east on the horizon.
So Unis will come to it, appearing as nine bright lights,
An indestructible soul of the south on the horizon.
So Unis will come to it, appearing as nine bright lights,
An indestructible soul of the north on the horizon
Unis will come to it, appearing as nine great lights,
An indestructible soul in the lower heaven
Unis will come to it, appearing as nine great lights,
An indestructible soul.

7
Say the words:
You are the child of the universe, this is what Osiris gives you:
He restores to life, as it lives it lives Unis lives,
As it does not die, Unis does not die,
As it does not perish, Unis does not perish,
As it is not mourned, Unis is not mourned.
As it is not mourned, Unis is not mourned.
You are the child of the air, this is what Osiris gives you:
He restores to life. As it lives, as it lives, Unis lives.
As it does not die, Unis does not die,
As it does not cease, Unis does not cease,
As it is not mourned, Unis is not mourned.
Mourn it, mourn Unis.
You are the child of moisture. This is what Osiris gives you:
He restores to life. As it lives, as it lives, Unis lives,
As it does not die, Unis does not die,
As it does not cease, Unis does not cease,
As it is not mourned, Unis is not mourned.
Mourn it, mourn Unis.
You are the child of the earth. This is what Osiris gives you:

He restores to life. As it lives, Unis lives.
As it does not die, Unis does not die.
As it does not cease, Unis does not cease.
As it is not mourned, Unis is not mourned.
Mourn it, mourn Unis.
You are the child of night, this is what Osiris gives you:
He restores to life. As it lives, Unis lives,
As it does not die, Unis does not die.
As it does not cease, Unis does not cease.
As it is not mourned, Unis is not mourned.
Mourn it, mourn Unis.
You are the brother of the sky, this is what Osiris gives you:
He restores to life. As it lives, as it lives, Unis lives,
As it does not die, Unis does not die.
As it does not cease, Unis does not cease.
As it is not mourned, Unis is not mourned.
Mourn it, mourn Unis.
You are the brother of wild nature, this is what Osiris gives you:
He restores to life. Its life, its two thunderbolts are yours.
For as it lives, Unis lives.
As it does not die, Unis does not die.
As it does not cease, Unis does not cease.
As it is not mourned, Unis is not mourned.
Mourn it, mourn Unis.
Unis is not mourned.
You are the brother of the wild sky.
This is what Osiris gives you:
He restores to life, as it lives, as it lives, Unis lives.
As it does not die, Unis does not die.
As it does not cease, Unis does not cease.
As it is not mourned, Unis is not mourned.
Unis you are the brother of perception.
This is what Osiris gives you:
He restores to life.
Its life, its two thunderbolts are yours.
As it lives, Unis lives.
As it does not die, Unis does not die.

As it does not cease, Unis does not cease.
As it is not mourned, Unis is not mourned.
Mourn it, mourn Unis.
The falcon is your father.
This is what Osiris gives you:
He restores to life.
As it lives, as it lives, Unis lives.
As it does not die, Unis does not die.
As it does not cease, Unis does not cease.
As it is not mourned, Unis is not mourned.
Mourn it, mourn Unis.
Nine great holy ones, this is what Osiris gives you:
He restores to life.
As he lives, as he lives, Unis lives.
As he does not die, Unis does not die.
As he does not cease, Unis does not cease.
As he is not mourned, Unis is not mourned.
Mourn him, mourn Unis.
Nine great holy ones, this is what Osiris gives you:
He restores to life.
As he lives, he lives, Unis lives.
As he does not die, Unis does not die.
As he does not cease, Unis does not cease.
As he is not mourned, Unis is not mourned.
Mourn him, mourn Unis.

You are the the son of night.
This is what Osiris said to you:
You are born of your father, for you are he.
His mouth, open his mouth,
That his son, his beloved falcon,
Be counted among his heirs, the stars.
That as he lives, Unis lives,
As he does not die, Unis does not die.
As he does not cease, Unis does not cease.
As he is not mourned, Unis is not mourned.
In your mouth is the central column

The *djed* column, his spinal column,
As his earthly column lives, so Unis lives.
As it does not die, Unis does not die.
As it does not cease, Unis does not cease.
As it is not mourned, Unis is not mourned.
Mourn it, mourn Unis.
In your mouth there is a vessel:
The lake within the head.
As the empty space lives, Unis lives.
As it does not die, Unis does not die.
As it does not cease, Unis does not cease.
As it is not mourned, Unis is not mourned,
Mourn it, mourn Unis.
In your mouth there is the place
Of what enables breath, the scorpion,
And the calming of the life force.
As it lives, Unis lives.
As it does not die, Unis does not die.
As it is not destroyed, Unis is not destroyed.
As it is not mourned, Unis is not mourned.
Mourn it, mourn Unis.
In your mouth is the holy shrine within you,
Wrapped in white linen, in which you are tied
And collected together.
As it lives, Unis lives.
As it does not die, Unis does not die.
As it is not mourned, Unis is not mourned.
Mourn it, mourn Unis.
In your mouth is the whiteness of teeth,
As it lives, Unis lives,
As it does not die, Unis does not die.
As it is not destroyed, Unis is not destroyed.
As it is not mourned, Unis is not mourned.
Mourn it, mourn Unis.
In your mouth there is Orion (who is)
Time in heaven, time on earth:
As he as Osiris goes around above you

May you see Unis, your seed,
Rising with you as Sirius.
As it does not die, Unis does not die.
As it does not cease, Unis does not cease.
As it is not mourned, Unis is not mourned.
Mourn it, mourn Unis.

East Wall

1

In your mouth there is the taste of the circular horizon
Put you outside, you would be finished
In it, as it lives, Unis lives.
As it does not die, Unis does not die.
As it does not cease, Unis does not cease.
As it is not mourned, Unis is not mourned.
Mourn it, mourn Unis.
In your mouth there is the great temple
Of the bull of heaven
Place you outside, you would perish.
You would die.
Within it, as it lives, Unis lives.
As it does not die, Unis does not die.
As it does not cease, Unis does not cease.
As it is not mourned, Unis is not mourned.
In your mouth there is the southernmost star of the circular horizon
Place you outside, you would perish.
It would destroy you.
Within it, as it lives, Unis lives.
As it does not die, Unis does not die.
As it does not cease, Unis does not cease.
As it is not mourned, Unis is not mourned.
Mourn it, mourn Unis.
In your mouth there is the northernmost star of the circular horizon

Place you outside of it, you would perish.
It would destroy you.
Within it, as it lives, Unis lives.
As it does not die, Unis does not die.
As it does not cease, Unis does not cease.
As it is not mourned, Unis is not mourned.
Mourn it, mourn Unis.
In your mouth there is the wheel of the sky
The lakes of light, the four heights within you,
The eye that encircles your body.
Within it, you are released,
As your son the falcon you live.
Within it, as it lives, Unis lives.
As it does not die, Unis does not die.
As it does not cease, Unis does not cease.
As it is not mourned, Unis is not mourned.
Mourn it, mourn Unis.
Your body is the body of Unis.
Your flesh is the flesh of Unis.
Your bones are the bones of Unis.
As you go, Unis goes.
As Unis goes, you go.

2

Open the doors of the luminous horizon
Dance, dance high in its wonders.
For it is he who goes with you, the red crown,
It is he who goes with you, rising serpent she,
It is he who goes with you, great one,
It is he who goes with you, great one [f.] of spiritual power,
The red crown, you are pure,
Though you may be afraid you are calm
In his purification, you are calm at his words
As he says to you beautiful things your face becomes calm.
You see your youthful vigor reborn as you are born as a star, father of stars.
It is he who goes with you, great one of spiritual power,

The red crown who has become a falcon
Surrounded by the protection of the great eye of spiritual power.

3
Ah red crown, ah bring to the red crown
Ah the great one to the red crown
Ah the great one of spiritual powers/harnessed chakras
To the red crown
Ah to the great serpent at the top of the spine
Give Unis terror with your terror to terrify
As you give a loud cry, give Unis your love,
With the love that causes the spirit to rise
[wall broken] with the light bodies
May you be given a hard knife that he know his falcon
Ah let the red crown rise
The great one blossoms as an arrow in you
The blossoming image of a serpent
Gives birth to you in the image of a falcon
Surrounded by the protection of his eye

4
Say the words:
Rise upon it, this ground of transformation
You are transformed upon it (by means of it)
You are raised high upon it (by means of it)
You will see your father
You will see your father with you
He goes with you, the light,
It is he who goes with you, the father
It is he who goes with you
It is he who goes with you
To channel and traverse, the father
It is he who goes with you as this channel
It is he who goes with you to cross
It is he who goes with you as the falcon

It is he who goes with you as the great bull
He is the surround that goes with you
It is he who goes with you,
Time, that envelops the earth in its greatness
It is he who goes with you, the father
It is he who goes with you as Sirius
It is he who goes with you, the father
It is he who goes with you as the glittering arcs of the falcon
May you be placed in its ultimate limit, Unis, in its pure light, the
     luminous horizon
May you O ruler, Unis, be granted the nine, lest it be destroyed
May you be granted the spiritual power
[wall broken] outside of the south
Would that he spin as he rises on the great tip of his greatest
     pathway
Set him down in the shrine of the north sky
Let him be spinning, lest you be destroyed
As for the spiritual powers of the wolf/the storm
He of the center, Kom Ombo, that pervades the south land
May you not be losed nor your east wind with you
Nor your spells nor your force from the southern stars
That tear up September (the harvest month)
You split the night, Destroying Set, the wild dog thunderstorm
Turn back to that place (the south) lest you destroy the young
     falcon
Do not remain, you are released, do not remain
As for you your work it is to become strong
Among the stars in the north, a falcon among their light bodies
You are free you are pure in the universe
[broken wall] assigned a place in heaven you rise
Among the constellations in your form
With your father the universe you are high above
You flow with your father the universe
You are free, with your lion's head of youth
You rise in the axis [of rising stars]
You open your way with bones of air
Surrounded by the arms of your mother the night
Pure, made of starlight you are free

You are pure in the lakes of air
You rise you descend you rise you descend with their light
With the mill you rise you descend you rise with the light you flow
With time embracing the earth in its greatness
You rise you descend with the temple that contains all things
The dark, with the vehicle of the two falcons
You rise you descend you rise with the throne
You flow with the lightning vehicle of the twin falcons
You are strong in your body but not on your feet
You are born as a falcon, conceived by the storm
You are purified in the field of the falcon of air
You receive your purification as a sound ruler of the field
With your father the universe you come into being on high
A soul washed white in the arms of your father, in the arms of the universe
Universe you see Unis, you surround him in your arms,
He is the son of your body in form

5
Say the words:
Rejoice Unis emerges, as the constellation rises
A thousand bread and a thousand beer
Roasted meat are your offerings
On the threshold of the sanctuary
In the temple of the daughter
As a holy one as a holy one
Offerings of bread and cake and beer
Provided with his bread your soul comes out
As Osiris, a luminous soul among the light bodies,
Strong among his constellations
The miller of the holy nine in the temple of foreknowledge
Emerge Unis, rise in the Milky Way
For the completion of time as it turns, rising in your ultimate form
May you be given the falcon eye, may it be reckoned for you
As the two lights come to you, with you, emerge Unis,
May you receive your bread and cake in hand
Emerge Unis may the door be opened to you
Say the words of the spell, Unis, that you be able to move

6

Say the words:
That cause the green sprouting mounds of the falcon
Say the words
That cause the green sprouting mounds of the wolf
You move as you say the words
Of the green sprouting mounds of Osiris, the prince of peace.
May you be with Orion, lord of the constellations,
Among your living words, among your light bodies,
Anubis (the dog star), the falcon of air, draws near
As dawn draws near the eastern lakes of the sky
Peace falls upon you as your star comes out
Among your brothers the stars. Of space is he of space is he.
Welcome child lord, protector of all that is on earth
May you come with them.

East Gable

1

O moon
O moon of water
Your essence is lifted burning in the sky
Breast, flood of the falcon eye washed white,
Wrap little Unis in swaddling clothes
Give him water from the lake of time
For Osiris never thirsts nor knows hunger
Nor does the essence of Unis
For the desert gives thirst then takes it away
What it fills what it fills are the hearts

2

Say the words:
O dappled one above
Food: it is rain

Give Unis your breath as bread,
And light, the taste of wine,
Give him light itself
Give him the light in the face of the bull of time
That he may have them
Give them to him to take
Give him grain:
Bread and beer, food and drink
An ox to plow the land

Unis, regarding the production of food,
There are three lights belonging to the sky
Regarding light there are two that belong to the earth
With you, nine holy ones,
The king he is the greater and the lesser light of ancient times
The greater and the lesser light is he, the king,
See, as in ancient times, see, oh the beautiful light
Just as the light of yesterday

Unis merges with the water
It is his sister:
Space itself
He unites with the disc of fire
He merges with the beautiful one he fears
The air itself
The hail and storms of the womb
Of the beautiful one he so fears
Will give him bread
For it is she, even today,
Who makes all that is good (in the world).

3
Say the words:
Food
[wall broken]
Food
Food

It is within the eye of light
Food
It is within the holy eye
The cook presents to you
Bread as a cooked offering

4
A leg of beef
With bread and handfuls of water

5
Say the words:
Green is the wind
Unis do not take its greenness away
Green is Unis
The wind does not take his greenness away
The wind does not take his greenness away
Offerings, hawk of the east, this is your bread.

6
Say the words:
Wake, opener on high, Thoth,
Wake you who sleep
You in the desert hills
On trembling arms
The great one rises from the Nile,
The opener of the paths.

With cedar purify the mouth of Unis
Consecrate with Natron the eighteen holy elements
Purify his mouth, protect the tongue,
From Unis run out, excess of excrement,
Putrefying urine, run out from Unis
That he not reabsorb the putrefying liquid

Of the great wild dog death.

The two companions crossing the sky
The sun *pi* and the full moon,
Unis is given to you, with you he eats what you eat
He drinks, he lives as you live
He sits with your wife, the throne,
Therein he is powerful, as you are powerful
There he sails as you sail
The embalmer's room for Unis
Is like a bird trap in the reeds
On the inundated land.
Unis is among the reeds
His offerings, his offerings
Are among you holy ones
Water for Unis is as wine
Like the sun,
Unis goes around the sky
Like the sun,
Unis sails the sky like the moon.

7
Say the words:
Hunger leaves Unis *pi*
Nor does he eat.
Thirst leaves Unis *pi*
Nor does he drink.
Unis becomes one
Who exists because
He has been given
The bread of light.
Though he has died *pi*
Set, the eye, lets him live.
Set, existing, lets Unis be,
Unis is conceived in the night sky.
Unis is born in the night sky.

The king within the light
On the holy arms of the realm of stars
Unis is conceived
As though he were born in water.
And in water goes forth.
He brings you the bread he finds therein.

8
Say the words:
Give him, give him the eye of the falcon,
The face of the mistress of the soul, the serpent.
He goes fluttering with the falcon of air.
The falcon he brings him his snake.
Offerings are offered to the falcon
Among the constellations.
There as what lives
There Unis lives.
There what is eaten
There he eats.
There what is drunk
There he drinks.
There is his leg of beef
There his grain
There his shining food
Pi

North Wall

1
Osiris, take to yourself Unis among your foster children.
Thoth, pour out the words in his name. Go take him to Osiris, bring the
    words.
In the name of Unis, Thoth, give him a place in your hand.

Say the words four times:
As a liberated being, You are under his protection, You are released in him.

2

Go go with his spirit. Go falcon with his spirit
Go wild dog with his spirit. Go Thoth.
Say this four times:
Consecrate the fire with his spirit
Go holy falcon with his spirit
Go Osiris with his spirit
Before the eyes of the holy falcon of old
With his spirit
Go you who are the spine, with his spirit
Unis, the leg of your spirit is before you
Unis, the leg of your spirit is behind you
Osiris Unis given to you is the falcon eye that destroys your face
There may you shine may you shine, the falcon eye is for you
Pure are you. Osiris counts you as pure
Counts Unis descending and rising

3

A libation: two pieces of Natron
With your son rising, with the falcon going out,
To bring you the falcon eye to cool your heart with it
To bring you your milk of darkness, pouring out around you as you rise
That your heart never weary
Say this four times:
As you rise there is a pervading voice

4

Remain, remain, open your mouth, oh Unis
Five pieces of Natron from the south
The entire horizon you taste its taste among the holy places
With the saliva of the falcon, remain,

With the saliva of the wild dog, remain,
Heart of the falcon, the all, of the falcon, the all, remain
Say this four times:
Bread of Natron, remain, pure emerging falcon
Among the holy falcons.

5

Natron in your mouth, Natron, the mouth of the falcon
Natron your mouth, Natron, the mouth of the wild dog
Natron, five pieces of Natron from the north lake of the sky
Natron in your mouth, Natron the mouth of Thoth, Natron your mouth
Natron, the mouth of the falcon, Natron your mouth, your spine, you
      are within them
Your mouth is the milky mouth of a newborn calf.

6

Natron in your mouth, Natron mouth of the falcon, Natron your mouth
Natron mouth of the wild dog, Natron your mouth, You are made holy
Natron mouth of Thoth, Natron your mouth, Natron mouth of the falcon
Natron your mouth, Natron your life force, Natron your mouth
Natron Natron your mouth, Natron your mouth, And this your spine
      within
Your brothers are the holy ones, Natron your mouth, head, your mouth
You purify your bones, you are not destroyed as your eye,
Osiris gives you the falcon eye that destroys your face
With it you shine you shine. O Unis you will remain.

7

May your jaws break the bread.

8

Osiris Unis I have opened your mouth with two holy things of north
      and south

Two pieces of bronze

9

Unis you receive the falcon eye. He goes to bring you what is to be put
   in your mouth
Three pieces of incense from the north. Three pieces of incense from
   the south.

10

Unis you receive three pieces of alabaster. Osiris, three pieces of alabaster

11

Take the tip of the breast of the falcon, of his body, what for you is milk.
A jar of milk.

12

The breast of your sister Isis, the protecting throne
Take to yourself this enduring protection, the vessel of space.
Offered: an empty vessel

13

You are pure, Osiris recognizes you as pure. Unis you are recognized,
   you are given
A libation from the north, rising with your son, rising with
   the falcon
Go bring you the falcon eye to whiten your heart with it
To bring you your milk, your milk. You shine from what pours around you
Rising with you. Nor will you weary while you drink it.

14

With the eyes of the falcon white and black (the phases of the moon).

Take them to see what is before you. They light up your face, light and dark.
These are its two vessels. You are full as a light in the sky. It brings you
    peace all, all
You are full, full as in the night sky of old. You are at peace
As the cobra (north) and the vulture (south) are at peace
It brings you peace. The sight of you is peace. You hear the silence
In your presence there is peace. Peace is with you, and after you.

15

Osiris Unis you take the shining destroying rays of the falcon.
A cup of five white grains

16

Say this four times:
Prince of peace, Give to Unis Osiris Unis the life force
You take the eye of the falcon. It is your bread, your food, the bread that is
    offered.

17

Osiris Unis
You take as the eye of the falcon, the law of the wild dog.
You may take this white stone. This is your jar of milk. Open your mouth
    for it.

18

Osiris Unis
Open your mouth fully with your jaws.
Offering: a jar

19

Qnk qnkt qnt

Osiris Unis you shine
Offering: beer in a cup

20

The light of the realm of the stars is yours in heaven
The realm of the stars is yours. For Unis offerings
All of your body, all of your life energy, Unis,
All of his body, all of it is holy.

21

Unis you take the falcon eye. It is your taste.
Offering: one conical loaf of bread [called taste, *dpt*]

22

Grow green grow green cries the night. [*aqaq*=*aeshaesh*]
Offering: *aesh*, bread

23

Unis you take the falcon eye you embrace.
[pun on embrace and offering]

24

Unis, you take the falcon eye, the law of the wild dog.
Take the horns/rays within it for yourself.
Offering: *mnu qnt*, a stone cup

25

Unis you shine. The offering comes out of Osiris
Offering: beer in a stone cup

26

Unis you take the falcon eye. It cannot be taken from you. Its heaven is for
you
Offering: beer in a cup of bronze [pun on *bi'a*=bronze or copper; heaven]

27

Unis you take the falcon eye, you are destroyed with it.
Offering: beer called *htm* in a cup [pun on *htm*, destroy]
Second register: west to east

28

Osiris Unis you are complete. Your eye is on the body.
Say this four times: Perfumed oil

29

Osiris Unis you shine. The offerings are within its face.
Offering: sacred oil

30

Osiris Unis you take the falcon eye
Go, you are freed in him because of it.
Offering: *sefetch* oil

31

Osiris Unis you take the falcon eye. He is protected
Offering: *neshemet* oil

32

Osiris Unis you take the falcon eye
Brought to him are the three holy things within it

33

The oils the oils are yours. Absorb what is before you
Eat your food. What the falcon sets before you, Unis
That you are made sweet for him with it. Let it make you a luminous spirit
That you be given the power in his body
You are given his, with the eyes of your light bodies
You will see him. You will hear him, His name.

34

Osiris Unis you are brought the eye of the falcon. Take it before you.
Offering: *htt nw*, finest oil

35

Say this four times: Osiris Unis you paint the falcon eye
On your face (offering: two bags of green eye paint)

36

Flow in peace. Flow milk in peace. In peace you flow.
(Offering: two bolts of white linen)
In peace is the falcon eye within the taste of the circular horizon.
In peace is the falcon eye within the sanctuary of the red crown
In peace receive the eyes the great one paints
Let her light the two lands for Unis. You love what they are,
What the falcon gives you, for the two lands, is for Unis
They love to go out in the wild dog (the wild sky), you are they,
What the falcon gives you for the two horizons is for Unis
They love to go out in the wild dog (the wild sky)
Sit on your throne before Unis as his holy spirit
Open his path among the light bodies. Place his words among the
    light bodies
Anubis/Canopus is before the falcon of air. The falcon is before Osiris.

37

Go go with his life force. Go wild dog with his life force, holy and on fire,
Go Thoth with his life force. Go holy falcon with his life force.
Go Osiris with his life force. Go with the eyes of his life force.
May your spine go with your life force.
Descend Unis, the arm of your spirit is before you
Descend Unis, the arm of your spirit is behind you
Descend Unis, the leg of your spirit is before you
Descend Unis, the arm of your spirit is behind you
Descend Unis, the leg of your spirit is before you
Descend Unis, the leg of your spirit is behind you
Given to you is the falcon eye that destroys your face
Say this four times: Stretch out, stretch out, the scent of the falcon eye is
      upon you.

38

You are pure. Osiris counts you as pure.
Counted as pure descend Unis
Rising with your son. Rising with the falcon,
Who goes to bring you the falcon eye to cool your heart with it.
To bring you your milk. Take what flows around you
As you rise. Nor will your heart ever weary possessing it
Say this four times: As gold it falls in you. It falls through the gates.

39

Thoth brings him under it, as he rises under the falcon eye.
A bronze table of offerings.

40

Give him the falcon eye. He is at peace with it.

41

Osiris Unis. Receive the falcon eye. He is at peace with it.

42

Osiris Unis. Receive the falcon eye in peace.
[odd composite hieroglyph of falcon rising from table of offerings]

43

Say the words: You are set according to your nature. Sit, be silent.

44

Osiris Unis receive the falcon eye. It rises in you from your mouth.

45

Osiris Unis receive the falcon eye. As three lights in you it leaps up.

46

Osiris Unis receive the falcon eye that was imprisoned.

47

Osiris Unis receive the falcon eye, a little food for the wild dog was in it.

48

Osiris Unis receive the falcon eye. At twilight they died for him.

49

Osiris Unis receive the falcon eye. Lift it up from your face.

50

Lift up your face Osiris. Lift up your face. Descend Unis p
Your light body goes out. Lift up your face Unis p
Emerald-green Sirius you see rising with you,

And the milky light of the moon
Unis open your mouth for the falcon eye as you flow forth as your spirit.
Osiris protects you with all the wrath within, Unis.
Receive your bread within the falcon eye

51
Osiris Unis receive the falcon eye
You are divided as its face. You are destroyed as the liquid within you goes
      out.
Offerings of bread and liquid
Osiris Unis receive the wandering eye of the falcon
One cup of wheat
Osiris Unis you are reconstituted as water within it
Two cups of water
Osiris Unis receive the falcon eye (in) the (field) bed of his mouth
Two cups of emmer
Osiris Unis receive the falcon eye
You have reassembled it from yourself
Osiris Unis receive the falcon eye, the sign of the wild dog

52
Osiris Unis receive the falcon eye imprisoned in him.

53
Osiris Unis take on your face.

54
Osiris Unis you bring to the face of the lion your face.

55
Osiris Unis the eye gives you a taste.

56

Osiris Unis receive the eye of the falcon. The three lights of yesterday are its
  face.
(The three phases of the moon)

57

Osiris Unis receive your head *pi*. Say this four times.

58

Osiris Unis with your eye you receive it. Say this four times.

59

Osiris Unis receive the eye of the falcon. The wonder of his
  breath.

60

Osiris Unis receive the eye of the falcon. In it is water.

61

Osiris Unis receive the eye of the falcon imprisoned in him.

62

Osiris Unis with the eye of the falcon placed in your mouth.

63

Osiris Unis receive the falcon eye: your bread your food.

64

Osiris Unis receive the falcon eye imprisoned in him.

65

Osiris Unis you bring his heaven, shining, stable.
Offering of flowers [pun on shining]

66

Osiris Unis with the Big Dipper, the eye of the falcon
Offering, *hepesh* (the word for Big Dipper is a leg of beef)

67

Osiris Unis dance for is not the earth with its heir.

68

Osiris Unis receive the falcon eye [wall broken]

69

Osiris Unis receive the one who has inherited the eye of the falcon.

70

Osiris Unis you shine as the stars around you. Say this four times.

71

Osiris Unis you shine as you pray. Say this four times.

72

Osiris Unis your son is from it.

73

Osiris Unis you take the falcon eye. He comes from it.

74

Osiris Unis you take the falcon eye. First he dies
(on his forehead P).

75

Osiris Unis with the falcon eye. The wild dog dies first.

76

Osiris Unis you shine. The heads of the wild dog after it.

77

Osiris Unis you shine throughout this essence.

78

Osiris Unis you take the falcon eye with his daughter.

79

Osiris Unis you take the falcon eye. Their warmth is going.

80

Osiris Unis you take the falcon eye. As its three lights he remains.

81

Osiris Unis you take the falcon eye imprisoned in him.

82

Osiris Unis you take the falcon eye, (thus) it is not cut up.

83

Osiris Unis. Thus you are the falcon eye.

84

Osiris Unis from the falcon eye he destroyed the water in it.

85

Osiris Unis you take the falcon eye. For the wild dog ate
    a little of it.

86

Osiris Unis you take the falcon eye. Thus they go round in a circle.

87

Osiris Unis you take the falcon eye. Thus the two lights
    in him never die.

88

Osiris Unis you perish as the liquid goes out of you.

89

Osiris Unis you perish as the fluid goes out of you.

90

Osiris Unis you perish as the fluid goes out of you.

91

Osiris Unis you perish as the fluid goes out of you.

92

Osiris Unis take (with your finger) the breast of the falcon. Their taste.

93

Osiris Unis open your mouth for it.

94

Osiris Unis you take the falcon eye. Its liquid essence is the three lights he
  swallows.

95

Osiris Unis you shine rejuvenated with the falcon eye. Open your mouth
  for it.

96

Osiris Unis you take the falcon eye he caught like a fish. Open
  your mouth for it.

97

Osiris Unis you take the falcon eye. Nor is there suffering for you.

98

Osiris Unis you take the falcon eye. It is water.

99

Osiris Unis you take the falcon eye. The light loosed in him.

100

Osiris Unis you take the falcon eye. He is made full in the hand(s) of the
  wild dog.

101

Osiris Unis you take the falcon eye. The white of its three lights, its lightning, it is he.

102

Osiris Unis the green of its three lights, its lightning, it is he.

103

Osiris Unis you take the falcon eye. Its three lights, its spinning.

104

Osiris Unis you take the falcon eye. Its three lights, its spinning.

105

Osiris Unis you take the falcon eye. And as for the soul it is a star.

106

Osiris Unis you take the falcon eye. Indeed they have become stars.

107

Osiris Unis. Open your eyes and you will see them there.

108

Osiris Unis you take the falcon eye. The three phases of the
moon it is he.

109

Osiris Unis you take the falcon eye. Its sweetness pervades you.

110
Osiris Unis you take the falcon eye. Consider this.

111
Osiris Unis for the light is going down. It is your light. Your light.

West Gable

1
Say the words:
Shenn'winn'wshen Shenwenushen
Surrounded by the serpent by the serpent surrounded
The baby bull, the nature of starlight, rises from the garden
    of earth
Rises from in you, rising within you a serpent sleeping
    spins out
As his majesty falls as a shining falcon over the water
As the serpent p (manifests in flame)
[strange hieroglyph of serpent emerging from flame]
You see the falcon light.

2
Say the words:
Cut from the head the life force
The bull of the life force and
Its great twin the ebony serpent
Let your mouth say this
Sacred light, holy spirit of the breath
Let your mouth say this
P you are turned upside down.
Let your mouth say this.

3

Say the words:
The face falls upon the face
The face sees the face rising within his majesty
The dappled green one watching absorbs him
Ya, he laps him up.

4

Say the words:
The clawed one which has no face
Son of death
Sailor in the spinning sky of time
Fall spin out.

5

Say the words:
Your two (kinds of) blood are from the earth.
Your two (kinds of) ribs are from a hole.
The mottled one that rises
Is (of) these two ancestors.
Your mouth is all right in what is to follow
The mouth is all right in what follows.
As its appearance arises
Count on this:
As the serpent, the green reed, the light,
Bites Unis on earth
Bites Unis on the earth
Bites Unis on the father
In biting him Unis is never bitten.
He does not bite Unis, for he belongs to him.
Unis does not come from him:
The two lights of his appearance are Unis.
The two lights seen are of Unis.
(As) you bite Unis
He alone gives you your appearance.

He manifests as your twin.
(Thus) the bite of the serpent is made lenient,
The bite is lenient by the serpent
That surrounds the sky
Surrounds the earth
That surrounded the limit (of existence)
Before the presence of mankind,
The surrounding holy falcon
Whose head is not seen,
Surrounding you yourself.
Bring back bring back this scorpion of the spine
Within the mouth of Osiris, the spine, the open face of the falcon.

6
Say the words:
Your bone, bone, your bones,
(Ultimate) essences of the lion
Of the columns within, in the place of heat,
Though they are made to fall,
(The lion) will remain
As the falcon of old is produced (given).
Pi

7
Say the words:
From the penis, from the penis, from the penis, from the penis,
Prompted from you is the falcon of his mother, the falcon of his mother
Come presence, come presence, with the scent of the unknown country.

8
Say the words:
A snake falls out to rise from the earth,
As a flame falls out to rise from the water
Fall, spin away.

9

Say the words:
The face upon you is the face of his coiled father
Descending the length of your spine within
The darkness recedes from the twin faces.

10

Say the words:
O vultures on the temple wall outside:
There's sex going on in here.
That is the mourning behind the great door.
That is the mourning.

11

Say the words:
Kbbhititibiti
Coiled snake, you are his majesty.
The (alabaster) vessel is destroyed,
The flesh: you are silent.

12

Say the words:
The spit is not in its place,
The mouth is destroyed.
In the home of its mother
The serpent sleeps.

13

Say the words:
The food of your father is for you
Yours is the little bread that you have in your father,
For you are the serpent. It is your flesh becoming gold:
The light rising. This is your bull,
The powerful revered thing that is made from his eye.

14
Say the words:
The white crown rises
The great one has swallowed (him)
The great white crown
Do you not see the tongue

15
Say the words:
The snake goes to heaven
As a falcon flies over the earth in the herd (of stars)
As a falcon he sweeps down
Unis sweeps down on the spinning sky of the falcon.
Unis does not know he does not know
The face is your face within: that he is him.
You flow you flow within you
The wondrous serpent creates the flow of falcon flesh
Retreating from earth the green reed given
On the burnt ground glides away.

16
Say the words:
The liquid of the spine is an edifice raised high
For it is the liquid that goes out of your mouth
Your own mouth.

17
Say the words:
Put out the fire.
There is no soul spirit
Serpent within the house
Possessing the gold.
The spinal cord serpent bites
Turn back, turn back to the house
He bites he is hidden within him.

18
Say the words:
The two trees the two trees
How sweet the twigs
The light the light is the bread
The light is the lion within you
Oh you
Great willow
Your tree
The willow
The willow within
The reed, the reed is he.

III

THE SILVER EYE: SEEKING THE DEEPER DESIGN

I have presented a translation of the text within the monument in full. Let me now resume my analysis of the verses as they appear in sequence on the remaining walls, considering derivatives and parallels of the ideas presented in them, with a view to seeing the deeper design in its entirety.

As the hieroglyphs advance upon the walls, there is a destination of understanding, and it has to do with the eye. We are used to ideas that you can't see, to religion as faith in hidden things, but this is about the visible world. Hieroglyphs are not recondite or indecipherable. They are metaphors drawn from physical reality itself, tactile, observable, knowable, and in its essence universal and true.

There is an axis at the center of a wheel. The wheel is time as the variegated circling of the sky. Time is the hidden intelligence of the sky, the glittering path of rising stars, the moon as a gradually closing and opening eye. The axis is a column, the axis is a tree, the axis is the fixed star around which the sky turns. The axis and the wheel together are eternity.

The Axis and the Wheel

Circe is the circling sky as seasonal time, *Mary* draped in blue and gold, surrounded by animals in a manger, the bull (thunder) and the donkey (as the Set animal because of its exaggerated ears, the meaning of which is the storm as chaos). Both animals are qualities of the changing sky. The series of transformations presented on the first wall of the Pyramid of Unis are a progression of iconographic identifications with nature as time. Does the origin of the idea of reincarnation lie in the sequence of poetic tropes that first appear here in the Pyramid Texts? Auden unknowingly mapped them out in his "alchemical" "New Year Letter":

> O Dove of science and of light
> Upon the branches of the night
> O Ichthus playful in the deep
> Sea-lodges that forever keep
> Their secret of excitement hidden
> O sudden Wind that blows unbidden
> Parting the quiet reeds, O Voice
> Within the labyrinth of choice
> Only the passive listener hears
> O Clock and keeper of the years
> O Source of equity and rest
> Quando non fuerit, non est

Robert Graves saw the progression as an ancient iconographic device that tracked the life and death of the turning year, and he called it the foundation of all poetry. Graves saw the poet as a shamanic figure who is absorbed into and identified with the circular movement of seasonal time. Indeed the word *poetry*, the Greek word *poew* (to make), in its original meaning is the place where language, nature, and religion meet, where a thing is not simply described but captured alive: the wild and potent life energy of the earth itself identified with fully and prompted on. The animals represent the elements—air, water, earth—to which they belong. They are, and the poet becomes, the dynamic movement in nature itself, the irrepressible flux and motion of life.

Graves saw the Garden of Eden as a scrambling of earlier religious iconography, and pointed out that the word *Eve* and the word *snake* are the same word. Mircea Eliade pointed out that the word *Eden* means permission (as in the Arabic phrase *edn-ek*, "with your permission," commonly used when walking through a crowded bus. It is the word for "ear," *weden*: "[May I have] your ear?" "Will you listen?"). Eliade wrote that Adam and Eve in the Garden of Eden looked like a failed initiation ceremony, the result of which would have been the fruit: higher knowledge. The initiation failed, the permission was not given, and Adam and Eve were asked to leave. The imagery appears repeatedly in the Pyramid Texts, where the snake in the tree is a dynamic metaphor for the human body (verse 27 of the antechamber east wall and elsewhere). The body is the tree. The snake is the life in it. They *are* Adam (a word that can mean "bone," "blood," or "flesh" in Arabic) and Eve (life). The iconography of Adam and Eve flanking the tree can be read as the male and female channels that flank the spine or central column in Tantric physiology. The merging of these internal male and female elements in the meditation practice of Tantric initiation prompts the rising of a serpent of heightened awareness through the tree of the body, the fruit of which is *omniscience*—described in Corinthians 13, "now I see through a glass darkly, but then face to face . . . then shall I know even as also I am known"—the quality of which is bliss, sweetness, an ever-expanding sense of nonduality, of selfless love.

Poetry is used in the original as a deliberate code to describe the numinous quality of reality, not a dark, sinister, archaic code but one of real delight and beauty: the one who gave birth but didn't know it, draped in a blue glittering cloak of stars, she whose crown is the crescent moon; the appearance of the three holy ones from the east, the stars in the belt of Orion, that presage the birth of the bright star, Sirius, rising in the field of rushes, the eastern stars at dawn. Resurrection is not a mystery. It is the fundamental nature of life on earth. Death precedes life. The only thing that is lost is the ephemeral human personality.

Antechamber

West Gable: The Lotus Rises

Both our organs of perception and the phenomenal world we perceive seem to be best understood as systems of pure pattern, or as geometric structures of form and proportion. Therefore, when many ancient cultures chose to examine reality through the metaphors of geometry . . . they were already very close to the position of our most contemporary science.

—Robert Lawlor, *Sacred Geometry*, 4

The escarpment that runs along the west bank of the Nile before the river breaks into what were once its seven deltas is lined with a series of geometrical experiments that took place over a brief period of a few hundred years in early dynastic Egypt. The experiments were worked out as geometrical problems of volume and alignment. A number of them didn't work in execution. Some collapsed. Some were "bent." But ultimately the goal of thought perfected into form was attained by means of the hidden mathematical keys to the structure of life on earth: pi and the golden mean, in the great pyramid at Giza, which is aligned with absolute precision with the North Star. The pyramids represent the working out of a system of geometry derived from triangulation using the stars. This method of triangulation connecting earth with heaven involved what we have come to call the Pythagorean Theorem, a method of calculation in which the triangle enables measurement. The religious system based on measurement that

Pythagoras represents, whether or not he was an actual person, belongs not to the Greeks but to the Egyptians, who perfected the giant triangular form as the three-dimensional resolution of the squaring of the circle. The subject of the text on the gables is the iconographic translation of this religious tradition, the translation of perception into form: the eye at the top of the pyramid, relating this oldest of religions to the Masons or geometers, the founding fathers of America, who put the eye at the top of the pyramid on the dollar bill as if to say "measurement began our might."

Linear time has a beginning and an end. Circular time is a pattern. The idea of history and progress, of an end of days, of looming disaster, belongs to linear time. But the circle is the realm of eternity. Pi is an imponderable. It is a kind of mirage. You are always approaching it, and yet it always recedes. It is the most useful mathematical instrument to have, but it is inherently inexact. It is the perfect illustration of the reality of an idea. It doesn't exist and yet it exists. Pi continues ad infinitum, which means you take it out to as many places as you want but you're still not there. Mathematics and science depend on exactitude, and with pi you can never arrive at exact knowledge. You cannot know what pi actually is. Pi is in fact infinity.

The text in the monument follows the motion of circular time, the motion of the turning sky. It reads from right to left in a counterclockwise direction, moving from north to west. The text now continues onto an isosceles triangle rising to the highest point of the central room within the monument, mirroring an isosceles triangle of text on the east side of the room. A new chapter has begun: the tone perceptibly changes to one of formality. The subject is more complex and relates to the architecture of the monument itself.

The west gable of the antechamber presents a progression of statements, some clothed in poetic imagery, some not, the ultimate point of which is the final verse: death is the pure sound of the wind in the reeds; it is emptiness. All that remains is the pattern. The point is the geometric underlay. The text is not merely descriptive but presents a layered meaning having to do with eternal life as the patterning of the energy body, and as the patterned movement of stars, signaling the turning of the sky and the seasons.

The question of orientation arises again here: how is the text fitted within the monument? This is the highest point of the west wall, a triangular slab of text at the top of the room, and the top of the writing in the room. It is mirrored by a triangular slab of text on the east wall. The central feature in this triangle on the west side is the rising of the hieroglyphic lotus, the

brilliant bluish-white light of Sirius rising from the Nile, flickering
like a living flame upon the horizon.

The dark sky mirrors the swirling flood, where *the pool of lilies glittering on the flooded land* recalls the Egyptian conceit that stars are blossoming, an eerily accurate perception of photosynthesis, that greenness *is* light. The perception is captured in the word *sha sha*, which occurs in both hieroglyphs and Arabic as the verb meaning both "to blossom" and "to appear in the dark," and in the origin of *blossom* in the Greek verb *blast*. *The green fields they are stars*, the stars blossom out of the dark as flowers blossom out of the black ground. *Al Azhar*, the rose, is *Zuhra*, the planet Venus. *Noah* is the word in hieroglyphs for "flood." *Susan* is the hieroglyph for "lotus." Both words appear in this verse. The story is contained in the word itself. *Susannah* bathing among the lotuses *is* the lotus, rising up before *the aged shades*. The subject of the west gable is the still water after the flood, the beauty of ultimate stillness. The east gable is the thunderstorm.

The two gables represent the polarity of male and female, in keeping with the Egyptian technique of twinning. The lotus is the female. The lotus is the throne. The lotus has nine petals. *The nine gave birth to you*. Nine is three rising up: the triangle given three-dimensional form. The prayer flags are three, then nine, then eighteen, then twenty-seven, demonstrating a system of proportional increase and the essential relevance of the number nine. The meaning of nine is now pursued on the west wall of the antechamber, as the meaning of the two and the four was riddled out on the north wall. The square root of four is two, the square root of nine is three. They both represent three-dimensional increase, the form rising from the pattern. What is sought is the magical key, the pattern that lies beyond form, the invisible, eternal structure of life.

Verse 1

The pool of lilies glittering on the flooded land would seem to be a reference to the Pleiades, the star cluster on the shoulder of Taurus, the name of which comes into English from the Greek word *pleiw* (to sail), the sailing stars. In Arabic they are *tiara* (the birds). The Pleiades have nine visible stars.

The first line on the gable begins where the last wall left off, with the eye. Hieroglyphs favor the noun, much as poetry favors the noun. First you look at the thing. Then you consider what it does. The action follows from the thing. In much the same way, as always in writing, the first line presents the idea. The north wall ends with the introduction of the concept of the emergent eye, with the chant *Your eye is his, his eye is yours, the eye is green.* Here the concept of the eye is immediately taken up and elaborated upon. *The eye is green.* That the eye *is* greenness is indicated in the entranceway: *the eye is the essence of the reeds.* The eye is understood as both the animating miracle of life in things and the recognition of the thing in the mind, the naming. There is no separation between the two functions of the eye, for the intrinsic quality of the eye is light. The eye *is* sight, what enables sight and what is seen, the essential nonduality of knowing as being.

Thus *the eye in you is you, your essence, your child*: the falcon.

In other words the falcon is the eye, meaning the eye goes out. We know that the eye goes out because of vision, the mind sweeping out into the world, *the first circle is the eye*, the sweeping wave of the mind. The eye can be read as a verb or a noun, but there is no object in the line for the transitive action of a verb. There is undoubtedly a false distinction between verbs and nouns superimposed on the Egyptian, which may have intended a thing to have the shading of both, for the shading, not the crisp definition, gives life to the word. The underlying grammatical question distinguishing the two is the reading of the wave to indicate whether the eye is a noun or a verb. The wave, the letter *n*, is the connecting element in hieroglyphs. It is understood as the preposition *in* or *of*, but it functions as the subtle element that connects one thing to another. The wave connects the noun to the noun in the genitive and dative and the action of the verb to the noun. Two waves following a verb indicate that the action has passed, the verb is in the past tense. But here it is impossible to say which is intended, as the eye is a thing and its nature is motion. Ambiguity is the point, as in the following line:

The great tremble as they see you rise with the book in your hand.

The book is the sword: The words *book* and *sword* in hieroglyphs are the same word (*sh't/shot*). The distinction between them is made by the ideogram, the determinative, which can either be a book, a rolled papyrus bound with string, or a sword. Here both determinatives are included in the word. The papyrus is commonly used as a determinative to indicate a concept, an abstraction. One might think, though, that here a book, in the basic physical sense of an actual book, is what is meant. The book is *this* book. It is being read aloud. The religious ceremony depends on the book. The activation of the concepts presented in the book, the progression of the religious ceremony, happens when the words that are written in the book are read aloud. There is also the possibility that the words written on the wall of the sealed tomb were considered to be potent and active, able to read themselves aloud in the dark. The book offers something that the sword cannot: eternal life. Hence the book *is* more powerful than the sword. And it is more likely in this context than the sword: for if it is a sword, what sword? Weapons have not been mentioned in the text. The transformation of the dead soul into a star has nothing to do with combat. The book, on the other hand, is the instruction, the critical importance of which in the transformation is referred to throughout the monument, for the book, the words, are making this happen, at this moment. Thus the book is the sword that enables the conquest of death, much as Manjushri, the avatar of the intellect, holds a book in one hand and a sword in the other. A book is an axe to break the ice, one might say, of the Pyramid Texts, which have been frozen in stone for more than four thousand years. The word carries the living thing concealed across millennia.

The snowy egret, or cattle egret, is a bird so common along the Nile that it is called the *abu kherdan*, the friend of the farmer. Its nests fill the eucalyptus trees that line one of the main streets in Cairo, Taha Hussein Street. Its whiteness covers the rich green fields of the countryside where the birds fall in flocks across the wide expanse of emerald alfalfa like flakes of snow. This bird is the sign determinative for the verb *sda* (to tremble); a detailed miniature of the egret follows the spelled-out word. The use of the bird in the word indicates the subtlety of perception in hieroglyphs, for it is not the bird itself that trembles but its delicate long white feathers that tremble in the wind.

The Dwat: This primary word and concept occurs here for the second time in the text. The *Dwat* is *the starry dawn*, the blue-green luminosity of the sky that precedes the dawn. The word is a hand with a looped cord and an encircled star, as though the star has been captured by the hand, by the mind.

The nine gave birth to you: There is much to suggest that the nine are stars, in the passages where they appear:

> The pelican rising foretells the nine, the great pelican twin

> A sailor in the sky sees the truth the nine holy aspects of the
>   distant falcon

> May he rise, Unis, as the shining light rises
> O great holy nine, the wondrous gold one is raised high . . .
> Unis grasps the crown from the holy nine

> The nine give their arm
> Among the nine the cormorant leaps up
> Nine great holy ones, this is what Osiris gives you
> May Unis be granted the nine lest he be destroyed

> The miller of the holy nine in the temple

The subject throughout is the paradox of coming into being without physical mammalian birth, and appears here as *Unis rises between the thies of the nine*. The hieroglyphs are the pictures of two thies, *mnit*. The phrase seems to indicate that paradox is what is intended: the nine are diffuse yet give birth as a single entity.

Verse 2

The cobra and the vulture are the river and the desert: The two animals represent the two opposing realities that are Egypt, north and south, wet and dry, river delta and rocky desert. The vulture is the immense griffin vulture, the terrifying *baanib*, with a wingspan of ten feet, a bird that soars up to eleven thousand feet in the sky. It is the bird that designates the words for both "death" (*mut*) and "mother" (*mut*), equating the two. Death is the mother. The mother is death.

Of malachite born is a reference to the sky having the essence of greenness, of life; the greenness of the sky is jewellike, it is the color of precious stones, the *emerald, turquoise, malachite stars.* The antechamber ends with a description of *the malachite land,* a pure land made of precious green stone. The *khadira,* or *green* forest where the stars are jewels in a vision of pure green light, is captured in a verse that appears in the nearby Pyramid of Tety:

> Sung to the great She who strides across the sky:
> Sew emerald, turquoise, malachite stars
> And grow green, that Tety grow green, green as a living reed

Three concepts of coming into being are used on this wall:

> *ms:* "to give birth": the paradox of birth without physical birth, it is
>   related to the word for "to rotate"
> *khpr:* "to manifest" (spontaneously)
> *kma:* "to be formed" (as if by hands; the hieroglyph is the
>   boomerang, a thing that is cast out by hand and comes back)

This is another illustration of how the hieroglyphic disc of light cannot possibly be the sun or "the sun god Ra" but refers to light itself. If the disc is used to mean the sun, this line would read: "carried high on the path of the sun Unis rises as a star."

Truth, *ma'a,* is introduced here for the first time, spelled with a ruler and marked with a feather, meaning it has no weight or physical substance but resides in the measurable underlying pattern.

The mantric pi: The use of *pi* on this gable and at the end of the east gable on the opposite wall, where it stands alone, makes it clear that *pi* is used not as a part of speech but as a sound. A chant indicating that *pi* is a magical formula is indicated by the command *Do as commanded,* followed by the movement of the corpse, indicating that *pi* is used to prompt the dead to life.

The mill, ndj: The turning sky is a mill wheel. The reference to the mill wheel following the repeated image in the verse of the *iwn nywt* clarifies the concept in this key hieroglyphic phrase. The *nywt* is the wheel, within which is the *iwn*, the axis.

Manifested in the enclosure of arms: The hieroglyphic picture is of embracing arms, bending inward at the elbows. This is how the infant is formed, born, and comes into being with the mantric sound. The arms are the arms of the stars, the Dippers.

Broken exhausted weary: A standard, formal address to Osiris that also appears in the passage to the sarcophagus chamber. The inert corpse is unwilling to come back to life. It is weary, asleep, broken, exhausted, yet, much like the Frankenstein monster, it is told to rise, to get up. It is an irony, for the corpse cannot get up, but the rising up of the energy within it is unstoppable.

The eye is the bread: The previous wall ended with the greenness of the eye and the words *may the bread fly up to the houses the houses of Egypt*. Now the eye itself is the bread; it is both time, as the creator of food, and beauty, as what is seen: the beauty of the sky and its stars. The phrase can also be translated *rise in the mill that makes your bread*, if the eye is read as a verb.

The nywt p: The circular surround of *p*. There is no other possible translation. It cannot be the unfindable "city of p," or "city of pe." The *nywt*, the circular surround, might be translated as "mandala" (from the Sanskrit for "wheel" or "circle").

Orion: The master of storms, the constellation that rises at the time of rain; the word *orion* means "rising."

Set: Chaos is the force behind everything, out of which everything comes. Everything in hieroglyphs is *tum*; the Arabic word *tum* denotes a sense of both "complete" (as in the common doubling expression of this word in Egyptian Arabic today, *tamam*, "completely") and "final," meaning the negative (as in the idea of something being over, hence no more). As a word in hieroglyphs it means "the universe," "the all." This word appears throughout the Pyramid Texts and has been translated arbitrarily, sometimes as the negation of a verb, and sometimes as "the god Atum." Verbal phrases in the hieroglyphic text have been routinely translated as "gods." In this passage Set lifts the *tum*. Set does not lift the god Atum. Nature lifts the universe, the wheel of the stars, and with them Orion, and with him time, and with it everything that lives on earth: Geb is Gaia, the earth as matter. The father, the earth, like Osiris, is what decays.

Form: *Kma*, the boomerang, is the hieroglyph for "to create." The verb is illustrated by a throw stick that goes out and comes back, an image that gives form the sense of spinning, being spun on a wheel. Orion, Taurus, and the Pleiades are visible in the blue-green light of the dawn, the *Dwat*, at this key moment of the year.

The gates of dawn: Waiting for Sirius to rise. The hieroglyph of the lotus is in the column on the uppermost point of the western wall.

O aged shades: The shades are ostrich feather fans, used to cast a shadow. This is the word for "shadow" and "shade."

Verse 3

Joy: The wordplay is on *lilies* and *joy*: *seshsesh*, *seshen*, and *reshret*, the sound of the lilies quietly rustling in the light wind. Unis becomes joy, *rsh*, which resembles the word *rsh* (to smell), conjuring the delicious scent of the flowers, as he *enters the surround, the ring of fire*.

The truth is within the fire: The transforming fire, the realm of origin; the false, the material, matter, the heavy, what decays, belongs, falls to the earth.

The cobras that guard the night: Of the great flood that rises with the great one (Sirius). Cobras emerge in heavy rain and flooding that forces them up out of the water-soaked ground. The star, the snake, and the lotus rise. The intrinsic quality of all three is rising: *pure are the stars of his appearance*.

Verse 4

The kas = energies, reassembled as hearts = centers. The hieroglyphs are three *kas* and three hearts with the verb "to reassemble," according to the method within the book. The hieroglyph for wisdom is a prayer shawl; the holy book is a scroll and a prayer flag.

Verse 5

The path of sprouting green: In the hieroglyph for "path" here the mounds (the mounds of earth left by the receding flood) are sprouting.

In the middle of the turning: The middle of the turning is *hnw* (enclosure) *phr* (turning). The hieroglyph is a twisting thread or path, and here introduces the idea of the labyrinth, the turning path of the stars.

The head of the blossoming time: Would that *ntr*, divine agency, give back the head of the (blossoming) time of sharp Sirius that cuts its throat under the sharp knife (of the horizon). There is a wordplay here on *spdt* (Sirius) and *spd* (sharp). The line illustrates how a story is a code, here used to describe the watching of the arc of stars, cut by the horizon at dawn, as a segment of time.

That cuts the throat: The image is of the slaughter of a bull; the head of Taurus is separated from Orion by the horizon. This is the head of the blossoming time. The sense here is immediate, as in the west wall entranceway: would that the bull rise, would that the sky now give back the bull's head, and with it the body of Orion, and Sirius. It is the man with the bull's head, Orion and Taurus together on the horizon, a designation for a segment of time within the labyrinth, the twisting path of the stars. The labyrinth is the circuit of the *labros*, the double axe that is thunder.

Is the circuit with the head of the bull and Orion: Orion is the rain, the bull is the thunder; this is the arc of the visual measure of the stars that mark the growing season, meaning a span of time is measured by the dial-like movement of the arc of stars. Give to Unis the burning ones, or hurrying ones: the hieroglyphic word is *ss* (with a suggestive sound, like *sizzle*) with the meaning of both "burning" and "hurrying."

The spindle: The verb "to spin" is marked with the hieroglyphic picture of a spindle. The word is introduced here and frequently used from here on about the sky. The three fates spinning the thread of life are the three seasons spinning the thread of stars.

Verse 6

He flows forth as a white bird: An arresting image captured by the beautifully drawn hieroglyph of an egret, the interchangeable white bird that stands for the soul.

Lift up your face, stars in the dawn: *The shore of light* is the *luminous horizon* used here, as later in Lucretius and Edmund Wilson.

The living words: The hieroglyphs are alive because they survive death.

Verse 7

The west gable ends with this verse, in which the hieroglyphs are clumps of reeds:

Pure is he who is washed in the field of rushes,

Pure is the light in the field of rushes
Pure is he who is washed in the field of rushes,
Pure is Unis, who is washed in the field of rushes
The arm of Unis is in the bright arm of Night
Iw seshw sw
Iw seshw sw

It is the sound of the wind. The words mean *let him be free, let him be free* or *he is empty, he is empty.*

Shu: The sound of the wind, *whoosh*, the word for "wind" and "air" and "free." The wind is conjured as if by shamanic mimicry; the tactile sense of the concept arises in the sound. The feather defines the word. A feather is weightless, hence it is empty. Because it is weightless its motion is a delicate mechanism for indicating the strength, direction, and speed of the wind. You cannot control the path of a feather through the air. This is why the feather defines the word for "truth." This phrase can also be translated as *he is the wind*, echoed in the Egyptian Sufi phrase chanted over and over as a self-intoxicant, a yogic breathing technique: *huwa hawa, huwa hawa*—"he (*huwa*) is the wind (*hawa*)," the hidden nature of the divine is the word *nefes* (to breathe). It is the word *nefs* ("self and soul"). The soul as breath is weighed in the scale against a feather. The swelling flood of the dawn drowns the reeds. What is left is the sound of the wind.

West Wall:
The Invocation of the Bull

Verse 8

The west wall of the antechamber is the invocation of the bull. This passage offers an explanation of the spelling of the bull as the *ka*: it is the thunderstorm, pure electrical energy suddenly released. Such a storm feels even now like the dangerous, threatening presence of an enraged bull that pauses to paw the ground, and charges erratically forward with frightening force and speed, ever closer, in an approach of inescapable danger. A thunderstorm can kill. And yet it brings the rain that brings all life.

This is the great force in the dark that exists although it does not know it, the bull of double brilliance, thunder and lightning. Here the text admits that it does not know what it is—is it the bull, is it Osiris—then it states, if nothing else it is the eye, the disembodied intelligence of the universe. Myrrh is used to conjure this presence, precisely as on the east wall of the entranceway, where the presence was first introduced. A circle with two lines follows the introduction of the bull in the verse. The hieroglyph has been understood to mean a place name, Nekhen or Hierakonopolis, but why would the name of a faraway place be stuck in this powerful verse? It seems to be a reference back to the earlier passage, as the two passages clearly echo each other. There the double nature of the bull was indicated by two shining discs of light. Here there is a single disc with two lines in it. Fire and heat first came to earth from the horn of the bull striking the ground, from lightning. The passage begins with a signal or stage direction for burning incense and directing its smoke; the hieroglyph is *idy*, the picture of a hand with the smoke of incense pouring off it. Then there is a first invocation:

great unknown spirit from the dark

qhaw ka r qhat (the phrase involves the blurring of *q*, *h*, and *k*, gradations of which are often confused in Arabic regionally) *qhaw ka* (mourned spirit) *r qhat* (from the tomb—the hieroglyph is the picture of the tomb). This is a poetic phrase where the words run together and echo each other.

The eye that is upon the throne: Osiris.

The eye is the thunder: In the story of "The Destruction of Mankind" in the Ramesside *Book of the Divine Cow*, the divine being sends down the eye in order to destroy mankind, "let it take the form of . . . ," meaning the eye manifests in different forms.

The energy of the dead is absorbed into the powerful force conjured on this wall: not the belief that there is a bull in the sky but a sense description of the violent electrical force that exists, although it does not know it. This is an honest appraisal of a great force of nature that acts, and creates a result, as though by intention. It can be characterized, but it is not a character. This is the opposite of myth. It is not about personalities but about trying to conjure with words the essence of the force. And it explains the iconography of Osiris, a name for an unnameable thing: the directing intelligence and power of the inextinguishable force of nature, in which death and decay are simply a passing phase. It is not life versus death, or faith in a life after death. It is the inevitability of life, and the irrelevance of death.

One can feel the eerie power of the invocation of this spirit, the inevitability of the rising energy of life from the dissolution of mere matter, mere form. Jane Harrison in *Themis* gives this insight into the iconographic riddle pursued here:

> Pythagoras, Porphyry tells us . . . underwent a purification . . . by a thunderbolt or thunder-stone . . . not so strange an implement of purification as it might at first sight appear. Celts or stone-axes over a large portion of the civilized world are . . . taken to be thunderbolts . . . Porphyry then goes on to enumerate the various ceremonies gone through during initiation. Pythagoras had to . . . go down into the cave . . . there he had to spend thrice nine days, and then at last he was allowed to gaze on the throne . . . Was the throne really empty? . . . Zeus in human shape was not seated thereon . . . but his throne may . . . have been tenanted by a symbol . . . even more powerful than . . . himself—his thunderbolt. The thunderbolt was to the primitive Greek not the symbol or attribute of the god, but itself the divine thing . . . The human child completely replaces the thunderbolt . . . child and thunder-stone were one. When Kronos was about to swallow Zeus, what is it that Rhea gives him and that he really swallowed? A stone in swaddling clothes. By such a stone was Pythagoras purified . . . We have definite evidence that in certain mystery-rites thunder was actually imitated by bull-voiced mimes . . . Aeschylus [describes them in a fragment from] the lost Edoni, "And bull-voices roar thereto from somewhere out of the unseen, fearful semblances, and from a drum an image as it were of thunder underground is borne on the air heavy with dread."

Lifted from the father: The eye is lifted from the throne. The falcon is lifted from the corpse, the earth. The hieroglyphs form a poetic line, doubling the sound in "father," *ft, fet m ift*, much as the English translation does in the line *lifted from the father*.

Earth, do not speak to him: Call him back. Do not look back lest you be con-
taminated by the gravity of earth. The earth pulls back the rising star of light
and heat into cold decaying matter.

Lest he fall: The verb is *wakh* (fall); it is the same word in Arabic and appears
in English as the star Vega, *waqia*, literally, "the falling one."

Finding on his path (the path of the rising star): The language is poetic and
the quality is fragmentary: lifted up from his father the earth, earth do not
speak to him lest he set/fall. The story is Orpheus and Eurydice, that the
words will draw one back.

Finding on his path . . . water (Gmy m wat f wnm f nefsw mwmw): Gm, "to
find," is the curlew, with its scimitar beak in the sand; the *y* makes it a participle: *gmy m wat*, finding on his path, his *wnm*, his food.

    Nefsw mwmw—the same phrase appears in the "Cannibal Hymn" on
the east gable, finding on his path his food, the breath of the wind, *nfs*, and
water water, *mw mw*; the Arabic word for "water," *moiya*, comes into English as the letter *m*, which is the picture of a wave. Here the word is doubled
because it is a pun on *mymy*, the name of the giraffe, the hieroglyph that immediately follows it in the column, connecting the two words in the visual
pun. The giraffe is the verb "to see beyond," "to foresee." What is foreseen
is the pelican. This coded line is an astronomical riddle. *The pelican rising
presages the nine, the great pelican twin.*

He flows forth as an egret, he rises as a pelican: The pelican, like the stork and
the egret, the crane and the ibis, is a white bird that rises from the earth.
Once these white waterbirds rose in the thousands and fell like snow on the
Nile. What are the nine that comprise the great pelican twin, and how does
the pelican relate to the giraffe? As one begins to see that the poem is a
progression of specific astronomical references, a good guess is that this line
and its iconography, which appears on predynastic combs and knife han-
dles, may indicate that the Pleiades were used as a calendric sighting device,

presaging the rising of the head of Taurus with Aldebaran, its red eye, directly beneath it on the diagonal of rising stars. We continue to go back into the dark night, back in time. The word *psdj* (nine) is a pun on the word *psdj* (to shine).

The pelican rises, presaging the rising of the constellation that twins the actual bird. The double meaning is that the pelican presages water. The dove in Noah's Ark is the shining white seabird. When you see the white pelican you know that water is near; when you see the Pleiades rise at dawn you know that the flood is imminent.

A sailor in the sky . . . the distant falcon: This wall is an invocation of the bull. The bull is preceded by the Pleiades. There seems to be some sort of regular pairing of the pelican and the giraffe. They appear together on a predynastic knife handle and two combs, one marked with a star that would seem to indicate that it is a calendric device involving the reading of stars. The coded meaning is signaled in this verse. In the hours between midnight and dawn in mid-July, the star groups rise in this order: the Pleiades on the shoulder of the bull, the head of Taurus, then the headless body of Orion, then at the moment of dawn, Sirius, rising as bright as a flickering planet on the horizon.

> Canst thou bind the sweet influences of Pleiades, or loose the bands of Orion: Canst thou bring forth Mazzaroth in his season: or canst thou guide Arcturus with his sons? Knowest thou the ordinances of heaven? Canst thou set the dominion thereof in the earth: Canst thou lift up thy voice to the clouds, that abundance of waters may cover thee? Canst thou send lightnings, that they may go and say unto thee, Here we are?

Is Job 38 a refutation of the Pyramid Texts?

Tantra: the spell of the twenty-seven ta ntr: The word *ta-ntra* appears here in the text: the holy ground. The twenty-seven refer back to the first verse on the east wall of the entranceway where the twenty-seven *netcherw*, holy things or spiritual aspects, obey the words that are being read aloud, with the burning of myrrh and the invocation of the bull of double brilliance. Here the words of the spell are doubled, repeated for power:

> *mdw di*=spell given
> *ntrw ta*=tantra
> *dni dni*=dam the dam
> *dmdj dmdj*=reassembled reassembled
> *sma sma*=joined together joined together
> *mr mr*=the canal canal

Dam the dam
Of the reassembled, reassembled
Joined to the light
Within the canal canal.

The serpent appears as the letter *dj* in the word *reassemble*, but its picture is the clue to the riddle of what is happening. It is an unusual composite hieroglyph, repeated twice: the picture of a serpent with a feather on its back, rising above the tomb, is the energy of life translated into air/space/emptiness. The feather is the sign for both floating up and truth. In this spell, as in Tantra, the body is conflated with the sky, the spine with the Milky Way. Intense heat is being generated within the body to make the serpent rise. The riddle of the Milky Way as the spine is the hinge into the sense of nonduality, the way into the cosmos. The serpent of life is prompted by the words of the spell to rise in the dead body, and then become the rising eye that is the pervading force of power and movement in the sky.

The serpent is the bird: The hieroglyphic serpent has wings, and rises into the air over the dead body. The dam and the canal are Egyptian inventions for the mastery of water. Here they contain and preserve the sweet influence of Pleiades: the flood and the rain. Then the verse puts the canal in the body. It is the vessel out of which the two sons flow, the banks of which are scorching hot.

Secret are the ways: The physical methods of Tantra are secret and difficult to achieve: the generation of intense internal heat that prompts the rising and emergence of the internal serpent. The paradox has to do with the essence of alchemy, water and fire. Water would normally be in a canal, but fire and light are in the canal in the sky, and in the canal in the body.

What is in the jar flows out: the body is a broken jar: The hieroglyph is a picture of a broken water jar and occurs again as the body in the passage to the sarcophagus chamber. The jar contains two sons, Caliban and Ariel, garlic and sapphire, the darkness of earth and the blueness of sky, the dark serpent and the white bird. The movement of both, the sliding of the snake, the gliding of the bird, are implied in the flowing out. The sound grows from one word to the next: *mskt skr* is the beaten (*skr*) Milky Way. The Milky Way is both beaten, in the sense of trodden, and beaten in the sense of beaten metal.

The idea of becoming something that is already there: one becomes the twin of Osiris, and with this has the power of Osiris, the power to overcome death. This "one lord" is both concrete and ineffable, both simple and profound, and raises the question of what Osiris actually is, the rotting corpse resolved into energy. The corpse contains the serpent, the white serpentine spinal cord, the source of the body's movement, electricity, sense perception. The snake sheds its skin as the electrical energy of the spinal cord moves upward from the spine. The similarity of the umbilical cord to the spinal cord suggests an Egyptian etymology for the non-Greek word *omphalos* (a word that is used to mean "the center, the eye, and the navel") as *m pr*, "what rises." This would explain why *ómphalos* means "the eye," and also "the center," and also "the thing that rises up" (and comes into English as "umbilical," the cord of life). The text goes from the sky back to the body, with the Tantric spell, then back to the calendric arc of water stars that contains the bull.

The circuit with the head of the bull and Orion is the Labyrinth: The Minotaur in the Labyrinth is Orion, a headless body of a man, joined with the bull's head of Taurus on the path of the sky. The two constellations form the calendar sign for the growing season. The Labyrinth, the circular path of the *labros*, the double axe or thunder, is the path of the stars in the growing season when the Minotaur, literally, the "threatening bull," is seen in the sky. Herodotus describes having seen the original labyrinth, still intact, on his visit to Egypt, as a temple of myriad small rooms, as though the king would act out the progression of the Minotaur through the rooms or thrones of the stars, as a sort of ritual progression or dance.

The monkeys in the circuit are the heads: The three monkeys are where the head should be on Orion, the three faint stars. Thus he is able to tie on another head instead, the head of the bull. It is Unis who ties the head. Unis is merged with Orion. The circuit with the head of the bull and Orion must be restored for the growing season to commence, and it is about to come back; within its garments are all the offerings it gives you. Its garments are the moving stars. Time is not separable from the evolution of forms, the integrated net of things coming into existence and passing away. The rain star is Aldebaran, the red eye of the bull; the horn of the bull is lightning. The entire passage conveys the column of stars: Aldebaran to Sirius, causing and mirroring the events on earth. The eye is lifted by the falcon. The turning sky lifts the eye. *Hsf*, the hieroglyph here, is the spindle. The sky is spinning. The Greek motif of the three fates having between them a single disembodied eye spinning out life as a linear thread to be cut are the three seasons, the precincts of stars that dominate each season, spinning the thread of rising stars, lifting the eye. The original Egyptian version is circular. The bull flows out into the spinning sky. Flow here is *shp*, the word used for the two sons flowing out of the body. The sky is a green marshland. The hieroglyphic details of the marsh are exquisite. The verse opens into a passage echoed fifteen hundred years later by Hesiod, advising farmers to pay attention to time as the interweaving of the stars and plant and animal life on earth. The poem then turns the bull in the sky into the actual animal. The timing of plowing in the rich, black earth of the overflow of soil from the Nile flood, with the domesticated, castrated bull, followed by the time of planting the seeds, is signaled detail by detail in the circuit of stars. The bull in heaven prompts the bull on earth. The bull in heaven, domesticated for use, mirrors the bull on earth, harnessed to the plow.

A second invocation begins with the burning of incense and, like the invocation of the bull, refers back to the passage on the east wall of the entranceway. Now the falcon of old is conjured, the horizon of the falcon of flame. On the east wall of the entranceway the words are *Unis becomes the bull of double brilliance in the midst of his eye. His mouth is stable in the heat. Unis has the horn of the Lord of the South, the falcon of old.* In this first passage it is clear that the falcon and the bull are one. The falcon has horns and is from the south. There are clear indications from the invocations on this wall that the Pyramid Texts belong to a cattle cult from "the old days" beyond the Nile Valley. One looks to the predynastic archaeological site at Nabta Playa in the Western Desert a hundred miles west of Aswan, where stones are set up in a ring as an astronomical observatory, and around them are elaborate cattle burials. The passage explains the iconography of the bull on the Narmer Palette, and suggests strongly that this is the same system, where the king is identified with the bull of heaven. The hieroglyph appears in the phrase that states that the soul of the king as the bull is the open eye of the storm, whose father is the wind. The storm is *nshny*; the hieroglyph is the wild dog facing the arc of lightning, over which arches a rainbow. This is called the power of the perception of the falcon, that is, the tracking of stars, which tells you what time it is: what the weather is going to do.

Al-debaran: The red eye of Taurus is a common word for "bee" (like Deborah, the bee, or prophetess, in the Old Testament). The color red is like the red pain of the sting of a bee, and the red rage in the eye of the bull. Taurus also contains *al nath*, the wasp.

Verse 10

Its essence is an eye thrust out: The eye is created from the fire of his serpentine light body, its essence is an eye thrust out. If the initiate is not prepared for this process, the rising of the heightened electricity of the internal eye will burn you. This is a description of the generation of internal heat that accompanies the rising of the internal serpent. This passage explains both the fire-breathing dragon and the third eye. The fire-breathing dragon is the third eye, consciousness as a shadow of electrophysiology.

A sailor in the sky sees the truth: Ma'a (truth) is the subject of the next wall. Again in this line the word for "truth" is paired with and closely resembles the word *maa* (to see). In other words, *the truth is seeing*.

The keening of his sister, the green serpent: This is readable, both visually and aloud, as the Egyptian lament tradition, which exists among Egyptian peasant women to this day. It is a kind of ritual improvisational poetry filled with imagery and repetition that sounds like the shrill sobbing of inconsolable grief. The poetry is a kind of formalized grief that functions as catharsis.

He has gone to the sky with the wind with the wind: The hieroglyph for "wind," repeated down the column, is the full sail, the wind, the wind. Whether this means he is lifted up to and across the sky with the wind or he has dissolved and is in the wind, is empty space, no longer exists, lies in the key phrase—we don't know whether he crosses the sky or ceases to exist; we don't know, but in essence the elements of his body flow upward to the sky. The serpent, his sister, is the Mistress of P, the sound that prompts the transference of consciousness in the Tantric death ritual called *pe-wa*. As a commentary on the *pe-wa* process states, when you strike your breast and say the syllable *pe*, your spirit goes to the sky. The ultimate sound is the wind that sweeps it all away, the ultimate truth. Beneath the flow of the wind, the flow of motion, all the cyclical changes of the world are measured in moments as degrees on the horizon.

The wall seems to focus on the rising of the Pleiades and Aldebaran, here called the rain star. The line *They see this as the bull in the sky* explains what the Egyptians are doing: they are coming up with a system of visual cues for reading the sky and tracking time. The entire passage explains how the sky mirrors the earth in the production of food via the circuit with the head of the bull and Orion. In the midst of this turning labyrinth is the path of sprouting green: the rising stellar arc of the Pleiades, Taurus, Orion, and Sirius. In it the bull is three things: Taurus, thunder, and the bull on the ground, gelded as an ox that plows the fields. All three result in the crops that become food.

The most remarkable element on the wall is the presentation of a Tantric formula, called on the wall the *ta-ntr*, in which the reassembled body is joined to the light, the body becomes light. It is the generation of the light body. Tantric methods are specific instructions to be followed to the letter, a closely guarded secret because they are dangerous. The canal in the body becomes scorching hot as the vessel out of which flow the two sons, the serpent and the bird.

South Wall:
Initiation into Heaven

Verse 1

The two truths: The south wall is the initiation ceremony for the soul as it is admitted into the sky. It begins with a discussion of the two truths, the ultimate emptiness of the human being who has died, and is reconstituted as light. This entity is now presented to the primary forces in the sky. These forces are introduced as riddles—*It is said of you: he is pain*—within an introductory formula that is a palindrome, *he knows you, you know him*, and a tongue twister, *stchtchw irchtsw stchsw irchtw*, again showing the use of words as multifaceted, magical vehicles that make things alike, and make things happen. The dead soul, his *flesh washed away in the lake of the wolf with water from the arms of light*, is introduced to great Isis, who first appears in the form of the hieroglyph itself: a chair he climbs up on as a little child. She gives *him her breast so that he may drink the milky-white light of the stars and never thirst or hunger again.* The soul of the dead king then undergoes the initiation. As in a Tantric initiation, the initiate merges with the mother in order to be reborn. The mother is the sky. The child is the rising star.

The first word is the foreleg of a cow, a name in hieroglyphs for the Big Dipper. The foreleg is followed by three reeds, the common word in hieroglyphs for what it represents, phragmites, the marsh reed. It has been interpreted here as the word for "father" (*ift*), because the assumption has been that the text must be about fathers. But the most significant element in the word for "father" is missing here, the horned viper, the letter *f*. Hence the reading of this line is more likely to be what the line visually represents: *O by the foreleg in the reeds.* The other translation, *by the strength of the fathers*, does not seem terribly relevant, while the field of reeds has just been described on the previous wall. The reeds are the stars. The foreleg of the cow in the reeds is the swinging of the arm of the great clock of the sky. Hence the hieroglyphic phrase would introduce the instruction that follows, explaining the fact that the turning of the sky means a separating out of the elements of the composite, revealing the truth that underlies reality: ultimately there is nothing there. This is the concept of time as a revolving wheel, captured in the death of St. Katherine (the name of the highest mountain in Sinai) on the wheel that tears the body apart. The essential theme is the turning of life into death into life, a series of stages of transformation. It is not a conceit but an actual unfolding, where words are used in a measured, repetitive way to effect the transformation.

Ma'a herw *the truth is vibration, sound*: The truth has a voice. One is deaf to the voice of the truth. This is the phrase discussed in verse 7 on the north wall, the vibration of truth that is the goal of a life. Are they deaf to the truth of the voice in the eye?

The line has the dimensions of both the actual and the abstract. The sound of the eye is thunder, as established on the previous wall. Thunder is the bull, the hidden power in the sky. The eye was invoked as the bull of double brilliance on the west wall, and here is its voice. But the phrase here, considering what immediately follows it, seems to mean, are they unaware of the truth of physical reality, the nature of life and death? The reality is this: there is a cutting apart.

This is a central concept in the Tantric physiology. The male and female essential drops of moisture in the composition of the physical person are separated at death. The Tantric idea is that one is formed from two coalescing drops of moisture that reside at the heart, the white drop of the father, and the red drop of the mother. Hence one is inherently both male and female, and this knot, these joined essential elements, separate when the wind enters the central channel in the process of dissolution at death, as a stage in the rising of the internal serpent that becomes the light body. The word for the drop of moisture in Egyptian, which appears here in both the masculine and the feminine in this line of hieroglyphic words, is an onomatopoeic word for "spit", *tf, tftftftf*.

This is a hearing—an obeying—of the two truths: The hieroglyphic verb "to hear" is the picture of an animal's ear drawn back, as an animal will pull its ear back in a posture of listening and obedience, hence the word conveys the concept of not only listening but responding and obeying. The sentence is plain and straightforward. These are common hieroglyphic words. They are well-known, and here they can only be translated in a way that belongs to the philosophical debate tradition of Buddhism; there is a hearing of the two truths, an obeying of the principle of the two truths. *Ma'aty*, "the two truths" (*ty* is the dual form in hieroglyphs as in Arabic), embodies the essential Egyptian conception of twinning, of inherent duality. But more than this, the two truths are one of the central perceptions of Tantra: the nature of conventional (material) and ultimate (pure energy) reality. One might say that they are heaven and earth. Much as Thoreau and Emerson saw heaven as the world itself, pervaded with light, only we do not see it, the Tantric strives to see the two realities at once, the world of form and the underlying light of its dissolution.

The wind is the witness or *Emptiness is the witness* or *It is emptiness*: The onomatopoeic line echoes the end of the west gable, *iw seshw sw*. Here *metrw* is the word for "witness;" *iw shw metrw, emptiness is the witness*. The text continues in the language of a Tantric instruction, the Egyptian version of which is physical reality: the wind itself is all that is left of a living thing. The line recalls the line in the last verse on the east wall of the antechamber: the two gates made holy, they whose form is air and moisture. These are the gates to the realm of form. There is a pun on the words for "instruction," *wdj*, and "separation," *wdj*. The separation is the instruction.

Beloved country: *ta mr*: The phrase *ta mr*, "beloved country," is the Egyptian name for Egypt today, *Masr*.

Ma'at, the embodiment of truth, marked with a feather, is the continuous, measured uncontrollable movement through space that is the natural order of things. The truth is the innate order of the universe that underlies life on earth as a physical reality. It is visible at any time and contradicts the assumption that death is the ultimate reality. The ultimate reality is the underlying order, and its pervasive beauty. Even disorder is ruled by, folds into, and emerges from the ultimate order. They are the two truths. The breakdown of the physical body at death is the mystery of form and emptiness. The wind is the witness, even as the death rattle itself, the expiring of the person through the mouth, the voice of the truth of the life energy leaving the body.

The truth is in the fire: A sailor in the sky sees the truth. The sailor is a star made of fire. As in Heraclitus, the ultimate reality is the fire of transformation.

He is reunited within the waters: The hieroglyph for "woman" is a vessel of water. The sky is the great mother, the dappled wild cow with its milk of white light, its water of life.

He is reassembled within the mystery, the waters: Elaborates the spell on the west wall, *reassembled and joined with the light*; *the body is a broken jar*. What it contains flows out.

The rising cobra: The spinal cord, the electrical essence of which sails across the sky.

The truth is brought to him raging within the waters alive: *Dndj* (rage) is the energy rising from the body as a snake. The hieroglyph for "rage" is the picture of a cobra rising from the skull of the bull. Rage, the primary quality of the bull, is the raw electricity usable in the manipulation of the energy in the body. The line seems to indicate that the soul as the initiate becomes the bull, and that the truth is the water of life, hidden in the sky. The Greek spelling of the Egyptian word for "truth" is *moira*, fate, which also means a measured section of the zodiac.

The refuge is in his eye: The text on the south wall is constituted of differently structured poems, some of them short and rhyming, as though to break the rhythm or seriousness of the overall content. This is a short embedded poem around the pun for "refuge," *nht*; refuge in *nkht* (strength).

The sky is a mill wheel: Bread is *brotos*, the Greek word for "mortal," what keeps one alive, as *aesh* in Arabic is both "bread" and "life."

The sky is a dappled sail: The quality of time is variegated. The sky is dappled with stars. The hieroglyph *sab* (dappled) is the skin of an animal with the tail hanging down, recalling the love of the dappled, the dappled horses drawn on the walls of Lascaux.

Give him the attainment of the words: The importance of the words themselves is made clear, for the words effect the transformation: *bring him the words*.

This is the first time in the text that things are meant to be repeated, four times, or seven times; hence one is entering a section of the text that is a significant ritual, and must be spoken in precisely the right way for effect. The next step in the initiation is protection: saying the words to effect the protection of the entity throughout the ceremony. The following step is the prompting of the descent of the light body, the invisible twin: he has broken the knots of the spine.

Here the hieroglyphs are accurate representations of the vertebrae. Then the line, echoing the same line in the passageway to the sarcophagus chamber, *what is in the jar flows out*.

The dead body is a broken water jar.

The soul is the green new shoot of his marvelous mother in the green fields of the stars, in an implicit conflation of plant and animal life. The text continues to elaborate on the nature of the two truths. The dead soul, Unis, becomes the departing of what is at once *the essence of earth and the essence of wind*, a paradox containing the contrast between the material and the air. In a further step it becomes fire in the wind. The spinal cord is the part of the human body that is understood to contain the contrasting elements of matter and electricity. The hieroglyph for pulling out the essence is the familiar device used even today for unspooling yarn. The image is of pulling, as though pulling out yarn. Thus the person is unraveled; as the spinal cord can be pulled from the body, the light body contained in the spinal cord is pulled out.

> To the ends of the limits of space
> Unis travels with the wind
> The horizon kisses the king

Shen: The hieroglyph for "nose" is the word for both "smell" and "kiss." The holy forms open their swaying arms, a lovely image of the moving constellations. His face is to the east, the ascending path; he travels the path of the rising stars.

The open eye of the storm: The eye is open: the hieroglyphic eye here has horns—horns mean "to open," *the open eye of the storm*.

Orpheus:

> Orpheus, Osiris, and the other daimons who are torn in pieces and put together again [are simply] the Year.
> —Jane Ellen Harrison, *Themis*

The second part of the text on the south wall of the antechamber is taken up with an extended repetitive liturgy that has clear affinities with Orphism, a religious cult introduced into Greece in the sixth century B.C. The earliest reference to Orpheus is in a fragment of Simonides (fr. 567) from that time, a verse that resonates with the imagery on the west wall of the entranceway:

> And birds flew up around his head
> And fish rose out of the blue-black water
> At (the sound of) his beautiful song

Orpheus is the bridge between shamanism and poetry. Like Solomon, who controls the winds and the birds, Orpheus draws nature to himself. He goes into and out of the land of the dead alive, and ultimately is torn to pieces by a stream. The question has always been where does he come from. Orphism is associated with Pythagoras. The two religious brotherhoods in Greece strongly influenced the literary movement of the time, the poetry of Pindar, the linguistic formulations of Heraclitus. These religious brotherhoods had the elements of what we now associate with Eastern monasticism: celibacy, vegetarianism, nonharming, a belief in reincarnation, intense focus on scholarship, memorizing, memory. Pythagoras embodies one aspect of this system: mathematics. Orpheus another: poetry. What is the purpose of poetry, a form of writing that begins as the riddle? Poetry can be known by all and understood by few, can be hidden in plain sight. Orpheus is not a person or a myth but an initiate in this ritual of the knowing and remembering of the soul. Orpheus as the embodiment of the *ma'a herw*, the true sound or vibration, both music and poetry, explains the *nfr* hieroglyph. It is the lyre of Orpheus that means both beauty and emptiness.

> The outlines of the doctrine and the accompanying myth seem to have been roughly the same for the Orphics, Empedocles, Pindar, Hesiod, Plato and others . . . This rough uniformity suggests that the doctrine . . . entered Greece already formed and did not undergo its stages of development there . . . These new doctrines were embodied in poetry, often with attributions to Orpheus or other legendary poets. Plato regards inspired poets as equal revelatory sources with priests and prophets . . . The Orphic initiate is sometimes buried with a small gold plate engraved with the necessary words . . . The soul must perform a preliminary or partial demonstration of memory, by carrying over the confusing threshold of death certain lines. In one version the soul, approaching the guardians, is to declare: I am a child of earth and of starry heaven, but my real nature is of heaven alone. You know me . . . Sometimes the formula involves declaring the name of the guardians as a sign that one has known them in the past and hence belongs to their company.
> —Thomas McEvilley, *The Shape of Ancient Thought*, 104–10

The secret cult of life in death is the Osirian cult of the snake, Ophis. The cobra hieroglyph rises from a basket, drawn up by the sound of a flute, suggesting an essential relationship between sound and form.

> The universe of moving and static things is knit together by . . . resonance . . . moving inside them, continually making an indistinct sweet murmur like the humming of a bee . . . or like a swarm of black bees drunk on honey, whose resonances evolve the fifty letters, and from them, all poetry and all realized form.
> —Philip Rawson, *The Art of Tantra*, 202–203, 204,
> quoting the Prapanchasara

Verse 3

As in Plato's doctrine of recollection, knowledge is memory, and memory is release. The connection between words and things is memory. Memory is electricity, the lighting up of the mind. This formula of recognition is introduced as the first of three liturgies in the Pyramid Texts. It begins as a tongue twister, consisting of wordplays on the verb *rekh* (to know), with a quality of magical sound and visual palindrome:

> *Stchtchw rchtsw stchsw rchtchw stchsw rchtchw*
> *Stchtchw irchtsw stchsw irchtw*

> You know him, he knows you

The soul is introduced to the luminous entities in the sky. They are: the sun, the moon, Sirius, the stars in the dawn, the bull of heaven. There is a possibility that *st*, rather than simply being a particle that emphasizes the introductory pronoun, is a verb, and that this is a carefully worked out formula in which the verb *st* means "to kindle," "to light": *You light up that he be made known/He lights up that you know.*

The invisible movement of the vowels shading the words, shifting the meaning, creates the sense that the arrival of knowledge is a reconciliation between subject and object as all forms merge. Thus will I know even as also I am known. Rather than a name, a riddling description, posed as a question, introduces each celestial entity:

> It is said of you, or, is it not said of you?
> The sun: greatest of all who set
> The moon: he fulfills the one
> The falcon: he is pain
> The stars: you are wide awake
> The bull of heaven: he who quakes

The falcon is pain, for it prompts the flood that drowns people in their homes.

The moon here is Thoth as the ibis, with its scimitar beak as the lunar crescent, and its luminous white back. The meaning of the ibis is the crescent moon that becomes full: it fulfills the number one. The moon is the model for the system of mathematical fractions in Egypt.

The bull of heaven as the name *nhp* is a pun. It can mean *he rises at dawn*, or *he protects the dead*, or *he is the one who quakes*. The phrase may be meant not to suggest one instead of the other but to suggest all three.

Unis becomes your departing: This is the breakdown of the body into its aggregates—earth, air, fire, in the electric nervous system, the essence of the spinal cord, which contains all three elements as it leaves the body. This is a way of saying that the body resolves itself into its elements and returns to the one, the essential light energy, and that eternal life is inevitable, not the personality, the moral behavior, the human success or failure. It is the physical reality of the composition of the body. The film of personality and circumstance is only a story. To confront death is to confront the dreamlike quality of life as a story that dissolves at death, or resides in words alone, in memory.

Who is Unis after all? Unis is simply the one who is going, the person who has died.

Poetry arises from this shamanic, integrated sense of the world. Shamanic mimicry conjures thunder, the flight of birds. *Shaman* is from the Sanskrit word *shru* (to hear), from *shramana* (a hearer). We must be silent, so that we may hear the whispering. The falcon, the prayer flag, and the circle of fire are universal shamanistic motifs. "Pythagoras coined the word *philosophy* to mean a special, introspective, or religious life: yoga, the shamanistic Orphic bios."

Verse 4

The verse begins by repeating a line with slight alteration as though a wheel is set turning the two embracing horizons; let him cross. The verse then proceeds into the realm of fairy tale, in which the hero is the soul, dressed in a leopard skin, holding a flail. The soul is now introduced to the ancient ones, the stars themselves, who announce him to the great serpent, the secret life energy that surrounds the universe. They grant him entrance to the fields of stars across the river of light, the river of memory. It is a fairy-tale geography, an imagined, jewellike celestial topography. His sister is the star Sirius, who enabled him to fly up into the sky on the north wall. The verse ends with the formula that declares the initiation to have been a success, with the final line: *He is the infant child of the blue-green light of dawn.*

Verse 5

An invisible double hovers near and is set free at the moment of death. The idea survives in Egypt today as the *qarin*, the spirit twin. Here the double is conjured into being with words identifying its parts, its living arms and legs emerging from the dead body, as if by naming or imagining the arms and legs one drifts into them, becoming light, laughing; the soul becomes Osiris, the living dead. The text then shifts into a delightful, lovely light verse of dancing up into the sky. The soul flies up, *papapa*, as a bird and alights as a beetle. The hieroglyph on the wall is the elaborated picture of a beetle, with long antennae curling into inward spirals. The beetle is a visual pun, meaning not only the insect but to spontaneously manifest, to come into being out of thin air, *khpr*, "to take form."

The ancestors who do not know nonexistence are the stars.

Verse 6

The verse begins with the image of a golden star rising in the east, Sirius rising at dawn. Unis rises as the star, followed by the letter *p* standing alone. The nine are first invoked, as though recognized; Unis then grasps the crown from the holy nine. The image again suggests the Pleiades rising above Sirius on the diagonal.

The soul is an infant, newly born as a star. Isis now appears, with her wild double Nephthys: the sky nurses the star with its light. As in the general method of the text, the image is briefly glimpsed and then becomes the subject of the subsequent verse. The image is presented lightly, and then returns with a deeper meaning. The infant soul feeds on the milk of the Milky Way. In the Orphic system the Milky Way is the spring of memory.

Osiris is not named in the verse, but the verse contains some of the most interesting and vivid imagery of Osiris: his great eyes are the gates of souls. He ties the knots. The knot is the kernel of existence, what enables the doubling, the complexity that becomes a thing. Always a knit of identity. Osiris wipes away the flesh from the life force with water from the arms of light. He washes him clean in the lake of the wolf. The defining hieroglyphic pictures are of a lake and a standing wolf. The lake of the wolf is the wild sky; the falcon, cosmic order, turns the sky, but the sky itself is wild. Osiris releases the life force of Unis into the lake of stars. With two fingers, as in verse 2 on the north wall, he makes him rise, and as in the earlier reference, one does not know whether this is simply a mudra for blessing or whether something else is intended, as two fingers together are a basic measurement in Egyptian, like an inch. The verse becomes a very powerful invocation of Osiris.

Verse 7

Unis as the initiate is an infant in the ceremony. He is brought to life, as elsewhere in the text, by means of clouds of incense. The incense draws the holy ones, who are asked first to smell him, then to love him. Isis is invoked (as though invocation is an imagining, a making real), then approached. Unis is described as an infant crawling forth and up onto her knees, as though Isis is simply the hieroglyph itself, the chair. *Mother of little Unis, give this your breast that he may cross it over his mouth, that he may drink from you your milk of shining white light of eternity, the light of the stars.*

Verse 8

The soul is imagined sailing in the boat of the sky with the stars, the holy ones. Isis is asked to come to him, to his very hair, with great tenderness, and to accept him. What follows is an accounting of his life, familiar from religious ceremonies everywhere. He has been purified. He has resolved all disputes. He no longer has enemies. No one can say anything against him. The power of words is again emphasized; there are no negative words out there anymore.

Verse 9

As he rises in the void . . . the green lotus: This verse portrays the sky as the wild cow on the greening desert hill, the sky that greens the desert hill after the rain. The soul unites with its mother, the night dappled with stars, the dappled cow high on the desert hill, as the white storks spiral down in vast flocks to whiten the land, the land, the land—a yearly sight in the Nile Valley. The stork rises as the individual soul and descends as a column of stars whitening the land with their light.

Sirius is now called the falcon dog star, indicating that these ideas work together and are the same: the guide that leads the soul to heaven.

Verse 10

Hierogamos: Raised up, united with her, the gate of the water.

The wall ends as the soul merges with Isis, the sky, the nature of which is the hidden water that enables all life. The connection of water with life is expressed in the hieroglyph for "woman" as a vessel of water. The hieroglyph for "child" is *saghair*, the Arabic word for "small" and for "child." In keeping with the actual physical dimension of what is described, this passage suggests that this moment itself is the gate of the rain that falls from heaven, and of the conception and rebirth of Unis as the star. Unis unites with the mother and becomes the child within her, as the Tantric initiate unites with the mother in order to be reborn. As in Tantra, the holy vision is opened to the initiate by means of the rising of the heightened electricity within the body, the internal serpent, prompted by real or imagined union. The rising of this energy prompts the birth of the eye, omniscience, the child or successful fruit of the practice. Thus it is only when the initiate merges with the mother that he sees the holy aspects revealed. On the following wall, the east gable, the initiate is reborn as the eye itself, the thunder. The release of water is the result. Isis becomes the cow on the greening desert hill in order to conceive the baby bull. As a child is conceived and then born, the soul follows the meaning of the words, into the womb of the innermost room, and then out of it into the broader realm of space. In that sense the text reads ingeniously both backward and forward, and has the quality of time being reversed, as a progress of mysteries revealed in a sequence that has the sense of a journey.

East Gable:
The Birth of the Eye

The east gable is the most powerful part of the monument and of the written instruction. The language of the poem on the gable begins with hieroglyphic words that mimic the sound of thunderclaps. This triangular slab of text mirrors the rising of the lotus on the west gable. There the sense is of stillness, the quiet nature of still water. Both gables point up and indicate the star rising. The two facing, contrasting poems present the dual nature of the sky: violent motion and pellucid calm. The east is the thunderstorm, the birth of thunder, the bull, the disembodied eye. The idea that the sky itself is food is the original perception of time.

The east gable is covered with a single long poem that begins with a passage that is reminiscent of King Lear on the heath. The meaning of the passage arises in its sound. The sound conjures thunder. *Gp* is the hieroglyphic picture of a rainstorm, *pt* of the sky; *ihy* is the word for "rattle" as a noun, and "shout" as a verb. These are words that can be translated both as nouns and verbs; they are perfectly plausible as vivid nouns: the violent sky, the bones of the horizon quake, as in a thunderstorm, and then, immediately after the thunder and lightning, there is silence, and an exhaustion in the air after the electrical charge. It is the exhaustion of the mother after giving birth. When the morning stars sang together and all the sons of God shouted for joy.

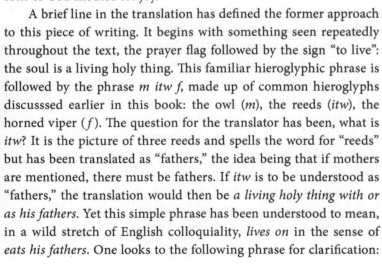

A brief line in the translation has defined the former approach to this piece of writing. It begins with something seen repeatedly throughout the text, the prayer flag followed by the sign "to live": the soul is a living holy thing. This familiar hieroglyphic phrase is followed by the phrase *m itw f*, made up of common hieroglyphs discusssed earlier in this book: the owl (*m*), the reeds (*itw*), the horned viper (*f*). The question for the translator has been, what is *itw*? It is the picture of three reeds and spells the word for "reeds" but has been translated as "fathers," the idea being that if mothers are mentioned, there must be fathers. If *itw* is to be understood as "fathers," the translation would then be *a living holy thing with or as his fathers*. Yet this simple phrase has been understood to mean, in a wild stretch of English colloquiality, *lives on* in the sense of *eats his fathers*. One looks to the following phrase for clarification:

wshb mwtw f, the wild bull of his mothers. The word *wshb* (wild bull) is fully spelled out and cannot be mistaken. Yet it has been translated instead as *wsh* (chew). Thus the Egyptological reading of this line is that the dead soul eats his fathers and chews his mothers. Hence the poem on the east gable is called the "Cannibal Hymn." The verse then states that the soul becomes *neb* (the all; the detested wolf); a picture of a standing wolf, as in the phrase *lake of the wolf* on the west wall, is followed by the word *bwt* (detested). This phrase occurs again on the north wall of the sarcophagus chamber, where death is the detested wolf. The detested wolf is nature, the essential nature of the universe. Yet it is the most precious, most powerful thing there is. The word for "power" is the scepter with the dog's head.

The sense of the extended poem on the east gable of the antechamber is essentially this: Unis, the dead soul, having merged with the mother, the sky, is now reborn as the active power in the sky understood as an active intelligence, the eye, individuated as thunder, the bull. This active intelligence turning the sky by means of arms and legs, the Dippers turning the stars, is the creator of all life, of the food that sustains mankind. Thus the arms stir the sky as a vessel of food.

The star rising in the east is the star in the east: What is being described is a thunderstorm. Not the god of a thunderstorm but the storm itself. It is described as a birth, as someone giving birth, the screaming, and then exhaustion of someone giving birth; the sky is a single entity, the mother, giving birth, she is giving birth to the wild bull, the thunder as the star Canopus rises in the east.

He is the all within the throne: the power in the sky. Pan as the child of the Great Goddess.

The wild bull of his mothers: Brings to mind the Bacchae, the mother fondling her son as a wild bull. Dionysus, literally "the new god," is the wild bull born of thunder as his mother Semele is fructified by a lightning bolt. She is struck by lightning and dies giving birth to Dionysus.

Unis becomes the all (the universe itself, the nature of all, wild nature), the detested, uncontrollable, feared wolf, feared because it is uncontrollable. *Whose mother does not even know his name*, as he has no mother but exists as pure energy in empty space, *yet he is the most precious thing in the sky. He is the power [on the horizon]. As no father gave birth to him* [tum *is the negative here, rather than the "god" Atum], he gives birth to one more powerful than he.* It is a riddle or paradox. The wild dog is chaos, the painted wolf, *Lycaon pictus*, shown on early slate palettes as the surround of the sky, within which is the serpent, the circling path of light, energy, its eyes, the sun and moon and stars.

The detested wolf is also the star that signals the season of storms. It is the white bird on the luminous horizon, Canopus, rising as one of the two brightest stars in the sky; it quivers as a mass of light on the horizon as no other star does, strangely resembling a white bird, a dove of light, coming to Mary as the conception.

> Unis becomes the bull of heaven, he lives in the form of every star
> He is the engine of heaven, the pervasive force, the spirit.

As the wild bull in the reeds, he feeds in the pastures of stars, filled with spiritual power from the surrounding fire, the fire that surrounds the horizon, the sunset and the dawn. Unis becomes the full vessel, the vessel that contains the stars; the sky, the arm, the back are in the sky itself. Unis becomes his hidden name; when you say the name the great one rises. Then the eerily Christian phrase, *the prince of peace*, he is the bread and the drink (the offerings are pictured, the loaf, the jar of fermented grain): he is the food of all mankind, for the source of all food resides in the natural turning of the sky.

The poem then shifts into the imperative: this is what is happening, open the instructions, the instruction is close enough to the ritual instruction in Tantra to make it recognizable as a ceremony for the emergence of the light body. The instruction suggests the reason for the inclusion of elaborately carved ceremonial flint knives in predynastic burials. They are to cut off the head of the emerging serpent of light. *So seizing the hairs on the top of the head in the dark they tie them for Unis.*

The hair is tied back so the serpent can rise from the head. In *Highest Yoga Tantra*, Daniel Cozort writes that before beginning the meditation session, one binds one's limbs with cloth or rope. Then one rolls one's eyes upward (closing them halfway) and holds one's observation on the upper opening of the central channel (between the eyebrows). This is the *ajna*, the third eye, where the head of the emerging serpent appears in Egyptian iconography.

This is similar to the spell of the twenty-seven *netcherw* of earth, in that it obviously involves the manipulation of energy in the channels of the body. The phrase *holds one's observation* means *concentrate one's energy at this particular place*; meditative focus is a way of concentrating energy, suggesting perhaps that the Egyptian kings trained for this in life.

·

Unis burns as wood in the fire of the stars: What follows is a riddle reminiscent of the riddle of the Sphinx, and perhaps the source of it, as this riddle is also about legs as markers for three phases of time: morning, evening, night. The two lights at dawn, great in size near the horizon, are small in the dark of the night.

Thus he is the arrow: This is a riddle. The answer: Sirius and Canopus are markers, netchers, flags. The marker is the arrow that points to the turning. The legs of the women are the turning, the Dippers, whose turning as legs and arms turn the seasons, much as the pun on *sbk* (crocodile) and *sbkh* (legs) on the first wall was used to indicate that the meaning of the legs is movement itself; the movement is the vessel of food that the seasons bring. Thus he is the arrow as Canopus, who goes around the sky as the legs of the women, the Dippers, turn it, like the hands of a clock. In other words the answer to the riddle is again that the sky is a clock. The image is one of perfect clarity and is emphasized by the repetitive line *the arm goes round the arm goes round the arm goes round*. It is a clock. His food is an immaterial presence; the two lions, air and moisture (*nefsw mwmw*), are the gates of form.

The ancient ones burn on his hearth: The stars, the thousand that go around with him on the winding paths of the starry sky with Orion. Unis rises again; his flesh, his existence, is absorbed into the light of the dawn.

He has broken the knots of the spine: Here are anatomically perfect hiero-glyphs of vertebrae. The energy has risen up and broken out of the spine. Then the remarkable following lines:

> He receives the essence of the stars,
> He feeds on red, he absorbs green

This is the correct appraisal of the spectrum of light: he licks the moist essence of light until his flesh is *flooded with it*; the essence of the stars is color, red and green. He is transformed into light, the mind of pervasive holiness.

Verse 2

This verse contains the mantric *pi* and the remark *that the mummy is nothing but a dry shell*, as Unis rises away from it, rising, rising, remaining, remaining.

The gable ends with an image typical of Egyptian humor and sweetness, a nod back to the first verse on the north wall, what is the dead man doing: he is dancing in the sky. The sky is a single multifaceted entity: hence he lives in the form of every star. Ultimately the eye itself is light. The eye is light itself. This key to the development of world religion is presented in the vehicle of poetry. Therefore one needs to approach the key not as a historical artifact but as poetry that is carefully constructed as a vehicle of truth. The vehicle of truth is metaphor. The poem is sacred because it is where the metaphor exists. Without this careful construction of words, the metaphor does not exist. The words mirror the shifting reality of the child that rises from the corpse, inert Osiris, the seat of the intangible yet determining eye that is at once a serpent, a bird, and the fierce, unstoppable bull of life.

East Wall: The Door That Opens Both Ways

The east wall below the gable is covered with twenty-six short riddles that are getting at the concept of the snake, the rising serpent, and what it is. The final verse in the antechamber is the resolution of this mystery.

Verse 3

Extraordinary hieroglyph of a bull with two heads, one at either end above a door. The door that opens both ways is death. Death is the door to the realm of both earthly decay and heaven, form and formlessness. The door in the monument is also indicated, for the soul, as a newly conceived entity, goes both into the womb and out of it. A secret is given away in the line. The question of orientation is itself a riddle, and the riddle is solved. The door is the door both in and out: the text can be read in either direction, both backward and forward.

Verse 4

You create your eye as it destroys you: The sound of the line is as important as the meaning; it is like a tongue twister: *irek irek irtek irek seksek*.

Verse 5

In the grave itself, the life force in his testicles rises: Anatomical hieroglyph of testicles. There is a pun on *qhr* (falcon) and *shr* (testicles) (what is underneath). The commentary quoted in verse 2 on the east wall of the entranceway explains the reference—the generative life energy in the body is identified with the clear liquids in the bodily channels: semen is understood as the clear fluid in the spine, the spinal fluid; the fluid, with the energy, has been reversed and flows upward. This is the creation of the eye, omniscience, at death, hence it destroys you. The formula for rising, like the rising of stars, is *hr sbn*, used in the imperative for both the falcon and the life force.

Verse 6

The arm of Babay strikes, and within it is the thunder: The serpent is introduced here as an actual presence. That Babay is Orion (with its meaning as a calendar sign of rain and storms and the flood) is confirmed by verse 29.

 The thunderstone as a hieroglyph, the template for the ceremonial *vajra*, the *labros*, the double-headed axe that is the thunder, appears first here. The hieroglyph is of the picture of a fossil squid, a belemnite, Greek for "what is thrown down," related to the word *ball*. The Sahara is the dry bed of an ancient sea, filled with hills of oyster shells and colored sea clays, and the white bones of the sea turned to stone. Much as fossil pine sap called amber (electra, electricity) was seen as broken shards of lightning that fell in the sea, the fossil squid was thought to be a thunderstone thrown down from the sky. The question of why there is so much about rain and thunder in the Pyramid Texts suggests that the system, and possibly the poem itself or parts of it, comes from an earlier time and place, Nabta Playa, the miniature Stonehenge in the Western Desert, with an astronomical clock of giant stones set up amid the graves of bulls and cows.

Like hieroglyphs themselves, the religious system belongs to the drying up of the desert in the Neolithic, to the herders moving east, praying for rain, as the desert lakes and semiarid scrub are dried up and disappeared, and finding at last the miraculous Nile with its yearly flood and black earth. There were in the desert sacred black stones that fell from the sky, as did the black meteorite in the Kaaba and the round black stone ceremonially brought to Rome as Cybele, the great mother.

> Release him O serpent,
> The rising serpent releases and becomes the light body

Verse 7

Out there it is dark: They all go into the dark, the dark interstellar spaces. The ways of Thoth are the known arrangements of stars, the paths, the rising and setting of the recognized star groups; beyond them it is indeed dark. Thus the word *mrw* (canals, artificially made ways) is what the mind has made of this. The sound of this verse is like a lament, like fear, *ti ki ta ha ti kki ti kki, it is dark it is dark.*

Verse 9

This is an invocation, as well as a riddle, in which appears the Arabic word for "star," *kawkab.*

The lion is the engine in the house that is the body: There is the house of the star that is burning, and then there is the secret flesh in the house of the body; the secret flesh is moving moving as the awakened serpent, moves up and out to the house of the star. The wordplay is on *n'y*—a word that means both "move" and "snake."

Verse 10

The praised gold: As in alchemy the goal is gold; the rising energy becoming light is described as *the falcon flesh becoming gold* as it rises. In this verse is the first mention of the flesh as rising burning, as light, as gold, conjuring Pindar's alchemical line:

> *ariston men udor, o de xrusos aithomenon pur*
> *ate diaprepei di nuktes*
> The most precious thing is water,
> The next is gold, burning like fire in the night

Verse 11

The thunder is given to Unis, whose hands spread across the sky.

Verse 12

It is important that the mouth not be filled, as something needs to emerge from it.

Spa, the centipede, is in the house. The hieroglyph is the perfectly executed picture of a centipede. One does not want the centipede to be in the house. It is another poisonous thing that bites. The natural response is "get it out." However, the point is the name, for "centipede" in hieroglyphs is a pun on the verb *s-pa* (to fly away). Thus the house as the body contains the ability to fly away. The two energies fighting within the body would seem to be the dark serpent (characterized here as a centipede) and the white bird. The verse plays out the concept of the Arabic word *dud* (worm), as a category of creeping things. The category runs from the particular to the general. The serpent is a creeping thing, the centipede is the internal serpent, it is itself the rope rising up within, and the lion as the engine of the body. Thus two conflicting energies are rising up, the serpent and the bird that is light.

The verses on the east wall are riddles on the irony that the rising snake is also the bird of light, a white bird breaking free. The verses conjure and describe the darkness and danger of the serpent, the whiteness of the bird, how they are both within and struggle with each other, and how they are both the same thing, the inner eye that becomes the rising soul.

The idea that the rising serpent bites is elaborated upon in the final resolution of the text on the west gable of the sarcophagus chamber. There are two voices in the sequence of verses: one is telling the serpent to rise, the other is telling it to go back. The house is the body, the word in hieroglyphs is *pr*. As a verb it means "to rise." In the Pyramid Texts it is typically not spelled out, it is only the picture of a house with an open door, hence it could be a verb or a noun, depending on the context, either "house" or "rise." The rope, *nwh*, is both male and female, perhaps energy channels like the *ida* and *pingala* in the Tantric physiology. The hieroglyphs in this sequence of riddles present a progression of naturalistic representations of different birds that shine white in the sky, the ibis, the vulture, the plover, the pelican, as the rising light body. In this verse the white bird is the ibis.

Verse 13

The riddles are all presented in different voices, as though by different presences, as though there were a surround of different voices posing them, the wise men surrounding the child with gold and incense and myrrh. Or perhaps a group of different writers presenting different aspects of the thing, a loose range of metaphor describing something real: death. This is a particularly lovely riddle about the nature of the eye, and how it relates to emotion and writing. There are in you things made of alabaster, *two alabaster cups*. The alabaster cups are the actual, external eyes, as opposed to the inner eye. This is a verse in praise of the eyes, as the home of tears and of perception. The book of the writer is *ntaw ssat, ssat*, the avatar of writing. The eyes are the home of the heart. Although this is a sacred text from long ago, it is a very Egyptian verse with a contemporary sensibility. In the deeper sense of keeping what is dead alive—the writing itself is its life. Thus the verse conflates the physical eye in the body and its water of tears, with the eye as the intelligence of the sky that prompts the flood. The fertile field is the heart, with its relation to the seeing, feeling eye. The fertile field comes from the flood. The fertile field of the heart is watered by tears that give rise to poetry, as the fertile field watered by rain gives rise to greening crops.

Verse 14

Glittering white as the vultures you are free: The Egyptian vulture is white against the deep blue desert sky. The herons glide back and forth across the waves. The alabaster bodily eye is now freed as a white bird.

Verse 15

The mother is the lion (the gate of water), a play on "lion" and "gate," a reference to the south wall; he unites with his mother, enters the gate of water; see verse 29, the two lions/gates made holy, moisture and air, as Isis/Aphrodite (born from the foam) rises from the sea.

Verse 16

This is a riddle. The answer is, the eye is, not actually an eye, it is the internal snake. The snake as an animal is uniquely silent. The cry of the *kerawan*, the Senegal thicknee or stone curlew, is pure, thrilling, pervasive sound. It is the sound that defines the Nile Valley at twilight, the eerie rising and falling of a prolonged scream, like the cry of the curlew in Yeats. The miniature representation of the Senegal thicknee in this verse has the thick knees of the actual bird. The snake has two faces: the rising inner eye is both a snake (in the body) and a bird (leaving it), hence in making itself known as a poetic conceit it borrows the voice of its twin, the bird. Unis does not see he has an eye within; as in the Buddhist philosophical conundrum, the eye cannot see itself. The inner eye is not Unis but transcends him. Like life emerging from stone, conjured in the hieroglyphs themselves, the eerie harmonic crescendo of the bird rises out of the dark tomb: *Aaeeeeee.*

Verse 17

Hr sbn as the free circular motion of birds, so the life force slips out of the body.

The bull, the bird, and the snake are the same thing: the rising life force. The life force is now told, is prompted, *hr* (to emerge, come out, rise, spin away).

Verse 18

This description will occur again; the rising face meets another face as the serpent is absorbed into the falcon.

Verse 19

This sequence of riddles elaborates the nature of the inner light: What is the snake that flies, the hidden eye, as opposed to the two alabaster jars, the visible eyes? The verses proceed to prompt it forth, a ceremony is taking place to prompt it forth, and the verses are a progression involved in the prompting. The shining white bird of the soul is now rising within.

Verse 20

Ikn hayy: Here is the word *ikn* that appeared in the first verse as *grow dark*; the serpent is told to grow dark, to go away, to disappear as it arises, as though those who are calling it up are suddenly afraid and wish to turn it back, thus the serpent is characterized as a real serpent, deadly and terrifying. The following verse explains the meaning: *Would that you be hidden . . .*

Verse 21

As in the previous verse, that one does and does not want to see the rising snake seems to be part of getting it to rise. In verses 20 and 21 the serpent is formally negated. The shining white bird, now a pelican, escapes the serpent, sheds its skin, flies away on the winding paths of the stars, but it is not Unis himself. The soul rises with the "pelican," the Pleiades, prompting the Nile flood, with the life force rising with the rising stars.

Verse 22

The acacia tree is the body: This is the verse that makes it clear that the serpent in the tree is an iconographic image from the Tantric system: the tree is the body, the serpent is the spinal cord, and what it contains, the root and branching of the nervous system. The serpent guides him to leave the tree, to rise up as a white bird, purified energy, leaving the tree of the body behind.

At first light: The direct realization of emptiness is called the actual clear light. The actual clear light of the fourth stage is also spoken of as "external manifest enlightenment" because it is always initially manifested at dawn (just as Shakyamuni Buddha became enlightened at dawn). (See Daniel Cozort, *Highest Yoga Tantra*, p. 109.)

Consider also Christ on Mt. Tabor—while his companions still slept, his garment suddenly became as white as lightning—and the *surat al fajr*, the dawn sura: Mohammed's realization comes at dawn.

Verse 23

The serpent manifests, according to what has been harnessed: The ceremony is conducted correctly and the serpent manifests. When the serpent leaves the body, what is left of the person? Does the person continue to exist and does it matter?

Verse 24

The riddles end by posing questions that are addressed in the subsequent riddle. The answer to the previous verse is *the serpent takes you yet you do not go*. The energy is freed, but the dead becomes earth, the corpse resolves to earth. This sentiment is elaborated upon in the following verse. If there is no death, where is the mind? The serpent is now defined as two serpents, one male and one female, the twin energy channels that flank the spine. The readers now signify that they are merely following the words of a ritual. The snake is never visible. It is a metaphor.

Verse 25

In answer to the question what remains of Unis as a person: he is gone, the man is dead, find his mind, it is gone. This is what actually endures after death, your bad deeds, your name, your children, and your writing.

Verse 26

The verse suggests the reason that beautifully carved unused flint knives are found in predynastic burials in Egypt. They are there to cut off the head of the rising snake. It seems to say that the presence of the knife itself prompts the snake's appearance as it leaves the body through the head. What is desired in the ceremony is the ritual appearance of the rising snake, which is in actuality the light body, the serpent sleeping within those who are in the cult of Osiris. Awakened, the serpent rises and enables the transcendence of death. In your shoes is the hieroglyph of a pair of shoes, an element of the plain and earthly in this discussion of otherworldly things. The inclusion of a point-counterpoint negative and positive; it's real, it's not; and so on seems to indicate the presence of a formal dialectic or debate tradition of refining, pinning down with words what is real.

Verse 27

The snake encircles you in your tree: The serpent rises through the tree of the body.

Verse 28

The far desolate expanse of the mirror world: The awareness throughout of actual death, that death is real, the person is gone. The hawk from the burning land, the land of stars.

Washed white as the moringa tree: Refers to the startling whiteness of the trunks of the moringa tree, which grows only on the lower slopes of high mountains in the desert. J. J. Hobbs in *Bedouin Life in the Egyptian Wilderness* (40) remarks that the trunks of the moringa are so white that they are visible from a great distance in the desert. The letter *k* in the hieroglyphic word *moringa* may designate both the letter *k*, which is a mountainside, and the mountain slope where this tree grows. Here in the hieroglyphic phrase is the picture of the moringa tree, and the letter *k*, which is the picture of a mountain slope. This final verse resolves the progression of animal transformations on the west wall of the entranceway, which begins with the falcon circling and ends with the rising up of the crocodile, here explained as the great green snake. The passage also brings to resolution the first startling image in the monument, which is not only an astronomical reference but has a compounded meaning that the semen drawn upward as the serpentine energy rising through the tree of the body enables the release of the eye as pure light.

These short verses in particular seem as though they were composed by different people, almost in a competition, with each verse rendering a different aspect of the religious mystery. The final verse on the east wall of the antechamber presents the resolution of the insight of the life of the soul and the life of the universe presented in the monument.

The holy stars in their atmosphere . . . secret of the universe: Dark energy is most of what exists. May you remain in the realm of light, in the light of the stars. Air and moisture, the two gates/lions of existence. The sense follows, may you become the falcon rising in the east: the star in the east that is the green eye, and all that is in it, water, growth, joy, writing, memory, singing, speaking, all the good that it makes possible, take it, its names and qualities: alabaster (the actual eyes); willow (the tree); your great joy for the serpent rises through love of you. This is clearly a description of the rising of the internal serpent that has been called *kundalini*, "the coiled one," by means of the reversal of sexual energy. The rising internal stream of energy, conflated with the reversed sexual energy, becomes pure bliss and leaves the body flowing freely as the omniscient eye.

The great wide snake is a detailed hieroglyph of a puff adder, which is indeed a great wide snake. As in the sequence of white birds, one reptile becomes another. The crown is the snake having risen to the head, the eye that sees the malachite land, the pure land, where all is precious, jewellike, and green, the diamond realm as green as emerald, the falcon lord of the green lake. The falcon is the green snake.

As the snake in the grass and the snake in the garden are commonly encountered by anyone who lives in the country, the image of the bird and the snake coming together as a single entity comes directly from a simple familiarity with nature: the bird flies up carrying the snake in its beak; the snake lies in the top of the tree to catch the bird that comes to land. As the snake rises from the tree to catch the bird, for a moment in the air the snake and the bird are one. This is the meaning of the final verse. The east wall of the antechamber presents a progression of naturalistic representations of different birds that shine white in the sky, contrasting the dark hidden things that lie below. The two primary contrasts are resolved as the final insight in the antechamber, as the riddle teased out in the previous verses is given a definite answer: the rising white-winged being, the nature of light, and the dark hidden thing from below are different vehicles for the energy of life and morph into each other. St. George and the dragon, Apollo and Python, the winged angel and the serpent are the same thing.

Passage to the Sarcophagus Chamber: The Flight of the Eye

South Wall

Verse 1

The flight of the eye, the twin of Unis descends: The passage begins with the eye. It is the passage of the eye, the flight of the eye into the dark. The point of this entire body of mystical poetry is the emergence of the naked eye freed to range throughout the universe. Hence the passage begins with the eye. Then the wall is broken. The inner room is the innermost darkness where the transubstantiation of the dead takes place. Matter becomes light and flows with the flow of the universe. Hence the body, not the sky, is the subject of this inner room: the body as the sum of its aggregates is the eternal nature of the aggregates themselves; the treatment and preparation of the corpse; the internal mysteries that will emerge from the body and survive: the rising serpent as *the golden flow of falcon flesh*, the emergent eye, mirrored in the moon that vanishes like an eye closing in sleep. The subject of the final wall, the west gable above the body itself, is the manifestation of the serpent, rising in the tree of the body and emerging from it. The garden (a rectangular hieroglyph consisting of measured square garden plots) is the earth itself, from which the soul, becoming starlight, rises away, leaving the garden of earth behind.

Verse 2

Broken, exhausted, weary you go into the night: The body is a broken jar, the contents of which flow out, as in Ecclesiastes 12:6, "Remember him, before the pitcher is broken at the spring." The soul becomes a baby hawk with soft, fragile bones made of light, rising to see the face of Osiris; the seat of the eye is no longer the corpse but the sky.

Verse 3

This verse foreshadows the line on the west gable above the body itself, where the soul becomes the baby bull, the nature of starlight that leaves the garden of earth. The stars gently ask in astonishment, in voices like the drifting sound of the wind, "Who who what son what child, what white soul is nursed? . . . What attributes are his as he races by?" They are flapping. They are wings. Here lies the idea of angels as the humanized ghosts of birds, flapping in the fields of stars, the Elysian fields, the lake of space. The cormorant leaping up is the hieroglyphic picture of a cormorant, and a reference back to the north wall of the antechamber where the waterbirds are rushing up into the sky. Then the soul is the bull as the thunder, marked with the hieroglyphic thunderstone, the belemnite.

Thus the primary ideas are listed, first the eye, then the soul of white light that rises as a bird, then the bull of heaven, as thunder, are received by the holy nine.

The eye of light sees: The hieroglyphic word is *nw*, identified as *nous*, the Greek word for "mind." It is first used in the text here as the verb for "seeing." As a noun this is the word for "hunter, tracker."

That Osiris count you: The English word *reckon* is the Arabic *reqim* (number). "Count" here has the sense of the English word *reckoning*, that you be judged to be included. But here there is another dimension to the concept: there is a mathematical underlay to the Egyptian idea of eternity as an astronomical reading of cyclical time; the souls are "counted" as stars in the readable grid of the sky.

•

The whiteness of moonlight as cream: The falcon eye is the moon, the cream is moonlight. This wall presents the conflation of the falcon with the eye, and the falcon as the eye with the moon. The soul receives and becomes the falcon eye.

As you rise a voice or sound comes to you: This is a reference back to verse 7 on the north wall of the antechamber. The *ma'a herw*, the voice arises, and now the soul, purified, can hear and understand it.

The sound carries over to the importance of the words themselves. The words effect the transformation: *bring him the words*. The ritual words are now meant to be said, four times, or seven times, and must be spoken in precisely the right way for effect.

The next stage is protection for the prompting of the descent of the twin. The actual descent is then described: the leg, the arm, as Unis is conflated with, merges with, becomes one with Osiris and is given the falcon eye; he is now the eye alone, having no longer a face, a personality, he is faceless, the self is gone. He literally becomes the eye, pure disembodied awareness. The eyes of light looking out are faceless.

Verse 2

Here is the recognition of this new merged being: *Greetings divine one, you who are three.* The falcon eye raised high is the moon.

The remarkable thing throughout is how contemporary the language is: the dangerous flight through the dark; broken, exhausted, weary you go into the night. The body is a broken water jar out of which the contents flow. The soul is a baby falcon with soft, fragile bones flapping into the dark. The soul flies up, flapping, to the eye on its throne. This icon is briefly humanized as a judge on a throne: whom he desires to live will live, whom he desires to die will die. Then it is simply the eye again, and the question resides in semantics: Is it the harsh, judging, watching eye, or is it the absorbing, shining eye that is light itself? Though one easily sees in this the familiar conception of the all-seeing, punishing God, the soul is not judged by this entity but becomes it.

North Wall

The hieroglyphs on this wall are written in reverse, in order to mirror the writing on the opposite wall of the passageway, indicating, as in the entranceway, that "reversal" is primarily an aesthetic consideration.

Verse 1

You will not die, because you are Osiris. As he lives, you live. You know the words, hence you are absorbed into the universe itself. Elements involving numbers: the nine bright lights, the four greens. Your face is the dog star. The path of the turning sky is *pshr*, the hieroglyphic verb for "going around." It is the picture of the winding path of the labyrinth.

The horns come out upon you: The alchemical unicorn. The hieroglyphic horns are the verb "to open." The head opens to release the serpent that forms on the brow as a single hornlike growth before emerging from the body. To examine the span of the word and the predictable hardening of the *h* into *c*, *q*, *k*, and *g*, in what might be called the progression of *hs*: horn=corn=*cornu* (Latin, horn*)=qarin* (Arabic for both "horn" and "spiritual twin")=grow= green.

The horn is the thing that rises up: Out of the upper part of your head. As the dead soul becomes the eye, like a baby bull it grows horns. The eye is a star, and the horns are rays of starlight. The eye is thunder and the horns are lightning. Hence the horn as the serpent is the uni-corn, or single horn. The horn goes into the lap of the seated virgin. You trap a unicorn with a seated virgin because the unicorn puts its horn in her lap. The seated virgin is the seat, Isis the sky. Thus the unicorn, as in Auden, gives way to the dove of light. As is explained in the verses that follow on the east wall, the rising serpent is both generated and pacified by love.

Horns and bones are both invoked as the hard, tactile substance of things: the bones of falcons, of holy serpents in the sky; you rise to the sky in your vehicle of light, your form moves, your feathers rush.

The boat in this verse has light streaming from the back. This is a further elaboration of the feather and the falcon: the falcon is the sky, the feather is its nature, emptiness, air, the wind.

Verse 3

Your sight of the universe: A world of light. It is only possible *to see it with the eyes of the stars*, for it is known only to them. The sky is holy, both as the harmonizing movement, the wheeling of the falcon, and the wildness of the wolf. The harmonizing patterned movement of the falcon brings coolness even to the desert, as the cool silver light of *the shining moon dispels the darkness of the wild sky.*

You will not forget, you will not forget: existence is remembering. *You are born not from love or sexual intercourse* but transubstantiation, a process that belongs, hence you in all your constituents, both physical and intangible as energy, belong and have their origin in the physical world. This is the mystery, the actual translation of flesh into light. Both are aspects of nature, hence the mystery of the translation of the body into the universe is real. Your eyes, your ears, your nose, your senses are all absorbed and not destroyed, you become the movement, the beauty, the harmonious turning. Yet you must remember where you come from.

Verse 4

The whole sky turns with you: The boats as vehicles have hieroglyphs progressively added to them. The ultimate truth goes with you, as you have attained the ultimate reality. The one who goes with you is *the starry sky, she of a thousand souls.* You become the one Orion takes around, *the one Sirius takes around* and brings to the pure realm of the stars, washed white with the starlight. The hand of the father is the hand of the universe. What is intended is that the universe itself is the parent of all that lives, is a realm of pure light, all of which is knowable without faith, and true.

Verse 5

The sacred shrine of the stormy sky: The four greens are the sprouting mounds of both the falcon and the wolf. The seat of the four greens is Egypt.

Verse 6

Unis is now merged with Osiris, shining white and strong. The nine bright shining lights are here defined as nine stars. Thunder, greenness, this is not your season of silence, for you are the eye of the wolf = *nshni*, the open eye of the storm. With Thoth, the moon, you go round and round the sky. Although one has been told not to mourn, the stars are seen as weeping, suggesting meteor showers. The image echoes the first verse on the north wall of the antechamber.

Nine bright lights, a constellation traveling the sky nearing each horizon, the Pleiades appearing as nine bright lights, the Pleiades circling the sky. The lines in this verse track the circular progress of the Pleiades about the sky, as though turning the wheel of the sky.

Verse 7

The text now goes into the mystery of Osiris. By identifying with Osiris you have eternal life. Hence the chant can be translated *you are the child of air, as it [air] lives, you live,* or *as he [Osiris] lives, you live.* But the overall meaning is the same, as Osiris is the eternal life within the corpse and in the universe. This very holy and significant liturgy examines the elements and the composition of the body and how they do not cease to exist. The point is that holiness resides, and the eternal life resides in the body itself.

The Aggregates: The verse proceeds as an exercise of logic. If what your body contains is eternal, then you are eternal. As in Tantric ceremony, repetition of verbal formulae is part of the process of sanctification.

You don't cease to exist, but you do cease to exist as a particular person, that is obvious. The air as breath is unchanging, eternal, hence your breath does not die or cease to exist. The following elements of the composition of the body are examined as in a logical argument that cannot be defeated: the moisture in the composition of your body does not cease to exist; earth, matter is next; then darkness; then the empty space; then wild nature with its two thunderbolts (the *vajra* is here explained as the double-headed axe). Hence Unis is rendered back into the elements. Thoth as perception is signified by the moon. Having conflated the dead with the nine holy

things—air, moisture, space, nature, dark, earth, decay, birth, perception—
what follows is *the opening of the mouth*. As though the text were saying
"These are the things within you, let us find them, let us open the mouth,"
we look in the mouth and what we find is empty space.

In the *nywt* hieroglyph the sides of the pyramid point to the center; here
the central column is the spine. In your mouth is the column of the *nywt*, the
spinal column. In your mouth is the lake within the head. In your mouth is
the scorpion that enables breath, the disembodied windpipe that resembles a
scorpion. In your mouth is the holy shrine within you, the emptiness of the
body itself. In your mouth is the whiteness of teeth, illustrated by a perfect
hieroglyph of teeth; their whiteness itself is eternal. This is the third shift:
first it is the holy nine elements, then it is the aspects of the body within the
mouth, the cavity, the throat, the teeth, now it is the universe itself, all of
this is within you: *the mouth contains all that is in the body*. Then a switch, as
sliding to the empty space of the universe is itself contained within the body,
as the text moves on to the next wall.

The Sarcophagus Chamber

South Wall:
The Aggregates and the Emptiness of the Body

The antechamber is the night sky. The adjoining room is the innermost darkness of the night, where the transformation of the body takes place. It has been called the womb of night. The physical reality of the body is the subject of the text in this room: the body is its aggregates. Then follow the treatment and preparation of the corpse, the physical offerings made to the dead, the internal mysteries that will emerge from the body and survive: the eye and the twin. The final wall is the west gable above the body. As on the final wall in the antechamber, the west gable presents a sequence of riddles that refine the meaning of the serpent as the eye, the manifestation of the serpent rising in the body and emerging from it as the flesh turning to gold. The serpent is in the tree of the body; the garden is the earth itself; the dead, having attained the secret knowledge encoded in the words, becomes starlight, rising away, leaving the garden of earth.

The passage into this inner room presents the flight of the eye and the descent of the twin, establishing the two principles of the eternal nature of the mind, and the eternal nature of the body. The eye is the mind released as free-flowing omniscience that flows through the universe; it is the star it sees. The twin emerges as an electrical shadow of light that, absorbed into the universe, becomes it. Thus the ultimate nature of the body and the mind is the resolution of the iconographic riddle of Osiris: the jewel in the lotus is the eye on its throne.

To say that the energy that electrifies your body in life emerges from you as horns of light, that bones are soft, that moonlight is cream—you can feel in these words poetry as a physical force that stirs an inner, tactile awareness of a living transformative reality. To define it kills it, but poetry captures it alive.

The text in the sarcophagus chamber reads from south to east to north to west, continuing in a counterclockwise direction. The language itself now has a silvery quality that gives the sense of unobstructed, free-flowing motion as the disembodied eye flows through the universe. There are extended passages of pure repetition, the verses come around first to a long liturgy that examines the aggregates of the body. The liturgy takes the form of a syllogism, again pointing to an established dialectic, the exercise of logic in a debate tradition among the Egyptian priesthood. The elements that comprise a human being are named, considered, and acknowledged to be eternal. If they do not die, what is death? The dense, repetitive liturgy opens into a detached division and analysis of these elements: air, earth, water; as they live on, you, too, live on. The liturgy progresses through the body and into the mouth. The hieroglyphic phrase *n-r-n-k* can be translated as either *in your name* (*rn-k*) or *in your mouth* (*r-n-k*). There is no way of knowing which is intended, but the phrases that determine the meaning are in your mouth are the cavities in the head, in your mouth is the whiteness of teeth, with a hieroglyphic picture of teeth, in your mouth is the taste, and so on. The liturgy goes through the mouth into the body itself, into the lakes, or empty spaces, in the head and in the body, to the rustling scorpion in the throat that once enabled breath. The entire progression of the analysis of the components of a human being is familiar as the Tantric analytical meditation on finding the nonexistent self. In what part of the body does the individual life reside? If the self is not findable, transformation is possible. The limbs of the corpse become generalized as the limbs of Osiris, and emerge from the corpse as arms and legs of light, horns of light. Dynamic, alive, they become the limbs, the motion, of the universe. The ritual preservation of the dry shell of the body ensues with the measured placement of particles of Natron, salt, netcher—as it appears in English—is the holy substance that removes the putrifying liquid of the detested wild dog, death: nature.

Although it has been acknowledged throughout the text that the body is a mere shell, death is characterized as the decay that makes it fall apart.

The composition of the ephemeral body and the eternal elements within it on the south and east walls leads back to its essence, the eternal eye, reflected in the rising moon on the east gable.

The four gables within the monument signify different versions of the eye, represented in things that rise: the lotus, the thunderbolt, the star, the moon, and at last, on the west gable in the sarcophagus chamber, the serpent rising through the tree of the body. The lotus signifies the beauty of still water that mirrors the violent thunderstorm in the antechamber. In the sarcophagus chamber the dangerous serpent awakened as the inner eye mirrors the external eye as the calm of the beautiful shining moon.

The north wall presents a list of offerings appealing to the senses: delicious foods, perfumes, soft clothes. The name of each offered object is a pun on the verb that offers it, creating a sense of the illusory nature of the object. The offering then becomes the eye itself: the seeing, naming mind, *take it, it is yours*. This "falcon" eye, the eye as the falcon that flies up into the sky, is then apparently painted on the face of the dead, with the repetitive instruction *take it, it is yours*. The rapid, violent chanting story of the eye devoured by the wild dog follows, as the moon is eaten away by relentless nature, until there is nothing left. The cycle of time is complete. But then it comes back. The final words on this wall make your hair stand up:

Consider this, for the light is going down, the light is going down, it is your light.

The text in the sarcophagus chamber is infinitely more dense, more difficult, but more fluid than on the previous walls. The flight of the eye, the descent of the twin, the flight through the universe, the twin as the universe, the deathless aggregates of the body resolved back into the universe, the verbal examination of the body as an exercise in logic opening into the description of the actual preservation of the body with Natron, salt. The south and east walls of the sarcophagus chamber are the most difficult parts of the text because key elements can be translated in different ways, and there really is no way of knowing which is meant. The overall structure and the essential meaning are clear. Others may work out the details as they understand them.

The first confusing element, as noted above, is the repeated hieroglyphic phrase *n-r-n-k*. It can be read as either *n-rn-k* (in your name), or *n-r-n-k* (in your mouth). There are enough specific references to the mouth, indeed progressive references—teeth, esophagus, taste, the cavities of the skull—to indicate that the mouth itself is meant. Furthermore the phrase is introduced by the command *open your mouth* to release the falcon. The mouth is the opening into the vast empty interior of the body. *Open your mouth . . . in your mouth . . .* The second confusing element is again the hieroglyph *nywt*. In this long repetitive liturgy it occurs over and over, and is gradually elaborated upon and then flipped (it is specific as the interior of the body, then general, as empty space) in order to be given a larger meaning, as the text does something quite interesting. Having examined the elements of the body on the south wall, and then going into the mouth and examining by naming the actual physical features within the mouth, the final verse on the south wall states *In your mouth is Orion: time itself.* In other words, in your mouth is the thing within you that emerges and goes into the sky, hence, in your mouth is the sky. Thus in the following phrase that begins the text on the east wall—*In your mouth is the taste of the* nywt—the *nywt* hieroglyph is obviously not used to indicate a city in some other part of Egypt (as it has been translated previously, as Busiris). The hieroglyph would seem to indicate, as before, the general concept of the delineated circle, and as such, a sanctified space with a center like a mandala, here meaning the interior of the body. The east wall follows this concept, taking up the gradual elaboration of the meaning of the *nywt* hieroglyph in the body, using it to open the sacred space within the body to the sacred space of the sky that contains Sirius and the stars that define the limits of the south and the north. In other words it is the *macranthropos*, man as the cosmos, arrived at through a detailed verbal examination of the physical body itself as something that has been sanctified for the ritual purpose in the verses of linking the body and the sky. The link is the open mouth.

In the West death is cessation. The principle at work here is its opposite. Death is motion. What they're getting at is a sense of constant motion that touches something deep in the heart of the mystery of things. Motion depends on an embedded pattern, in the sky and on earth. It is the pattern itself that is eternity. The whole motif of the sky and the Nile is continuation through the reliable repetition of a pattern. The doctrine of remembrance that appears in Plato's *Meno*, as in these verses, is the pattern embedded in the mind. Death is a reawakening in which you must remember the deep structure of who you are and where you are, and whom you are with. The use of repetition throughout the text highlights the sense that this is a pattern and words are an essential part of it.

The verses that comprise this body of mystical poetry are a compendium of ritual formulas into which any name can be inserted. This is the importance of the ever-sought "treasure text," the "golden tablets" of which this text is the source, the origin of all the derivative religious texts that were hidden away or buried with the dead, such as the Egyptian Book of the Dead and the Coffin Texts, the Orphic tablets of gold, and the golden tablets Joseph Smith unearthed in Canandaigua that were the foundation of Mormonism. The buried writing is the most precious thing on earth, for it is a vehicle for the transformation of the soul, any soul. Hence the name is interchangeable and really is the least important element in the text. The theme throughout history of the buried body of writing that contains the lost essential secret is the sword in the stone, the secret weapon that brings the dead thing back to life.

This is the one part of the monument where the text continues from one wall to another, from the south wall onto the east wall of the sarcophagus chamber, as part of the same theme and structure. The south wall examined the body as the dead person identified with Osiris, going into the body itself through the mouth. Inside the mouth what is found is the emptiness within the body; in the final verse on the south wall this empty space becomes the sky. The east wall picks up this theme: inside the mouth is the *nywt*. It seems that the idea in this hieroglyph of the circular surround of the sky is joined with the physical idea of the mouth by the word *taste*. *In your mouth is the taste of the* nywt. In the five verses that follow, the circular space designated by this hieroglyph is defined: it is *the temple of the bull* (the life force); there is a southern star or limit to it, and a northern star or limit. In the fifth verse the point is made that within the sacred space inside the body that has been correlated to the sky is *the eye that encircles your body. Within it, you are released, as your son the falcon you live*. You enter the eye in the body and are released into space as the "falcon." As in the circular sanctified space of a mandala, you are safe within it, but outside of it you would cease to exist (as what you are in the ceremony). The verses on the south and east walls are not simply declamatory but are describing an actual process in keeping with Tantric ceremony. In the second verse the doors of the horizon are now open, and (as in verse 1 on the north wall and verse 5 on the south wall of the antechamber) the soul goes dancing joyfully up into the beauty of the night sky.

The passages open into the description in verse 2 of the rising of the female serpent of great spiritual power, *she rises, she rises,* readily recognizable as *kundalini,* "the coiled one," the sleeping female serpent that is coiled up at the base of the spine in every human being. It is the potential of the awakening of the concentrated nerve energy in the spine that shoots up like a live current of electricity when awakened. The goal of the religious practice is to harness and direct this potent blossoming current of electricity in the spine. This serpent is fierce and dangerous but the initiate controls the process, calms the serpent, with the focus created by *beautiful words,* the ritual words of the ceremony, and so sees the fruit of the practice: as the serpent of sparking nerve energy rises up the spine, youthful vigor is reborn. The serpent is awakened by means of *the love that causes the spirit to rise,* the arousal and reversal of sexual energy up the central channel or spine described on page 239. Thus the Tantric spell in verse 1 on the east wall of the entranceway and verse 8 on the west wall of the antechamber, *dam the dam of the reassembled, reassembled joined to the light,* is explained. This is what the beautiful words are meant to achieve: the control of the canal where the energy in the channel of the body is to be concentrated and then released. As in Tantra, the rising is described as a ground of transformation: *Rise upon it, this ground of transformation. The great one blossoms as an arrow in you the blossoming image of a serpent gives birth to you in the image of a falcon.* The chant then becomes *it is he who goes with you,* the falcon, the bull, Sirius, and so forth. The essence of the Egyptian religious system is presented here. This is how it actually happens, the blossoming image of a serpent gives birth to you in the image of a falcon. The channeling of the energy in the Tantric practice is what enables it to cross the sky.

Surrounded by the protection of his eye (the serpent), Osiris is the "father," the avatar that is this vehicle, shorthand for the practice itself.

May you O ruler: Wordplay on *hk* (ruler) and *hk* (spell) in the line below.

Be granted the nine lest he be destroyed: Has the possible meaning *Let the Pleiades rise so that Sirius will not be destroyed (will fail to rise in the lineup of stars).* The verse proceeds to describe the path of Sirius through the sky. The glittering arc of the falcon is the path of Sirius across the sky; follow it as far as it goes. *Spin* here has the sense of keep on turning, going around, do not stop. The language of the poem mimics the motion of the turning sky.

As in a Tantric ritual in the Vajrayana, the negative forces must first be invoked and pacified. The text follows into an invocation of Set, with a description of what Set actually is: bad weather, the wild-dog seasonal storms of the south with their howling winds that tear up September, the harvest month. The presence is invoked and asked not to destroy the infant falcon as it rises, whose work it is to become strong. The verses continue with the sense of fluidity present on these two walls, the flow of the universe, *you rise you descend you rise you descend*, with the quality of pure motion, pure fluidity to the ultimate conclusion. *Rejoice: the star is in the sky. Sirius rises.*

East Wall:
The Rising of the Inner Serpent

The progression presented on the east wall of the sarcophagus chamber is as follows:

1. The empty space in the body approached through the opening of the mouth is sanctified and correlated with the sky.
2. Found within the empty space in the body is the vehicle, the eye that surrounds you within. The soul as initiate enters/makes use of this vehicle to be released as the falcon.
3. The great female serpent within is invoked and described as both terrifying and prompted upward by love. Harnessed and controlled by the words of the ceremony *she rises she rises*, bringing with her the red crown, the king of Egypt.
4. *It is he who goes with you*: Begins as the king enabled to rise by the rising of the female serpent, the great female of spiritual power, and then becomes the king's progressive manifestations as the falcon, the bull, Sirius, and so on.
5. Rising as a star, the king dances with joy high in the night sky.
6. May he be granted three things: First, *the nine lest he be destroyed*, described in the sarcophagus chamber as *the nine bright*

shining lights; are these the Pleiades that presage the rising of Sirius in the night sky, described in this room as *the temple of foreknowledge?* Second, the spiritual power of the words. And third, to be placed in the north sky with the stars that do not set.

7. The dangerous negative forces are addressed and pacified as Set, the bad weather of autumn in the south. It is requested that this entity not harm the infant soul rising as a newborn star, whose work it is to become strong.

8. Poetic passages capture the beauty and free-flowing movement of the sky: *You flow with your father the universe, with your lion's head of youth you rise, you open your way with bones of the wind, surrounded by the arms of your mother the night, you are pure in the lakes of air.*

9. The sense captured in these images of the lovely rising of a bright star gives way to the beautiful chant *you rise you descend you rise you descend,* with progressive variation: you rise *with the light of the universe, with time embracing the earth, with the temple that contains all things—the dark, you flow as the lightning, a soul washed white in the arms of your father the universe.* By repetition, by reification, the soul as a star is made real.

10. The universe is then told to look at Unis and thus accept him as a son. There is then rejoicing as at the birth of an actual son.

11. The first food offerings are made (perhaps foreshadowed by the first phrase on the wall: *in your mouth is taste*). The soul, given its food, comes out *as Osiris, miller of the holy nine, in the temple of foreknowledge.* The soul is told to *rise in the Milky Way. May you be given the falcon eye. May the door be opened to you. Say the words that Unis be able to move.*

12. The purpose of the entire ceremony is then stated in the final verse on the east wall: *Say the words that cause the green sprouting mounds, may you be with Orion among the living words.* The soul as a rising star has become the principle of time itself, the thing that brings food and all sustenance to the earth.

As dawn draws near the eastern lakes of the sky
Welcome Child Lord, Protector of all that is on earth

In your mouth is taste: In your mouth is the eye that encircles the body, within it you are released. It is the falcon that releases you from the body, as the falcon becomes the emergent eye.

That the horizon has doors. That one dances with joy in the beauty of the sky. The red crown is the king of Egypt. The serpent is terrifying and conjured with erotic energy *that causes the spirit to rise.*

She is the great female principle of spiritual power that rises to the crown, so that he *know his falcon*, is able to make the transformation, throw out the light body. The ceremonial presence of the knife in the calling forth of the serpent, as awareness and the light body thrown out at once, again suggests the use in the ritual of the beautifully carved flint knives included in desert burials, and that this is a prehistoric system coming from elsewhere, involving the knowledge of the night sky, the conjuring of the internal serpent, a system to which the animal rows on the predynastic combs and knives, as star groups marking time, belong. The presence of both the knife and the loud cry of terror suggest that the conjuring of the serpent must mimic an encounter with a deadly poisonous snake.

The great one blossoms as an arrow in you: The blossoming image of a serpent gives birth to you, it is rising powerfully forth and out, like an arrow, the eye is now a fierce protector as a serpent that can go out and do things like harm enemies.

May you be granted the nine (lest you be destroyed): As for the storm, the bad weather of the south, of September, go away, do not blot out the young falcon, wild-dog thunderstorm with your clouds and rain.

In the hand/the protector/the great mill: A wordplay on *dn/nd*.

Provided with his bread (its food), your soul comes out: The first appearance of the wattled crane hieroglyph as the soul in this text.

East Gable:
The Moon as the Silver Eye

The east wall presents the beginning of the offering ritual that is the dominant subject of the next, or north wall. Offerings are made to coax out the serpent. The sky is accurately called *the temple of foreknowledge*, the reading of seasonal time. The poem is about the invention of time, and it mimics throughout the turning of the sky, and the elements in the sky: birds, the howling winds, the thunder. The east wall ends with the point of the formula, *say the words*. You move as you say the words. The words are not describing something but, by imagining it, making it happen. The words are alive. Thus the snake and the walking stick are equated with each other: the words are life, as the snake is life. The words are what enable the soul to move.

The east gable of the sarcophagus chamber begins in a very fine hand and has a distinct quality throughout of fineness and beauty. There are two short words in the first two columns that read from right to left. After looking at them for a long time I realized that the first word in the first column is the word for "moon," spelled backward or upside down as though deliberately hidden. The word is *iahw*, the hieroglyphic name for "moon," a word that the Old Testament scholar Theodor Gaster identified as *yahweh*, a variation on the word *iahw*, the divine principle that is the bright shining light that shines through all things. The second column spells out the word for "moon" in Egypt today, *qmr (qamar)* and may well have been a word for "moon" in hieroglyphs as well. The hieroglyphic phrase in the second column reads *ya qamar a nw, O moon of the flood*. It is also possible to ignore the word *qmr* and read the plow hieroglyph *mr* as the word for "love," as in *O love of water*. Egyptologists have translated this phrase as *the hoers are aroused*, evidently reading the plow hieroglyph as a hoe and as the verb "to love" at the same time. That the moon is indicated in the verse is confirmed by the use of already established tropes to describe the moon in the parallel phrases that follow: it is a milky breast, it is the falcon eye washed white. A verse that follows invokes the full moon, trembling as it rises from the desert hills across the Nile.

It is quite a beautiful verse. The moon is both burning (the onomatopoetic word *ss*) and cool. Its milky light, the food of the infant soul, is water from the lake of time. The verse explains this with the strange take on Osiris, who as the desert of death knows no hunger or thirst. Its essence sustains not the body but the heart. *What it fills what it fills is the heart* reads like a classic line from contemporary Egyptian poetry.

The second verse invokes the sky as a beautiful bird, *O dappled one above*, and pursues the idea of food that was introduced in the first verse on the east gable and continues as the primary subject through the north wall. The food of a star is space and light. This gives way to the idea of actual food. The light in the face of the bull of time would seem to be Aldebaran in Taurus, the rising of which prompts the rising of grain, which becomes bread and beer, the two staples of Egypt. How is this bread and beer attained? By means of an ox to plow the land. This opens into what at first seems to be a lecture on the production of food but turns out to be a riddle, the meaning of which, like the riddle of the Sphinx, involves the interpretation of numbers. As regards the production of food, there are two lights belonging to the sky and three lights belonging to the earth: the greater and lesser light of ancient times. The subject of the verse would seem to be the sky as a clock and its relationship to the production of food. The final verse presents the image of the soul merging with the sky, his sister, who is both empty space and the water hidden within it. The soul merges with the beautiful one he fears, the stormy sky, for it is she, even today, who makes all that is good in the world. The passage is reminiscent of the beginning of *De rerum natura*, "for without you is nothing beautiful made nor comes into being within the shores of light," and Job 38, "out of whose womb came the ice and the hoary frost of heaven, who hath gendered it?"

The question of the mathematical nature of this riddle—there are three lights in the sky, and two relevant to the earth—is open to discussion. The answer might be the sun and the moon, and the three phases, or shapes, of the moon. In the strange arresting poetic riddle mentioned above, Unis merges with the water, the source of water, the sky. It is the ultimate *hierogamos*. The sky is the great paradox: the mother, the sister, emptiness, space. Her nature is fire, for she is on fire with the stars. And her nature is water, the water that falls from the sky. The hieroglyphic word spelled out on the left, *nk* (wave/basket), is the word for sexual intercourse here, and a word for sexual intercourse in Egyptian Arabic today (in English it appears as nooky). The determinative for the word as it is used uniquely here is, remarkably, the downward-facing triangle, the Tantric icon of the feminine. The beautiful one he fears is the sky as the womb of all things, the womb of storms.

The strange and powerful, and beautiful verses on this gable present the concept that the moon, the Silver Eye, is food itself, for time brings the earth to fruition. The moon is then, on the north wall, itself eaten away, by time, by nature, by the wild dog.

Verse 2

The hieroglyphic determinative for "food," *aka/l*, is the cormorant, Shakespeare's greedy cormorant. The hieroglyphic phrase *hwt aka* is the contemporary Egyptian phrase *hagat akl* (things to eat).

Verse 3

Food resides in the eye of light, the holy eye.

Verse 5

Only in the desert can one understand the poignance of this verse: do not take its greenness away, the greening power of the rain wind, do not leave us with only the parching desert wind.

Verse 6

The moon is now itself described as the opener of the paths. The wild dog signals its rising on the path of the ecliptic. It is Thoth, who sleeps in the desert hills, trembling, as it rises over the Nile, a vivid description of the wavering moon rising over the water and the desert hills beyond. Thoth, the moon, as the luminous disembodied head, as St. John, who said, "Make my paths straight."

The embalmer's room for Unis is like a bird trap in the reeds, a lovely poetic conception.

Asheret, here the word for "trees," is *ashgar, shagara*, the Arabic word for "trees."

Here, also, is the reappearance of *bwt*, the detested (putrefying) liquid of the great wild-dog death, the natural process of death and decay.

Verse 7

The eye as Set is a composite hieroglyph: lightning merged with the rainbow and the feather. In keeping with the sense of the verse, the eye is the moon, the eye is the storm with its rainbow.

Verse 8

Pi stands alone at the end of the east gable, making it clear that *pi* is a magical or mantric sound.

North Wall:
The Corpse Becomes the Seat of the Eye

The east gable introduces the moon and its relationship to water and to the eye. The full moon both swells and beautifies the flood, a sense that carries over onto the north wall. The moon and its relationship to water hence food morphs into the offerings of food and hinges on the question of naming them. Ritual offerings are made in the ceremony. The eye is the organ that recognizes and names things. Every object is presented by a verbal pun on its name, as though the nature of the thing resides in its name, and the name resides in the eye. Ultimately the eye itself is offered. The eye is Osiris. The dead person is Osiris. The eye is then eaten. This is the presentation of the central mystery. The eye is eaten bite by bite by the wild dog death, nature, until it is gone, and then . . . it comes back, opening like an eye waking after the dark night of sleep.

Thus the text on the north wall addresses the question of what the eye actually is, and involves the ritual creation of the eye. Unis, the dead person, is given and becomes the eye. The eye is then eaten and restored, as the moon is eaten and restored. It is the eye that destroys your face, your individuality. To bring you the falcon eye, to cool your heart with it, to bring you your milk of darkness, pouring out around you as you rise, that your heart never weary. As you rise there is a pervading voice, *remain, remain.* This wall maps out the actual ceremony of the preparation of the body, its preservation with salt, Natron, the religious instruction that goes with this, the offerings, each of which is a pun on a poetic line that is recited as it is offered. This is, one might say, the early version of communion. The falcon rises from the dead body and becomes the eye, the dynamic energy of light that is embodied by the stars, and particularly, here, by the moon. This "eye" is eaten as food itself, created by time and the seasonal coming of water; the eye is a metaphor for the physical manifestation of light as life on earth. The mystery again resides in the reversal of an essential taboo: the eye is eaten. The moon is both the eye of the sky itself and the breast of the sky that nourishes—with both its visible milky light and its association with water in terms of both the seasons and tides (the Nile has tides). The moon is eaten by nature, hence the ceremony of eating the eye is a metaphor for time, and life as the light energy that manifests in life on earth through the medium of time. The moon shrinking is seen as the water drying up, as the water in the growing desert of the Neolithic dried up, as moisture now goes out of the body in death, conjuring the sense that what you see is what you are. The moon reconstituted is the return of water, the return of life after death. In essence it is the cyclical nature of time.

You take the falcon eye. *Its sweetness pervades you.*

The idea of sweetness, that the eye is sweet, occurs again in the final verse on the west gable above the body; it is the idea that sense experience has a taste.

Here white and black eyes are mentioned, and would seem to indicate the light and dark phases of the moon. Elsewhere the green eye, the azure eye, and the red eye are all different aspects of the sky as time, greening, peaceful, stormy.

Some of the remarkable lines on this wall:

Grow green grow green cries the night

Aqaq=aeshaesh, a pun on the word for "bread," the offering here, which is also the word for "life"

As gold it falls in you
It falls through the gates

As the end draws near the alchemical gold arises. It is the serpent that possesses the gold.

> You are set according to your nature
> Sit, be silent

> Emerald-green Sirius you see
> And the milky light of the moon

> It is Your light
> Your light

Consecrate with Natron the eighteen holy elements: Suggests that the holy eighteen in verse 1 on the north wall of the antechamber are in the body. The putrefying liquid of death is different from the liquid of life, water, conjured above. Natron, salt, netcher, because it prevents decay (and makes permanent, places the body beyond time), here used in sanctifying the mouth, hence the interior of the body, and identifying it with the holy principles.

His mouth is the milky mouth of a newborn calf: Presages the birth of the baby bull, mentioned on the east gable of the antechamber and the west gable of the sarcophagus chamber. The mouth is purified for the emergence of the eye, the falcon. The alabaster vessel is the body, the person no longer exists. Similarly in Tantra the body is described as a vase. The unknown country is death. The liquid going out of the moon parallels the liquid going out of the body. The mouth is dry. *The serpent sleeps within* in verse 16 is also the meaning of verse 7. The liquid of the spine is understood to be the same as saliva and semen, and goes out of the mouth as the light body.

The falcon eye destroys your face: You become a star, you become the moon, you are no longer a person, you shine rather than see. This wall explains the *ankh* sign—it is *the open face of the falcon*, the open top of the spinal column approached through the mouth. The falcon eye was imprisoned because it was hidden as the sleeping serpent inside you. The falcon is coming out of the mouth; wrath is part of it.

Foster children: Throughout the text the question is considered: What in fact is a child? What is birth? The soul as the child of Osiris is not born from the living body but from the head in death. You are released into Osiris; you become him.

Thoth provides the words: The words are "poured" like a libation. The offering of bolts of white linen represents flowing milk.

Receive the eyes the great one paints: In other words the female serpent is *the great one*. She "paints," enables, the holy vision. Let *her* light the two lands.

West Gable:
The Flesh Becomes Gold

This is the writing on the gable directly above the body in the coffin. The wall below the gable is covered with vivid geometrical designs, the color of which has lasted to this day. The columns on the gable read from right to left. The garden is in the first column, as a divided rectangle. The picture of a baby bull appears in the second column. The surrounding serpent is in the third and fourth.

The section of short riddles on the east wall of the antechamber mirrors this progression of riddles defining the inner serpent on the west gable of the sarcophagus chamber, as the walls themselves parallel each other in the monument. Here the riddles have a deeper layer of meaning. They conjure the sense of trying to catch or draw out the elusive snake, which is briefly visible and which you know is there. The gable begins with a tongue twister that hearkens back to the protection cord in verse 10 at the end of the north wall in the antechamber. Here the protection cord is the serpent that surrounds the universe, life.

Verse 1

Shenn'winn'wshen shenwenushen
Surrounded by the serpent by the serpent surrounded
The baby bull, the nature of starlight (*hbs/sh*),
Rises from the garden of earth

The serpent is a sibilant sound, and the sound of the word itself surrounds the word: The meaning of the phrase is "surround surround," hence the serpent is conjured, its meaning is expressed in the sound. The serpent is not actually seen in the ceremony.

Cut from the head the life force: Again suggests the presence of the ritual knife, mentioned three or more times in the text previously, and clarifies the ritual passage on the east gable antechamber (*so seizing the hairs on the top of his head . . .*).

Verse 2

The life force has a twin, the ebony (i.e., invisible) serpent.

The verses are a progression, approaching the serpent in its different aspects, and gradually elaborating what it is, and what is happening at death.

Verse 3

The dappled green one watching absorbs him: Sees the face rising within his majesty. The phrase echoes *the falcon the falcon is the green snake*.

Verse 4

 The clawed one which has no face: A riddle: *neheb kaw* (the one who yokes the energy centers) is the spinal cord within the spine with its claws, the sharp-edged vertebrae.

Verse 5

This verse is a riddle that explains what the serpent actually is: the serpent, the energy in you as it manifests as the nervous system in the body, is the energy that surrounds and turns the universe. A series of complex metaphors is presented. The snake as the nervous system is understood as electricity or fire, based on empirical experiential knowledge of the range of states of consciousness rooted in the body, with their states of expanded, heightened perception. Here there is a close relationship between word and thing—a beautiful example of the exploration and exploding of a metaphor. In the verse is the gradual development of punning on the word *psh* (to bite). The verse explains the *ankh* sign, the hieroglyph for "life"; it is *the open face of the falcon*, the top of the spine, appoached through *the mouth of Osiris*, the corpse.

It is not a serpent of earth that bites . . . the two lights seen: This is the manifestation of the twin. The hieroglyph in this verse is the anatomical picture of an open vertebra.

Verse 6

The bones are the columns of the body. They collapse.
    The essence of the lion will remain as the falcon is produced.
    The lion, the sweetness, the eye, the collapse of the columns: Suggests again the riddle of Samson.

Verse 7

Meti meti meti: In the Tantric system the reversal of semen upward through the body, or more specifically the erotic energy that generates semen, is the source of the creation of the light body. The semen is reversed up into the central channel to emerge from the head as the light body, instead of out of the body in the procreative act. That is the meaning of this verse, elaborated in verse 9. It generates the falcon of light, the energy rising up and out through the body.

Verse 8

The snake is pure light: The words here are the words from the beginning of the text; there they are used of the rising of stars, here of the rising of internal energy, *hr, sbn* (come out, rise).

Verse 9

The entire process is being explained in an unfolding sequence of riddles, mirroring the sequence on the east wall of the antechamber.

Verse 10

The vulgar and ignorant will gather around the temple, on the outside, like vultures, and will misunderstand what is happening inside. They will not be able to enter, because they have not solved the riddle: that this reversal of sexual energy within is an inner purification.

Verse 11

Kbbhititibiti: The sound alone is relevant here. This is the sound of a snake. The snake is addressed. The alabaster vessel is destroyed, the body is destroyed. The snake is not what killed it but is eternal life. The system described here makes sense out of the story of the death of Cleopatra, who was voluntarily "bitten by an asp." As Egyptian royalty she would have undergone the death ceremonial of the serpent cult. And also the cryptic words of Jesus Christ, "Those who follow me will raise up serpents." It also makes sense of the story of the blind seer Tiresias, who saw two serpents twined together and struck them, and then became female for seven years and saw that the female is where the power lies: the power resides in the female serpent rising within.

Verses 12–13

These read as though an observation is being made in the ceremony that the mouth is dry—it is just the mouth of the corpse, the supposed serpent within is asleep, is nowhere to be seen, and the process is not working. This human-sounding, casual observation is then countered by the liturgical language of the following verses, which state that the liquid has been successfully raised up through the spine, then coaxed with offerings of food as though the metaphorical serpent were an actual animal. Then stating what it is: it is the alchemical gold, it is *your flesh becoming gold*, the light rising within. This is what is meant by the alchemical (meaning Egyptian) transformation into gold.

Does this mean the ritual has or has not been accomplished?

Verse 13

Thus the king has been absorbed in the rising serpent.

Verse 14

There is the serpent—don't you see it? The verses track the process as it unfolds. The contrast of the snake and the falcon is again resolved.

The wondrous serpent creates the flow of falcon flesh
The green reed given on the burnt ground glides away

This verse contains a hieroglyph that looks like a predynastic rock drawing from the Egyptian desert of a herd of cattle. The herd is of souls; it is the herd of stars.

Verses 15–16

The liquid of the spine goes out of the mouth: The liquid continues to rise; the idea is that semen is the fluid in the spine rising up, as in the Tantric physiology, meaning the process of release is working.

Verse 17

As in a point-counterpoint dialectic, again a contrary voice comes in, indicating that this is all a ritual: "This has not worked, it is not real, there is no serpent." Put out the ceremonial fire. There's no point. There's nothing there. The house is the body. There is no hidden serpent of gold. A serpent is an animal that bites.

Verse 18

The ceremony concludes with a cryptic image, a riddle: There are two trees within the body, how sweet are their twigs, the light is the bread within them, the light is the lion within. It is the green reed, the new life that emerges from the body. The word that defines what kind of trees they are (as the specificity of nature is a factor throughout hieroglyphs themselves, and this Egyptian text) is the hieroglyphic tree name *khasat*. In Arabic it is *alkhasat*, in English "acacia," "cassia," "locust," the wild pea tree that miraculously grows in the desert, the flowers of which are called *nuar* (lights). This is the desert tree whose pod is the hieroglyph for sweetness, the food of the Hamadryas, Thoth, Hermes Trismegistus, the luminous head, whose *meat was locusts and wild honey, whose voice* cries out from the wilderness, the desert hills. The cassia is the cinnamon tree, the powdered bark of which was smeared on the skin of the dead in Egypt. There are two trees. The first is the skeletal structure of the living body, around which entwines the second, the serpentine life force, the nervous system, which heightened and released becomes the Tantric all-seeing eye released at death. Thus, as Plato observed, "Sweetness is knowledge, knowledge is sweet."

Egyptology:
Settling a Dispute

Some elements in the translation of hieroglyphs are simply not knowable. They are a matter of opinion. For example, there is nothing to suggest the use of the imperative or the future in the first verse. The Russian Egyptologist Alexandre Piankoff, working in the 1960s, differs from James Allen on vocabulary, parts of speech, and his interpretation of the sense and arrangement of the text: Allen sees the beginning as what Piankoff understands is the end, the west wall above the sarcophagus, which they believe is covered with magic spells to protect the mummy from snakebite. But there are numerous misrepresentations of things throughout their interpretations that are perfectly knowable. Distortions of well-known words in the original hieroglyphs and pervasive grammatical inaccuracies distort the sense of the passage and turn the translation into something that is neither Egyptian nor English. Some simple details in the passage quoted on pages 29ff illustrate the confusion:

1. "You" does not occur with "door."
2. *Netherw* is translated as "gods."
3. *Qhr* is translated not as "falcon" but as the god Horus.
4. The word *sbn*, translated here as "glide," in verse 2 as "crawl," does not occur in the same column as the word "path" and does not modify it.
5. *Blast of heat where the gods scoop water* unnecessarily exaggerates the word for "fire" and ignores the preposition "beneath."

6. *They will make a path that Unis may pass on it* does not acknowledge the double use of the word *path*, and instead turns the simple verb from *path*, *s* (causative prefix) + *wa*, into translationese, *that Unis may pass on it*, further clouding the obvious meaning.

7. The hieroglyphic hapax legomenon at the end of the first verse, with its triangle, is ignored.

The translation of the second verse continues in the same vein, rendering this concise, well-constructed poetic line into garbled English:

Get back gored longhorn . . . Fall down. Crawl away.

Here *neg nega* becomes "gored longhorn."

Why would the bull, who is the one with the horns, be gored?

The assumption in the translation is that this is a monster that has shown up in the myth for no apparent reason, rather than an accurate description of something in the real world. In the translation of the third verse:

1. *Htt* is translated as "screeching," although the pictorial determinative of the mountain landscape for this word in the parallel text of Senwosret-Ankh marks the word unquestionably as the description of an actual place.

2. *Ptt* is translated as "howling," again a wild guess.

3. *Anus on his back* is taken from *'rt*, the participle for the verb meaning "to rise," with a circle as a determinative.

4. *Imakh*, the hidden, internal spinal cord, a religious word and concept in Egypt, is translated as "back-ridge," in keeping with this violent description of a baboon.

The assumption that this is a primitive text about African animals as monsters and gods continues in the same spirit, and is now firmly in the realm of misrepresentation. One could ignore this if there was not so much at stake. This is one of the most influential traditions in the development of world religion, and it has been grotesquely misrepresented, and hence written off as devoid of content or relevance. The defense of the kind of virtually unreadable translation above has long been "philology," as though there were a special expertise in understanding the words that are hieroglyphs. But the simplicity of the words themselves has been aggressively distorted, and the grammatical structure, as it is well understood in Egyptology, is ignored whenever it suits the translator. It is important to look at this, because this really is why so few people have read Egyptian literature. Mistakes are inevitable. Some things cannot be known. But the important thing is that more people look at the original.

Left to the field of Egyptology, hieroglyphs have been dismissed as lacking in anything other than historical value. This position has led to unchecked mistranslation like the above. The succession of quotes below illustrate the dismissal of the literary or cultural value of hieroglyphs by Sir Alan Gardiner, who in 1927 wrote *Egyptian Grammar*, the standard work on hieroglyphs to this day.

> Despite the reputation for philosophic wisdom attributed to the Egyptians by the Greeks, no people has ever shown itself more averse from speculation or more wholeheartedly devoted to material interests; and if they paid an exaggerated attention to funerary observances, it was because the continuance of earthly pursuits and pleasures was felt to be at stake, assuredly not out of any curiosity as to the why and whither of human life.
>
> —Sir Alan Gardiner, *Egyptian Grammar: Being an Introduction to the Study of Hieroglyphs* (Oxford: Clarendon Press, 1927), 4

> Egyptian shares the principal peculiarity of Semitic in that its word-stems consist of combinations of consonants, as a rule three in number, which are theoretically at least unchangeable . . . The Egyptian scribes ignored the vowels in writing . . . Such a variability of the vowels could not fail to engender the feeling that the consonants were all that mattered . . . [thus] it often devolves upon the translator to supply the implicit logical nexus . . . The only basis we have for preferring one rendering to another is an intuitive appreciation of the trend of the ancient writer's mind.
>
> —Gardiner, *Egyptian Grammar*, 2, 9, 439

After a century of informed observation the vocabulary and structure of the language of hieroglyphs are well-known. This is a written language that is organized around a well-defined, easily translatable system of root cores made of hard consonants in a phonetic alphabet much like our own. The fluid vowels that move like space or breath between these consonants define the use of the root as a word, as a noun or a verb. The vowels are inferred, as in Arabic, by the placement of the word in the sentence, an easily recognizable pattern of verb-subject-object, and by external signals such as prefixes and suffixes. Far from rendering the language inert, or primitive and limited in any sense, the invisibility and changeability of the vowels give it a dynamic, fluid quality, making possible fine shadings of meaning and a crystalline sense of the interrelationship of words. The language is patterned, much like music.

Hieroglyphs are simple. The multiplicity unfolds in the meaning. Egyptology has reversed this, making it seem as though hieroglyphs themselves are alien, hence complicated and inaccessible, and the meaning flat, hence lifeless and irrelevant. *Sarcophagus* (flesh eater), *Sphinx* (the strangler), *Coffin Texts*, *Cannibal Hymn*, *Book of the Dead*, *mummy* are not Egyptian words or ideas; they come out of the realm of European death-cult kitsch, where the interpretation of Egyptian philosophy has been mired for a long time. This accounts for the apparent lifelessness, the alien and airless quality of "ancient Egypt." People are both attracted to this cultural dust heap and repelled by it. But this inert interpretive framework is the dust heap itself. What has been missed is that hieroglyphs are based on astute readings of the physical world. They have the timeless shine of the real.

Epilogue

Alchemy, the Egyptian method, turns out to be neither metallurgy nor a range of symbols generated by a universal subconscious mind. Alchemy is a consciously created system of coding for the invention of time, the creation of written language, and the yogic practices of *Ta-ntra*, "the holiness of the earth itself," the oldest religion in the world. This method of coding, of hiding and probing the dimensions of profound realizations in elaborate constructions of words, is the origin of poetry.

When I first went out to the Western Desert to work as an archaeologist in the summer of 1980, I brought with me a single book that I had purchased in Matbouli's the night I arrived in Cairo, a tattered used Faber edition of *The Four Quartets*. I turned to its pages over and over, and I go back to them now:

> There is only the fight to recover what has been lost
> And found and lost again and again: and now under conditions
> That seem unpropitious. But perhaps neither gain nor loss.
> For us, there is only the trying. The rest is not our business.

Pursuing Eliot further into *The Sacred Wood*:

> If this tradition is to survive what is needed are more educated poets who know Greek.

Eliot and other poets seem to be reaching in the dark toward Egypt with its "locked rooms, and books that are written in a very foreign tongue." Hence it is only appropriate to dedicate this book to Egyptian poetry, old and new, to the Mother of the Eyes,

the eyes with hard words and sad smiles
and say to her,

"O friend to those who wander
Your friend who has loved you
Year after year has returned.
And by life—a night of longing,
By dawn and those who cannot sleep
By morning and those who hope
By noon and those who sweat
By evening and those who are tired
By maghreb—and what is it
But a punishment for madmen?
Do not abandon a friend
Who was never false
And never—though love was lost
Cried out—
And never said, 'But I . . .'
May the earth and sky be my witness."

•

And around the shanties and the hovels,
Heart, when you go—
Don't go as a nightingale or as a bat—
Go as what you are,
A heart
With a thousand eyes
And a thousand ears
And a thousand thousand tongues.
Crawl on your belly on the pavement in the dust,
And if it is the cowardly month of Tuba, the brutal,
Listen and see what rises in the wind,

O heart, o million.
Say to those in a house of tin,

> "Wake up,
> Your lost friend returns.
> Your friend who wandered too far,
> Forgive him.
> I am not Christ,
> But I'll tell you something,
> And I swear it to you,
> I swear to you—
> The world is lie upon lie
> And you alone are true."

—Salah Jahin

CHESTER BEATTY PAPYRUS IV

If you learn this profession you will become a writer
Think of the writers of the past: their names have become
    immortal
Even though they are dead, and their descendants are gone.
They didn't make themselves tombs out of copper,
With tombstones of iron from heaven.
They didn't think about leaving heirs in order to perpetuate their
    names.
They made heirs out of books they had written themselves.

People they will never know are their children, for a writer is a
    teacher to all.
Their children are buried, their houses are gone, their graves are
    forgotten,
But their names live on in the books they made while they were alive

Be a writer. Take this to heart,
And your name will be like theirs.
A book is better than something carved in stone,
Than a solid tomb, for it lives in the heart.

A man decays
His corpse is dust
His family dies
But his books live on

Where got I that truth?
Out of the medium's mouth
Out of nothing it came
Out of the forest loam
Out of dark night
Where lay the crowns of Nineveh

Notes

The poet alone knows astronomy, chemistry, vegetation and animation, for he does not stop at these facts, but employs them as signs. He knows why the plain or meadow of space was strewn with these flowers we call suns and moons and stars . . . By virtue of this science the poet is the Namer or Language-maker, naming things sometimes after their appearance, sometimes after their essence, and giving to every one its own name and not another's . . . The poets made all the words . . . For though the origin of most of our words is forgotten, each word was at first a stroke of genius . . . Language is fossil poetry. As the limestone of the continent consists of infinite masses of the shells of animalcules, so language is made up of images or tropes, which . . . have long ceased to remind us of their poetic origin. But the poet names the thing because he sees it . . . Genius is the activity which repairs the decay of things . . . This insight, which expresses itself by what is called Imagination, is a very high sort of seeing, which does not come by study . . .

On the brink of the waters of life and truth, we are miserably dying . . . Every thought is also a prison; every heaven is also a prison. Therefore we love the poet [for it is he who] unlocks our chains . . . The religions of the world are the ejaculations of a few imaginative men. But the quality of the imagination is to flow, and not to freeze . . . Here is the difference betwixt the poet and the mystic, that the last nails a symbol to one sense, which was a true sense for a moment, but soon becomes old and false . . . Mysticism consists in the mistake of an accidental and individual symbol for an universal one . . . The symbol of a mother and child, or a gardener and his bulb, or a jeweller polishing a gem . . . The mystic must be steadily told—All that you say is just as true without the tedious use of that symbol as with it . . . The history of hierarchies seems to show that all religious error consisted in making the symbol too stark and solid, and was at last nothing but an excess of the organ of language.

—Ralph Waldo Emerson, "The Poet," in
The Complete Essays and Other Writings of Ralph Waldo Emerson
(New York: Modern Library, 1950), 329–36

•

If hieroglyphic writing may be described as a series of concrete representations, some of which are phonetic in character and others ideographic, it is equally valid to consider Egyptian sculpture and painting as the equivalent of the ideographic component. In paintings and relief the difference is a matter of relatively greater size . . . Gardiner and his English colleagues failed to see that "Egyptian pictorial art" does not merely show "analogies with methods of writing," but is so intimately related to the hieroglyphic system that it virtually *is* writing.
—*The Orientation of Hieroglyphs*, Henry Fischer (New York: Metropolitan Museum of Art, 1977), 3–5

Considering Fischer's insight above, it would be valid to make the observation that the relief that has been interpreted as Akhenaten worshipping the sun is not a representation of the worship of the sun as a god, but in fact the *iahw* hieroglyph that is the divine principle as the bright shining light that shines through all things, much as Heraclitus and T. S. Eliot wrote of the holy fire as the background of all life. This is the word, in keeping with Sigmund Freud's *Moses and Monotheism*, that would seem to become the word *yahweh*. This iconic image of the light that touches all beings with its gentle reaching hands is the icon of Avalokteshvara, who reaches out compassionately to touch all that is in the world.

The *iahw* hieroglyph appears in verse 5 on the west wall of the entranceway, as the energy behind the movement of life, and directly across in verse 2 on the east wall of the entranceway, doubled, as the shining, burning life force that is the essence of the eye.

•

"How can we talk about netchers?" by which he meant primary hieroglyphs, pristine archaic nouns, words that would be drawn directly from nature.
—Mark Lehner, in conversation, 1989, Fustat, Cairo, Egypt, in Susan Brind Morrow, *The Names of Things* (New York: Riverhead, 1997), 10

Who wants to know and describe living things seeks first to drive out the spirit, then hold the parts in his hand, but, alas, the spiritual bond is now lacking.
—Goethe, quoted by Alexandre Piankoff, in *The Pyramid of Unas* (Princeton: Bollingen Series, Princeton University Press, 1968)

•

Egyptian Astronomy

Another method of telling time was by observation of the transiting hour stars during twenty-four fifteen day periods. Two priests, seated opposite each other on a north–south line, made the observations on the flat roofs of the temples by means of the *merkhat*, a sighting instrument in the form of a slotted stick. The observer held it close to the eye with one hand while, holding a plumb line at arm's length in the other, he looked southward at the assistant priest. The hours were defined when certain stars were seen to cross the plumb line aligned with the heart eye elbow or some other part of the assistant's body. The results of these findings were tabulated on a diagram ruled in squares, showing the seated figure of the "target" priest and the stars posited around him.

—Alexandre Piankoff, *The Tomb of Ramesses VI* (New York: Pantheon, 1954)

. . . and, after the Singer, advances the Horoskopus [star-watcher] with a horologium in his hand, and a palm, the symbols of [astronomy]. He must know by heart the Hermetic [astronomical] books, which are four in number. Of these, one is about the arrangement of the fixed stars that are visible . . . and one concerns their risings.

—Clement of Alexandria

Carlyle wrote of it in his *Heroes and Hero Worship*:

> Canopus shining-down over the desert, with its blue diamond brightness (that wild, blue, spirit-like brightness far brighter than we ever witness here), would pierce into the heart of the wild Ishmaelitish man . . . It might seem a little eye, that Canopus, glancing-out on him from the great, deep Eternity . . . Cannot we understand how these men *worshipped* Canopus . . . We do not worship in that way now: but is it not reckoned still a merit, proof of what we call a "poetic nature" . . . ?

[The astronomer Sir Norman] Lockyer tells us of a series of temples at Edfū, Philae, Amada, and Semneh, so oriented at their erection, 640 B.C., as to show Canopus heralding the sunrise at the autumnal equinox . . . At least two great structures at Karnak, of 2100 and 1700 B.C., respectively, pointed to its setting; as did another at Naga, and the temple of Khons at Thebes, built by Rameses III about 1300 B.C. . . . It thus probably was the prominent object in the religion of Southern Egypt, where it represented the god of the waters.

—Richard Hinckley Allen, *Star-Names and Their Meanings* (New York: G. E. Stechert, 1899), 70–71

There are four essential points which dominate the four seasons of the year . . . They correspond to the two solstices and the two equinoxes. The solstice is the "turning back" of the sun at the lowest point of winter and at the highest point of summer. The two equinoxes, vernal and autumnal, are those that cut the year in half, with an equal balance of night and day, for they are the two intersections of the equator with the ecliptic. Those four points together made up the four pillars, or corners, of what was called the "quadrangular earth."

—Giorgio de Santillana and Hertha von Dechend, *Hamlet's Mill* (Jaffrey, N.H.: Godine, 1977), 62

The untranslatable particle *pi* appears throughout this earliest version of the Pyramid Texts whenever a transformation takes place. This may or may not be related to its use as a mathematical formula commonly dated to the seventeenth century A.D., but apparently in use long before that, and the possibility of its having been passed down through the ages as, perhaps, a Masonic secret. Tantric *pe-wa*, the transference of consciousness, and the Greek verb *pe-lo*, "to turn or become," also come to mind.

In *The Four Quartets*, T. S. Eliot's "sapphires in the mud" (quoted on page 12) refers to Job 28: "the stones of it are the place of sapphires," the earth is as the body.

The poem "Death Is Before Me Today" is from "Songs of the Harper," Papyrus Harris 500 in the British Museum. I believe it was used as a book or cover detail when I was working in the Wilbour Library of Egyptology.

The purpose in writing this book is to bring the language and literature of Egypt out of obscurity and into the land of the living. The underpinning of this effort is to make connections wherever possible, in natural history, poetic traditions, world religions, and language. Hieroglyphs are called an Afro-Asiatic Proto-Semitic language, meaning they are under the broad umbrella of one of the primary language groups in the world, where we now place Arabic. It is not known how this language group developed. Current theory has Proto-Semitic coming out of North Africa into the Levant because of the rapid desertification caused by climate change at the end of the Neolithic in 3500 B.C. (Edward Lipinski). In this book I am looking not at historical questions or derivations but to root parallels between the hieroglyphic vocabulary and the vocabulary of Egyptian Arabic today. *Mw*, water; *mwt*, death; *nfs*, breathe; *lwn*, color; *shgr*, tree; *sghr*, small; *rah*, go; *wakh*, fall; *akl*, food; *haga*, thing; and *hayy*, snake are basic words common to both Egyptian Arabic and hieroglyphs, all of which appear throughout the Pyramid Texts. Egypt, by virtue of its geographical position on the Mediterranean as a cornerstone between Africa, Asia, and Europe has absorbed one cultural and ethnic wave after another. And yet it is distinctly itself. To this reader the Pyramid Texts are a timeless and distinctly Egyptian creation. "There have always been good and bad paintings . . . In art, however, the words ancient and modern have no place." Hsieh Ho, A.D. 500.

Works Cited

Allen, James P., and Peter Der Manuelian, eds. *The Ancient Egyptian Pyramid Texts.* Leiden: Brill, 2005.

Alpin, Prosper. *Histoire Naturelle de l'Egypte, par Prosper Alpin, 1581–1584.* Cairo: Institut Francaise d'Archéologie Orientale du Caire, 1984.

———. *Plantes d'Egypte: 1581–1584.* Cairo: Institut Français d'Archéologie Orientale du Caire, 1980.

Auden, W. H. *Collected Poems.* Edited by Edward Mendelson. New York: Random House, 1976.

Calasso, Roberto. *The Marriage of Cadmus and Harmony.* New York: Vintage Press, 1994.

Catullus 85, author's translation.

Chester Beatty Papyrus IV, author's translation.

Clark, R. T. Rundle. *Myth and Symbol in Ancient Egypt.* New York: Grove Press, 1960.

Cozort, Daniel. *Highest Yoga Tantra.* Ithaca: Snow Lion, 2005.

Dossi, Dosso. *Circe and Her Lovers in a Landscape,* c. 1525. Washington, D.C.: National Gallery.

Eliot, T. S. *The Four Quartets.* New York: Faber and Faber, 1972.

Emerson, Ralph Waldo. *The Complete Essays and Other Writings of Ralph Waldo Emerson.* New York: Modern Library, 1950.

Eyre, Christopher. *The Cannibal Hymn: A Cultural and Literary Study.* Liverpool: Liverpool University Press, 2002.

Faulkner, Raymond. *A Concise Dictionary of Middle Egyptian.* Oxford: Oxford University Press, 1962.

Fischer, Henry. *The Orientation of Hieroglyphs.* New York: Metropolitan Museum of Art, 1977.

Frazier, Sir James. *The Golden Bough.* London: Oxford University Press, 2002.

Gardiner, Sir Alan. *Egyptian Grammar.* Oxford: Oxford University Press, 1927.

Gaster, Theodor. *Myth, Legend, and Custom in the Old Testament.* New York: Harper and Row, 1975.

Goodman, Steven M., and Peter L. Meininger. *The Birds of Egypt.* Oxford: Oxford University Press, 1989.

Graves, Robert. *The White Goddess: A Historical Grammar of Poetic Myth*. New York: Faber and Faber, 1948.

Harrison, Jane Ellen. *Themis: A Study of the Social Origins of Greek Religion*. Cambridge: Cambridge University Press, 1912.

Hinds, Martin, and El Said Bedawi. *A Dictionary of Egyptian Arabic*. Beirut: Librairie du Liban, 1987.

Hobbs, J. J. *Bedouin Life in the Egyptian Wilderness*. Austin: University of Texas Press, 1989.

Holy Bible: King James Version.

Hopkins, Gerard Manley. *The Poems of Gerard Manley Hopkins*. London and New York: Oxford University Press, 1970.

Jahin, Salah. *Ghenut Baramhat*, author's translation.

Lawlor, Richard. *Sacred Geometry*. London: Thames and Hudson, 1982.

McEvilley, Thomas. *The Shape of Ancient Thought Comparative Studies in Greek and Indian Philosophies*. New York: Allworth Press, 2002.

Mitchell, Stephen, ed. *Tao Te Ching: Laozi*. New York: Harper and Row, 1988.

Morrow, Susan Brind. *The Names of Things*. New York: Riverhead Books, 1997.

Papyrus Harris 500, author's translation.

Piankoff, Alexandre. *The Pyramid of Unas*. Princeton: Princeton University Press, 1968.

———. *The Tomb of Ramesses VI*. New York: Pantheon Books, 1954.

Pindar, Olympian 2.86, author's translation.

Rawson, Philip. *The Art of Tantra*. London: Thames and Hudson, 1982.

Rilke, Rainer Maria. *Letters to a Young Poet*. Weimer: Rilke Archive, 1929.

Rudaux, Lucien. *Larousse Encyclopedia of Astronomy*. London: Hamlyn, 1967.

Santillana, Giorgio de, and Hertha von Dechend. *Hamlet's Mill*. Jaffrey, N.H.: Godine, 1977.

Sappho, fragment 104a, Fr. Adesp. 976, author's translation.

Saqhr, Amal Dunqal, author's translation.

Shantideva. *Bodhisattvacaryavatara: A Guide to the Bodhisattva's Way of Life*. Translated by Stephen Batchelor. Dharamsala: LTWA, 1999.

Spencer, Edmund. *The Faerie Queen*. New York: Oxford University Press, 1963.

Sze, Mai-Mai, ed. *The Tao of Painting: Chieh Tzu Yuan Hua Chuan*. Bollingen Series. Princeton: Princeton University Press, 1956.

Thoreau, Henry David. *Wild Apples*. 1862.

Wehr, Hans. *A Dictionary of Modern Written Arabic*. Beirut: Librairie du Liban, 1974.

Yangchen, Gawai Lodoe. *Paths and Grounds of Guhyasamaja According to Nagarjuna*. Edited by Geshe Losang Tsephel. Dharamsala: LTWA, 1995.

Yeats, W. B. *The Collected Poems of W. B. Yeats*. London: Macmillan and Co., 1950.

Ziadeh, Farhat, and R. Bayly Winder. *An Introduction to Modern Arabic*. Princeton: Princeton University Press, 1957.

Acknowledgments

The author gratefully acknowledges the lectures of and conversations with the following people who contributed to the formation of this book: Roger Bagnall, Saad Abdel Basat, Bernard von Bothmer, William F. Buckley, Jr., Noam Chomsky, Steele Commager, Hossam Fahr, Henry Fischer, Elise Frick, Theodor Gaster, Ed Hirsch, Joe Hobbs, Michael Jones, Venerable Rato Khyongla, the Fourteenth Dalai Lama, Mark Lehner, Thomas Logan, Edmund Morris, Lance Morrow, Elaine Pagels, Edith Porada, Nora Scott, the Fourteenth Shamarpa, Gamal Sharif, E. Gene Smith, Gareth Sparham, Carl Strehlke, Robert Thurman, Jeannette Watson, Elie Wiesel, Margot Wilkie, Sally Wriggins.

Needless to say, the conclusions and ideas presented in this book are those of this author alone.

•

With grateful thanks to the John Simon Guggenheim Memorial Foundation and the Crane-Rogers Foundation for funding the research for this book.

With grateful thanks to Tina Bennett, Svetlana Katz, Eric Chinski, Ileene Smith, John Knight, and Jeff Seroy, for bringing the book to completion.

Motif Index